# 'LAST ORDERS, PLEASE'

T0314633

# 'LAST ORDERS, PLEASE'

## ROD STEWART, THE FACES AND THE BRITAIN WE FORGOT

## JIM MELLY

EBURY
PRESS

First published in Great Britain in 2003

Ebury Press

Random House, 20 Vauxhall Bridge Road, London SW1V 2SA

The Random House Group Limited supports The Forest Stewardship
Council (FSC®), the leading international forest certification organisation.
Our books carrying the FSC label are printed on FSC® certified paper.
FSC is the only forest certification scheme endorsed by the leading
environmental organisations, including Greenpeace. Our
paper procurement policy can be found at
www.randomhouse.co.uk/environment

MIX
Paper | Supporting
responsible forestry
FSC® C018179

Printed and bound in Great Britain by Clays Ltd, St Ives PLC

The Random House Group Limited Reg. No. 954009

www.randomhouse.co.uk

A CIP catalogue record for this book is available from the British Library

ISBN 009188618X

Typeset by seagulls
Cover Design by PUSH, London

Printed and bound by CPI Antony Rowe, Eastbourne

Addresses for companies within The Random House Group Limited can be found at:
www.randomhouse.co.uk/offices.htm

Jim Melly is of Irish parentage but was born in Guys Hospital in South London in the year that England won the World Cup. He managed to live through most of 'yer actual' youth subcultures and survive. He was the singer, songwriter and producer of a highly acclaimed (yet averagely selling) 'Indie-Pop' band in the early Nineties and was later the editor of *Inside Edge*, a national, monthly (and averagely selling) cricket magazine. He has also appeared on television and national radio as a commentator on popular culture and sports. Still a Mod, he now lectures on popular music, popular culture, politics and stuff like that. The proud father of a glorious daughter, he currently lives in North London, way too close to Arsenal for a Charlton supporter. He is a bit of a Faces fan.

# CONTENTS

# ACKNOWLEDGEMENTS

As ever, any book is only marginally the product of its author, who usually only gets to write it. Credit for this book is due to many people, only some of whom appear on its pages.

Immeasurable thanks are due to everyone who agreed to be interviewed for this book. It wouldn't have been the same without you, and your memories made it the book it is – any flaws in this work are entirely due to me. Readers should note that some of the names of interviewees have been changed; this is because indiscretions regarding their pasts would make their present positions difficult.

Special thanks are also due to Jane Turnbull, my agent. Jake Lingwood, my long-suffering editor, is also due gratitude, not least because his comments were always prescient and his patience was always unending and unrequited. I raise a glass, too, to Lucy O'Brien, because it was she who ultimately convinced me that I could do this and helped me out when I thought I'd lost the plot.

Even more thanks (I know, it's starting to read like an Oscar acceptance speech, but pay your debts, that's what I say) are due to those who had to endure a year of fretting and lent a hand when they least expected to: Annie and Adrian who were endlessly patient; Carol and Sid, who did their best when I was at my most flaky and unreliable; Chris, Diana and Maya; Duncan and Roy, who've been through madness with me before; John and Joanne; Karen, Gerry, Emily and Hannah; my mother, who berated me in the best way possible; Rob Matheu, all-round top geezer and Faces fan to the end; Sara, the ultimate exponent of Kenneth Tynan's theory of aestheticism and abstract art, who endured everything I could throw at her and still smiled at me because she always knew better; and the Valley North Stand crew, who bought the programmes when I could not. Oh, and Smudge the cat, who gave pet-therapy without ever knowing that she was.

This book is for my mum, who wasn't sure I'd finish, and for my dad, who didn't live to see me start. It is most especially for my daughter, Sid, whose humour, beauty and general brilliance kept me sane through the three-day week of my soul.

# INTRODUCTION

It is the late Nineties, on an ordinary autumn night in London – cold, but not too cold, the streets still damp from earlier rain. Despite the imprudent weather no-one feels too bad, really – the worst ravages of Margaret Thatcher's Britain (and the banalities of John Major's Britain) have more or less been laid to rest by the relatively recent election of Prime Minister Tony Blair's 'New' Labour government. Unemployment is gradually declining, inflation is under control and he/they have promised to do something about the state of the National Health Service.

As if by accident, it feels like a weight has been lifted from everyone's shoulders. It's not like it was after the 1992 election, when it was difficult to find anyone who would confess to having voted for John Major's flaccid party. Now everyone is happy to say, 'They're bastards, but at least they're our bastards' – so now, on this dull, autumn night, no-one has to think about politics any more. Which, after the past twenty years, is a burden lifted, a relief, a relief that is reflected in the media: the television, the radio and the newspapers speak almost solely of football and celebrity. Which is all one ever wants, really.

On that cold night, in a smart but crowded venue in Camden Town, the leading lights of the South-East's Mod fraternity have turned out to watch a piano player and his new band. The bar area is busy and drinks are difficult to get (and not cheap). The atmosphere is very smoky, and one or two of the punters are sporting haircuts that haven't been seen for … oh, twenty-five years. The people standing around tend the occasional pint, but more usually the measures are small. Jack Daniel's seems quite popular. And, on the whole, the less-than-demonstrative-yet-excited males are explaining to their girlfriends why they should be paying attention.

Among the luminaries in attendance are – apparently – Rolling Stone and guitar legend Ron Wood; former Who drummer Kenney Jones; and – it is rumoured ('and it's really only a rumour') – former (and occasionally current) tabloid regular Roderick 'the Mod' Stewart, with or without his latest blonde. Obviously, others among the Mod hierarchy are here to pay their respects. Paul Weller, recently crowned the 'Godfather of Britpop', formerly of The Jam and The Style Council, is here (it is said); as is Glen 'I used to be a Sex Pistol but I'm over it now' Matlock.

The piano player is here to promote his new album, but the crowd aren't really, truly interested. Instead, their biggest cheers are reserved for two old songs, two very old songs, songs that the piano player once played on bigger stages in what must seem a previous life. The first is called 'What'cha Gonna Do About It', originally released in the Sixties by a band of sharp, young Mods called The Small Faces. The second – which starts with a smart riff on his piano followed by shuffling drums and a neat guitar riff – is called 'Cindy Incidentally' and was released in early 1973 by a band who were then on top of the world, The Faces.

Rumour has it that a few of the members of that band are in the audience. Certainly only one of them, Ian McLagan, is on stage, playing the piano and belting out songs that someone else used to sing. As

'Cindy Incidentally' starts, the crowd – well, those of the crowd old enough to remember – are drawn back to another, different, perhaps slightly more brutal time. Some of them see the constant embarrassments which were youth club discos; some of them see football ground terraces, packed with waves of Mandrax-fuelled young men, ready to be taken by force; some of them see pictures on dodgy black and white television screens of flying pickets, bread and candle-queues, and bomb-blasted shop-fronts.

One of them sees a council flat in a tower block overlooking Glasgow's Citizens' Theatre. He can still see the theatre's name picked out in red neon lights, just as he can still see his parents and his uncles and aunts getting ready to go out for the night (he can probably see a couple of other tower blocks, maybe a few people walking purposefully down the road and a few randomly parked cars as well, but somehow they never quite fit into the moment quite so appropriately). And while the relatives prepare themselves for a night out in Glasgow with some well-chosen clothes, some seemly make-up and a couple of tins of Watney's Pale Ale, the music on the newly purchased stereogram is made by The Faces, and then Rod Stewart, and then more by The Faces.

And then they're gone, and it's all crap TV (there are only three channels, after all) and crisps and lemonade and cream soda and bedtime. But then it's later, they're back, and it's The Faces again and illicit sips of Watney's from a can and nicking chips from the grown-ups' fish suppers, and suddenly bags of peanuts and more crisps and even more Watney's and everybody's laughing at the kid tottering in his pyjamas...

This is the story of The Faces, from start to finish. And most places in between.

# ONE

# NEVER HAD IT SO GOOD

The story of The Faces begins – began – in London at the end of World War Two. Despite the end of the war, life in London barely changed, the only obvious relief being the cessation of the 'doodlebug' Flying Bombs which had peppered London through 1944 and early 1945. Otherwise life was pretty much the same – the bomb sites, which had once been houses and factories, remained, places where small boys searched for shrapnel and played war games among the rubble.

The rationing of food and other goods imposed during the war remained in place, the new Labour government and the British state too impoverished by the cost of war to be able to import goods in any great numbers. Mothers would fastidiously save up the coupons from the ration books to get a treat for Sunday dinner – a leg of lamb or maybe some beef. Even clothes were rationed, and even if they hadn't been, the absence of cloth of any quality meant that everyone's clothes would have been the same, drab colours and styles.

The new Labour government had been elected in a landslide, a political earthquake, premised on their promise to implement Beveridge's plan for a welfare state, and it was to this that the government turned its attentions. And in its attempt to create the welfare state Attlee's government's attitude was personified by Attlee himself, whose strange but very British brand of socialism and austerity frowned upon anything which could be described as 'lavish' – it was said that his own ministers and their wives were terrified of invitations to Chequers because there would be no heating in the bedrooms and the sherry was served by the thimbleful.[1]

And in addition to the rationing which had continued from the war, in the summer of 1946 bread was rationed. It hadn't been rationed during wartime, and it came as a blow to families all over the country. Though it only lasted two years, it was the first obvious sign that winning the war didn't mean that things were going to get better. On the plus side, however, by 1948 the new welfare state was up and running, with National Insurance to cover unemployment and retirement, and the National Health Service which gave ordinary people reasonable access to health care for the first time. Without having to find extra money to pay doctors, families could now ensure that the many illnesses which afflicted their children would be treated. And as the men who had been off to fight in the war returned, kitted out in their government-supplied 'demob' suits, Britain turned to something approaching normality.

In the late Forties and early Fifties, things like oranges and bananas were exotic, unattainable items. In an attempt to stave off ill-health and promote healthy growth, the government gave free milk to all children of school age – it came in small glass bottles, each containing a third of a pint and was kept at the back of each classroom in crates, growing ever warmer, until it was given out in time for morning playtime. It was common for working-class families from London to go on working holidays into Kent and the counties surrounding London doing jobs like hop and fruit picking.

There was no television to speak of, only radio, and that was limited to broadcasts from the BBC's three channels. Though BBC TV began broadcasting again (having gone off-air during the war) in 1947, it had no competition until the advent of a commercial channel, Independent Television (ITV), in 1955. Financed by the revenue from advertising, it was famously described as 'a licence to print money'.

So in the absence of any recognisable mass media, there remained a tradition in working-class homes of 'making your own entertainment'. Everyone had a 'turn' they could produce at a party, most households contained at least one musical instrument (usually a banjo or ukulele, though possibly a piano) and at least one household member would be proficient at it. Everyone would know the same songs, passed down through generations and through music hall. And music hall was the defining tradition in British popular culture, from comedians, writers and musicians. If Britain had a popular culture in the late Forties and early Fifties it was this, along with American and British movies which were shown at local picture palaces.

Following the end of the Second World War and the defeat of Germany, the Soviet army had occupied Poland, Czechoslovakia, Hungary, Albania, Bulgaria, Yugoslavia, Austria (which they ultimately withdrew from) and Eastern Germany as far as the River Elbe, including the surrounding of Berlin. Though Churchill had declared as early as 1946 that an 'iron curtain' had descended on Europe, the first real signs of trouble arose in January 1948 when Soviet troops began harassing food convoys into Berlin (which was held jointly by Britain, the USA, France and the USSR), eventually enforcing a total blockade which was to last a further 325 days. The Western powers responded by airlifting supplies into the city until the blockade was lifted.

From then on, the two sides – the USSR-dominated East and the American-supported West – faced each other down over the borders, caught up in a vortex of spiralling military spending that neither side could afford. Though the stand-off was subsequently premised on each side's retention of nuclear weapons, there were to be relatively few direct flashpoints between the two main Superpowers, the USSR and the USA. However, the threat of nuclear war overhung the decades that followed.

Though the Labour Party were ejected from office in 1951 (in an election where they gained more votes than the Conservative Party), the new Conservative government – under an increasingly ailing Winston Churchill – continued many of the policies of the Labour Party, most importantly the welfare state. As the early Fifties continued, the restrictions on private life – essentially the rationing of food and other goods – were gradually lifted.

The economy, boosted by the massive introduction of public money into a major house-building programme (the Conservative government were committed to build 300,000 new homes each year) as well as the NHS which was becoming an increasingly major employer, was beginning to thrive. By the election of 1955, Anthony Eden (who had become Prime Minister due to Churchill's retirement on health grounds) was able to tell the country that they 'had never had it so good'.

Television had spread into many homes largely due to two entirely separate conditions – first, the Coronation of Queen Elizabeth

II in 1953, broadcast to the nation for the first time on flickering, dark and very small screens; the second impetus for television was the ability to rent. Most housing was rented, and so people didn't feel any impetus to buy expensive items. Televisions were very expensive to buy, and it was possible to rent one for a small weekly sum from companies such as Radio Rentals. Radios had made their way into households during the previous twenty years in this manner.

However, between the welfare state and the growth in the economy, life as a kid during the Fifties was not all bad. Families and locales were important, and it was a time when kids were still allowed out to play in the street. While education was limited and very few working-class people went on to university (which was almost exclusively the preserve of grammar school children), there was no lack of work following secondary education at age fifteen. Men being demobbed from the army were helped to find new work or returned to their old jobs as women left the factories and went back into the household.

The growth of the clerical sector meant that working-class men could find themselves office jobs, and National Assistance (the dole) meant that it was possible to stay out of work and learn a different trade: playwright Joe Orton famously lived off national assistance for almost ten years as he honed his writing skills. Throughout the country, writers, musicians and artists used the time afforded them through their new-found access to higher education and the dole to learn their craft.

These were also the days before supermarkets. Any high street would have a butcher, a baker, a newsagent. Grown-ups smoked Players and Embassy cigarettes without filters, and the men drank beer – not lager, which, if it was consumed at all, was drunk by women. People still went to church on a Sunday, they got married and they stayed married. Families, still not used to the fact that most of their children would survive due to the NHS, had three or four kids. Within the social and legal constraints of the day there was increasing freedom, at least in economic terms.

'When I came here first, it was great,' remembered Jimmy O'Malley, an Irish immigrant to Britain in the late Fifties. 'If you were in a job and you didn't like it, you could just jack it in and you'd have another one by the afternoon.'

Harold Macmillan was correct – to some extent – when he announced in 1955 that people had never had it so good. But even as he was speaking, the world was about to shift from under Macmillan's generation.

Sociologist Dave Phillips remembers the time as being the cusp of change. 'My parents died when I was very young,' remembers Phillips, 'but that generation got a pretty raw deal from their children in a way, 'cos they had been through a very hard time – through the war and austerity – so it's hardly surprising they wanted things to be stable, to build their homes and their families. Then all their kids were complaining they were bored and wanted to dance in the street and be rebellious and all the rest of it.'

By 1955/56 a new kind of music was being heard on radios all over Britain. Not played on the BBC channels, it was overheard from other, European stations – especially Radio Luxembourg. It came from America and it sounded like nothing British listeners had heard before. Rock 'n' roll – American black southern slang for sex – was an exciting new amalgam of black rhythm and blues and white country and western with a souped-up backbeat, sung (at first) by a white southern boy named Elvis Presley. As his voice spread through the Western world, it was followed by others, and sometimes even by the original black artists themselves. The first big hit in Britain came for

Bill Haley, a rotund gentleman prone to wearing checked jackets and with a flick of hair for a fringe. 'Shake, Rattle And Roll' lit a fire in British youth, who until this point had been wondering what they were going to spend their new-found wealth on.

At the same time, young people were discovering their own ability to make music – Lonnie Donegan had fuelled the skiffle craze of the mid- to late-Fifties. Skiffle was a mixture of jazz and traditional American folk music, and was remarkably easy to play. With the craze in full swing, all over Britain groups of young men were taking up acoustic guitars, tea-chest basses with wash-boards for percussion. It was the first DIY-rock, preceding Punk by twenty years, and everyone was at it. And what made it suddenly dangerous was that Elvis Presley, who looked and sounded like promiscuity on legs, played the guitar. It instantly became the instrument of musical revolution.

'I was born in 1945 and spent my childhood moving into the Fifties,' remembers Dave Phillips. 'Music was what you heard on the radio on the "Light" programme [on the BBC], *Family Favourites* and so on. I can remember the first time I heard "Heartbreak Hotel" on *Family Favourites* – I was ten or eleven – and I thought, "Bloody hell, that's an amazing sound." But I also liked things like "Singing The Blues". My experience was from the late Fifties to the late Sixties there was always a musical soundtrack to what we were doing, so it went with politics and it went with being bolshie. It was just the way that our generation was – the musical soundtrack was wonderful.'

The mid-Fifties also saw the emergence of a new group of authors and playwrights. Linked only tenuously by the media and critics, their work was epitomised by John Osborne's *Look Back in Anger*. These writers became known as the 'Angry Young Men', and as much as they railed against anything, they railed against the cosy, middle-class world of the mid-Fifties. They were against privilege and for the gritty, working-class communities that were gradually being broken up by the slum clearances first effected by the Luftwaffe in the Forties. They provided an intellectual backdrop for the new music, fashions and consumption that were to follow.

And, just as importantly, the 1948 British Nationality Act gave Commonwealth citizens the right to come to Britain to live and work. The reason for the Act was to attract immigrants from former British colonies who would work in the newly formed National Health Service and on public transport. The immigrants, who would become an important force in British youth culture, were often placed in the worst areas of Britain's cities in terms of housing and were subjected to racism, sometimes malicious but more often casual. It was not uncommon to see signs outside boarding houses which read, 'No blacks, no dogs, no Irish'. As a result, the late Fifties saw a series of civil disturbances in the Notting Hill area of London between the immigrants – who felt they were defending themselves – and local, working-class youths.

'I suppose what was happening was that the British Empire was coming home to roost,' says Dave Phillips. 'What had been a very undifferentiated and homogenised culture which didn't recognise its own origins was having to come face to face with the fact that we had all these exotically coloured and cultured people from other parts of the world coming here to live.'

Among the bomb sites, building sites and corner shops, children in the Fifties grew up in a world very different to that of their parents: unworried by cares over employment and ill health (or at least finding the money to pay the doctor), their horizons broadened (however slightly) by television, radio and the new, outspoken authors, theirs would be a world of opportunity. That is, if they chose to take it.

★

Rod Stewart was born on 10 January 1945, the son of a newsagent in Archway, North London. German V1 and V2 bombs were still falling on North London, and when Rod was born, the Whittington Hospital and the Archway itself (a huge, Victorian bridge which spans the Archway Road and still revels in the nickname 'Suicide Bridge') were about all that was left standing in the Archway Road. The youngest of five children, Rod was often indulged by his parents, Bob and Elsie Stewart. Bob, a hardworking Scot who had had a life as a merchant seaman before settling in London, was obsessed by two things outside of work – music and football.

As Rod grew up through the increasingly prosperous Fifties, he took on his father's passions, and was a good enough footballer that he went on to represent both his primary and secondary schools, as well as his borough and county sides. Whether he was good enough to have gone on to represent Arsenal FC, the local First Division (now Premier League) team and Stewart's first footballing love, is a moot point; suffice to say that by the time he was old enough to leave school at the age of fifteen he was offered apprentice terms by Brentford FC, but he quit after a few weeks of early mornings spent cleaning professional players' boots.

'It worked like, you had a three-month trial and played a couple of games for the "A" team and then got through to the reserves,' remembered Stewart in the Seventies.[2] 'I don't think really I was that good at it. I wanted to get into the music business. It wasn't purely a choice thing – I was too bloody lazy to get up and trek over to Brentford and I didn't want to be cleaning the first team's boots any more. It's a terribly underpaid sport. I was talking to one of the guys with Leyton Orient and I said what a take on football is. This guy gets seventy to eighty quid a week. And I said, "But you entertain 28,000 people a week." For me that's really underpaid.' Without making a conscious career decision, Stewart had decided to become a musician. That is, if he could get anyone to take him seriously.

In an attempt to remain a world power – and, as a side effect, to end the universally unpopular National Service – the Conservative government in the mid-Fifties decided to build up Britain's nuclear arsenal. The idea was to retain world status at a lower cost and nuclear weapons don't need to be trained, fed or clothed and never complain of being bored. In response, the Campaign for Nuclear Disarmament (CND) was formed in 1958. Each year, CND organised a three-day march from the government's Atomic Weapons Research Establishment at Aldermaston to a rally in London's Trafalgar Square.

'My first CND march [to Aldermaston] was in 1962,' remembers Dave Phillips. 'Before that I'd marched locally, up and down the High Street with those little CND "lollipops".' The Aldermaston march became a focal point for London's growing 'Beat' population. Such as they were, the London Beats were based on a vague idea of what was actually going on in America. With writers such as Allen Ginsberg and Jack Kerouac gaining intellectual and cultural significance on both sides of the Atlantic, semi-intellectual and culturally aware young men and women in London sought to emulate their lifestyles. However, since they could not readily emulate the adventure of a road-trip from New York to San Francisco (London to Hull doesn't really have the same appeal), they took on the other affectations of the American Beats, learned in Paris in the early Fifties – hanging around in cafes, drinking coffee, talking about books and being precious about what constituted culture. To this end, jeans were out – too common – rock 'n' roll was out – too earthy – but folk music was in.

It was into this scene that the young Rod Stewart thrust himself in the early Sixties. He had grown up with a strong folk music tradition at home, sharing with his father a love not just of Scottish folk music but also of the strong folk tradition from America – Woody Guthrie, Big Bill Broonzy et al. Whereas today Stewart prefers to remember his time marching with CND as just another way of picking up girls, he had in fact inherited from his father his concern over social issues: his father was a vehement Labour Party supporter, and was naturally inclined to support pressure groups such as CND. In addition, the Cuban Missile Crisis of 1962 – in which the USA led by President John F. Kennedy faced down the USSR led by Nikita Khrushchev over the latter's policy of siting nuclear missiles in Cuba – reinforced for young people the very real threat at the time of a nuclear war.

Picking up on the new wave of American folk writers and performers such as Joan Baez and the nascent Bob Dylan, Stewart began writing in a folk style, and took to performing folk songs from America in London bars and on street corners. He also had a series of day jobs – picture-framer, sign-writer, gravedigger, helping out in his father's newsagent shop – but none of these held his attention for very long. The young Stewart instead took off on various road-trips of his own, hitching his way to France, Italy and Spain, sleeping rough outside the Nou Camp Football Stadium in Barcelona, and trying to earn enough from busking on the Paris streets to pay for food. When he eventually arrived home, Stewart had no job and no money, and the clothes he stood up in were in such a bad state that his mother took them into the garden and burned them.

★

While Rod Stewart was living a Beatnik idyll and looking for his big break in music, on the other side of London Steve Marriott was already engaged in a career in showbusiness. Born on 30 January 1947 to Bill and Kathleen, Marriott lived in Manor Park in the East End of London. He was – according to his mother – always a performer with a passion for music. His first break came when his mother saw an advert in the *Daily Mirror* inviting children to audition for a part in Lionel Bart's musical *Oliver!* Marriott was spruced up and taken along to the audition by his father, where he performed Buddy Holly's 'Oh Boy'. Bart was taken with the lad and gave him the part. For the next fourteen months, Marriott performed every night except Sundays, marking him out from his school friends' more ordinary lives and showing him that it was possible to make a living that didn't involve any outdoor work or heavy lifting.

Though he was still required to attend school during the day, Marriott's attendance began to fluctuate, and it finally came to an end when he inadvertently set the school alight due to the unfortunate conjunction of a cigarette and a leaky gas pipe. He transferred to the Italia Conti drama school in Islington, where he spent two years taking any acting job he could get to help towards his tuition fees, and thus appeared on television with star British actors like Sid James in *Citizen James*, Jack Warner in *Dixon of Dock Green*, and Peter Sellers and Eric Sykes in the movie *Heaven's Above*.

Following the movie, work began to dry up for Marriott, and this, along with Marriott's dislike of the hours spent waiting around on set, governed the sixteen-year-old's decision to give up acting for a career in music. Initially this meant forsaking a guaranteed six-month run with the Old Vic Company in Chichester for the dubious pleasure of forming a group called The Moonlighters which came to nothing. He returned to film work, appearing in *Live it Up* (with David Hemmings) and *Be My Guest*, both of which were minor British films cashing in on the new pop music phenomenon.

In 1964 he worked for a short time as a harmonica player with Andrew Loog Oldham's 'Andrew Oldham Orchestra' before forming another group, The Frantics. Marriott's musical taste had developed since the skiffle boom of the mid-Fifties, and he was now enamoured with American rhythm and blues. Any spare time and cash were spent seeking out imported R&B records from small shops in and around Soho in London's West End. Marriott would soon find others to share his obsession.

By the late Fifties, the reforms introduced by the 1944 Education Act – which gave schooling to all children until they were aged fifteen with the possibility of further education after that age – were beginning to take effect. Ordinary children were now encouraged to stay at school and get the education which would get them jobs in the ever expanding offices rather than in the factories. Needless to say, many ordinary kids, enthused by the advent of skiffle and rock 'n' roll, were using this extra time at school to get themselves a musical education.

Elsewhere in Marriott's East End of London, Ronnie Lane was also deciding to try and make a living out of music. Born on April Fool's Day in 1946, by the time Lane became a teenager, he had always felt like he was an outsider at school, claiming that 'I got into a lot of fights and got picked on because I was small … when we had games I did the odd jobs like oiling the tennis posts.'[3] By the time he was fourteen, Lane had started to play the guitar, simply because playing a guitar could mark him out as 'different' and give him an identity.

When he was sixteen he left school to enrol on an art course at Lister Technical College. In what today would seem like an odd move, he also joined the Green Jackets Rifle Brigade – part-time boy soldiers – where he met a squaddie called Kenney Jones while out on manoeuvres. Moreover, he got himself a job working at Battersea Fun Fair, where he fell in love with the nomadic romance of the fairground and soon quit college to pursue a career managing the Roll-a-Penny stall and working on the Big Dipper. However, fairground work is seasonal, and the season finished in September. 'You know, a fair when it's closed is the saddest sight in the world,' he said later.[4]

Following on from his stint at the fairground, Lane formed his own group, The Outcasts, later renamed The Pioneers. Though finding a bass player and a singer wasn't a problem, The Outcasts – like all new bands – had a problem finding a drummer. The reason for this is pretty simple: despite evidence to the contrary, playing the drums even moderately well is not easy. It takes a lot of practice – much more than playing the guitar, which can be mastered in its most basic state in a couple of weeks – and the practice itself is very, very noisy. And, to add to potential drummers' problems, drum kits are expensive and difficult to move from one place to another. And to round it off, the drummer tends to sit at the back of the group, and most girls' attention tends to be aimed towards the singer or the guitarist. Therefore, half-decent drummers are always in short supply. Lane was lucky, then, when his brother said that he knew someone who played the drums. The drummer turned out to be Kenney Jones. After some discussion, initially between Lane and Jones, and subsequently between Lane and the other band members, Kenney was in.

Born in Stepney on 16 September 1948, Kenney Jones shared Ronnie Lane's working-class background. Jones's parents, Violet and Samuel, sent him to school in Cable Street, the road made famous in the Thirties as the final bastion of working-class and Jewish defiance against Oswald Mosley's Union of British Fascists. Jones remembers the place as 'a really tough school'. He hated it and would go into the school in the morning to register his name before cycling over to another school where his friends were. Jones's first interest in playing music was aroused by the skiffle boom and he wanted to play the banjo, but ended up playing drums because that was the only instrument available when he and a friend decided to be skiffle stars. However, he found that he liked it, and after pulling a minor confidence trick on his parents (he bought a drum kit on a hire purchase agreement which required his parents' signature, and had it delivered to his house along with the agreement which his parents were then morally blackmailed into signing) he got down to practising.

Jones would watch every drummer he could on TV and endlessly played along to the only records his parents owned, two 78rpm discs of '12th Street Rag' and 'Rawhide'. 'I never want to hear those records again,' he says today.[5] For Jones, as with many young, aspiring musicians since the development of the mass-produced record player, playing along with records was the obvious way to learn, since instrument lessons cost money and they didn't teach you what you wanted to learn anyway – how to play like your heroes, from Elvis onward.

Like most underage British teenagers Jones had started to sneak into pubs and he soon became a regular in the British Prince pub in Stepney where he would avidly observe the resident drummer. The drummer, obviously freaked out by Jones's incessant staring, asked him what he was doing. Jones explained that he was trying to pick up tips from him, and Jones's next visit to the pub resulted in his first proper performance, sitting in for the drummer he had been studying. It was this performance that led Ronnie Lane's brother – who was working behind the bar at the time – to recommend Jones for The Outcasts.

★

And over in West London, a young Ron Wood was genially making his own way. Born in Hillingdon on 1 June 1947, his family were much more liberal than most, and were open to new forms of music and art. Parents Lizzie and Arthur, along with older brothers Art and Ted, were very supportive to the young Ronnie, and his talent for drawing was noticed and nurtured early, and he went on to win prizes for his drawing and painting. Art and Ted were obsessed with music, and formed groups long before Ron got round to it; but he was exposed to a number of instruments including saxophone, clarinet and drums before settling on guitar. In addition, his musically mature older brothers gave Ron a schooling in blues and jazz, allowing him a head start over most other young musicians.

One of the things that deters young people from learning to play an instrument is the idea that it is intrinsically difficult, as though there is some secret, magical trick to picking up a guitar and strumming a few chords. The ease of access to musical instruments, along with the attitude in Wood's household that anyone could play them, undoubtedly helped the youngest Wood. When he was sixteen, Ron followed his brother Art into Ealing College of Art, and it was while he was there that he formed his first group, The Rhythm and Blues Bohemians, who fell apart only to become The Thunderbirds, later renamed The Birds.

Ron Wood had decided he was going to be a guitarist. By 1964 he was well on his way.

# TWO

# A CHAOTIC LESSON IN BULLSHITTING

By the time each of the Faces had left school, they were – with the exception of Rod Stewart – all firmly paid-up members of the Mod youth culture. Mod had emerged in the late Fifties/early Sixties as a reaction to the Beatniks and Teddy Boys who had been prevalent earlier. Teddy Boys came out of strong, working-class communities in the East and South of London. Dressed in a parody of early twentieth-century Edwardian dress – long, drape jackets and 'drainpipe' (very tight) trousers – they oozed a very genuine threat of violence. They listened to rock 'n' roll, idolised Elvis Presley and Gene Vincent, and were aligned to the 'Rockers', motorbike gangs who modelled themselves after Marlon Brando in the movie *The Wild One* (released in 1954).

The Beatniks – who hung out in coffee houses in Soho, Chelsea and various university campuses – were considered a bit 'worthy' by the young working class, though part of the Beat attitude was incorporated by the new Modernists who were starting to appear. These Modernists were working-class young men revelling in a new affluence due to relatively good wages paid by the new clerical jobs. Where Teddy Boys and Rockers liked rock 'n' roll and the Beatniks liked traditional jazz and folk music, the Mods (as they became known) preferred rhythm and blues and Jamaican ska. Where the Rockers drove huge, oily Triumph motorbikes, the Mods preferred Italian scooters, Vespas or Lambrettas. And clothes were everything to Mods, who – in their own parlance – aspired to be a 'Face', the best dressed Mod around. The very concept of Mod was that they would be sharper than anyone else, wearing traditional English clothing but with an Italian or American 'preppy' twist.

'Up until the Sixties you couldn't buy clothes other than your parents' clothes,' remembered McLagan. 'Before that all you had was the same clothes your dad wore. Life suddenly was colourful.'[1] Kenney Jones also remembered the difference that Mod made. 'I remember everything being black and white, growing up,' he recalled, 'and then suddenly everybody started to wear colourful things. That's what I loved about the Mod movement.'[2] As an early Mod, Richard Amos also saw the subculture as a reaction to the Fifties. 'The Sixties were good,' he recalls. 'I went to school in the Fifties, away to school, boarding school. And it was pretty austere. I can remember sweets when they were rationed. I must have been about ten. And I think the Sixties must have been a reaction to that austerity. It took a long time to get over the war, I guess. It was a complete "other side of the coin".'

Dick Hebdige, the author of *Subculture: The Meaning of Style*, points out that whereas Teddy Boys were obvious and obtrusive in society, Mods invented a style which allowed them to 'negotiate smoothly between school, work and leisure and which concealed as much as it stated'.[3] For Hebdige, a former Mod himself, the way that Mods (and later Skinheads and others) chose to undertake their consumption was more than the mere flexing of economic muscles. By dressing apparently normally, the Mods 'undermined the meaning of "collar, suit and tie", pushing neatness to the point of absurdity'.[4]

'You can stylise Mods as wearing rollneck sweaters and that,' recalls Amos, 'but it was just clothes that you wore. I certainly wasn't a Rocker. They always looked slightly dirty to me. I started liking modern jazz when I was at school. And just continued with it afterwards. And when I was home from school you used to go to jazz clubs. I saw the Rolling Stones at Richmond, a couple of times, before they'd even made a record.'

Des Sadlier, a Mod in the mid-Sixties, felt that being a Mod was more of a life choice. 'I worked for a bookmaker during the week,' he recalled. 'We would get suits made at Burtons and then wear them at the weekend, on Saturday nights 'cos we had to work on Saturdays. We'd stay up for two nights and get back for work on Monday mornings. I went to see The Who at the Marquee and was so impressed that I bought a drum kit. I wanted to be Keith Moon. I wasn't very good, though.'

Dave Phillips, then a student at university, remembers that subculture was something reliant on income. 'I was more a Mod than anything else but students weren't anything 'cos we were too poor,' he remembers. 'I went to the University of York in 1963, and most of the intake were from minor public schools. This was an era when people wore tweed jackets and Bedford cords – this was the break-out from school uniforms, it was an experimental time.

**19**

'The big change was who wore Levi's and who didn't, which happened in 1964/65. Life used to be quite simple – if you were Mod-ish you wore Levi's and a brown suede jacket … a brown cord jacket and blue jeans was very popular for a long time. It was all very simple dress. We were Mod-ish and we had tag-collar shirts and pencil ties. One or two guys took it very seriously. A concert I went to in early '64 was initially headed by John Leighton of "Johnny Remember Me" fame and on the bill as a supporting act were the Rolling Stones but by the time the tour was happening they were the main act on the tour. On that tour were groups like The Hollies, the Swinging Blue Jeans, possibly Billy J Kramer & The Dakotas. They all wore extraordinarily shiny trousers.'

Sociologist and cultural commentator Dick Hebdige also found himself attracted to the Mod lifestyle. 'I was a "wannabe" more than a bona fide Mod without the necessary cash or panache to purchase high end gear or to hang out properly in Soho,' he recalls. 'I did grow up in the Fifties and Sixties in Fulham, a Mod centre and from 1962–9 went to a grammar school which served as a kind of concentration camp for West London Mods who'd passed the "11-plus" exam. It was situated next to Wormwood Scrubs, a few miles west of Shepherds Bush.

'My very first memory of Mod was seeing an edition of the *Tonight* show on TV in early 1962 when I was 11 and still at primary school. At this point, I wanted to look like Billy Fury or Robert Mitchum in *Night of the Hunter* and used copious amounts of Brylcreem to elevate the forelock in an attempt to impress the ladies, even at one point affecting Mitchum's heavy-lidded postures to the audible amusement of adjacent female classmates. Two years before Margate, Clacton etc., Cliff Michelmore, the show's host, introduced the British TV-watching public to Mod–Rocker enmities. A Mod and a Rocker, hauled, allegedly, straight off the streets of Soho, were wheeled in front of the camera and were asked to give an account of themselves. The Mod, I remember, looked like Adam Faith. Michelmore, assuming the role of the indulgent but firm Boys Brigade leader, invited them to shake hands. They refused: Michelmore gave that patronising, exaggeratedly bemused look that marked the dead centre of the generation gap and that was that. The next day I was eager to hear what the girls thought. Didn't the rocker look great? No, they said, they much preferred the Mod. From that moment, the dye was cast.

'1964 was the year a bunch of 16-year-old school-leavers in parkas churned up the rain sodden playing field on their scooters. I remember anarchy at lunchtime: older boys bringing bullets into school and detonating them with bricks in the confines of the "cage": the fenced-in area into which we were all herded after swallowing school dinner. I remember the pain and shock of getting nutted for the first time, aged around 12 by a Hammersmith Mod named John Stratton. I remember a kid we used to call "Knitting Wool Face" (though not to HIS face) slashing another boy's neck with a sharpened steel comb. I remember a Rocker, the only real rocker in the school, implausibly named Bill Bailey, an unrepentant Ted from Fulham Palace Road with an elaborate Elvis-scale quiff and a Victorian "macer's" rolling gait fighting off all-comers and getting suspended for refusing to shave off his sideburns – the school regulation was no hair beneath the top of the ear. I found Bill Bailey's solitary embodiment of the opposite principle, and his refusal to back down under any circumstances, heroic and fascinating – if not actually imitable.

'I remember flicking Hassidic style sidelocks over my ears at the school gates every morning in order to avoid Bill Bailey type suspension/expulsion during the era of Steve Marriott haircuts. Aged 14, we used to go to local church youth clubs after school and we formed – with a bunch of friends – an R&B and Motown covers band called

Cacophony (I "sang") that played a couple of true-to-form tuneless gigs at a youth club on the Wandsworth Bridge Road and an even more disastrous Girl Guides dance near Putney Bridge where the rhythm guitarist destroyed a speaker in homage to Pete Townshend. The drummer, stricken with nerves, got stuck in a military band tattoo holding- pattern during the drum solo in the course of which we were supposed to stand at the side of the stage nonchalantly smoking Peter Stuyvestants. Steve Bonnett, the bass player and a flamboyant mod from Putney actually went on to become a successful professional musician. There was a drug raid on another youth club near Eelbrook Common behind Fulham Broadway when I was 16 where the police wheeled in institutional-style fabric dividers and made the boys strip on one side, the girls on the other as pills and, it was rumoured, one or two clunky old glass syringes fell to the floor. I remember "Black Bombers" and "Dexes" [Dexedrine] in matchboxes and an almost metaphysical terror of heroin. I remember sitting, aged about 15 (this would be in 1966) in the flat of a prematurely liberated classmate (his parents had divorced and the flat was some kind of compensation) and feeling sick as I watched him shoot up. I remember rumours of hard Mod villainy – of a guy threatened with castration by some speeding nutter with a cutthroat razor as he stood in the gents at some club.

'I remember watching the older Mods in floor-length, tan and butter and moss-green leather coats lining up to get into the Pontiac club on Putney High Street. I remember John Marks, the brother of my first real early adolescent crush getting off his Vespa and walking into his mother's ground floor flat in Sands End on a Sunday evening with eyes like saucers. One morning I found John scouring the flat for broken appliances – a non-functioning dansette record player, an old Fifties radiogram – to strew about the bedroom floor after a Morris Minor piloted by a drunk driver had slammed through the decaying brickwork (the house faced a T-junction) before coming to a stop in the middle of his bedroom. His racing thoughts were tightly focused on a hyperinflated insurance claim. Later in the Sixties when we started going to pubs aged around 17 I met other older local Mods like John Tidy and Jumbo who really did live the ideal, West-End Moddy lifestyle. Jumbo was involved in the little reported scooter charge on Buckingham Palace on 5 November 1966. I remember listening to the Rolling Stones' first EP with 'You Better Move On' on it in a record booth in Shepherds Bush market with a mate called Thoms; then looking at a pair of basket weave black leather shoes in Raouls (later Ravels).

'The main impetus behind Mod in London was territorial. Fulham, at the then rough end of the Kings Road, was a Mod centre and Mod style defined the local paradigms of cool, from the Italianate "bumfreezer" suits and chisel-toed shoes favoured by my brother and his mates (four years older than me) to the eye-challenging psychedelic combos which came briefly to the fore around 1967 to the neo-skinhead/rude boy look which I affected in the early Seventies. To a certain extent subcultural affiliation tended to be territorially determined in those days. There was a lot more bullying, more "bundles" and more sadistic peer group coercion than tends to be acknowledged in rosy tinted retrospect and the kinds of analytical accounts students of subculture like myself have, in earlier incarnations, tended to concoct. The local girls all favoured Mod fashions and Mod boys more or less exclusively. To deviate from the code would be to hazard ostracisation and, likely, a punch in the mouth. Once entered into, the imagery of Mod could become a fascinating universe unto itself, where tiny variations in style (be)spoke volumes.

'There were, however, local and regional variations within the Mod style, too. A common affiliation to an approximately similar clothing style would not make much difference if you encountered a group of Millwall fans on a Friday night, their hearts set on a 'bundle'. East End Mods in particular were considered rivals and potential enemies by South London Mods, particularly after the supposed Kray Twins–Richardson brothers contest. The Mod style did intersect closely with the world of Sixties Soho, East End and West London gangsterism and professional villainy.'

By the mid-Sixties, the rivalry between Mods and Rockers (Teddy Boys had largely disappeared by this point) was exhibited in a very explicit manner: on bank holidays, large groups of Mods and Rockers would meet in coastal resorts such as Brighton and Southend, places where ordinary families from cities would go for a day-trip. Among the families camped on the beaches and through the narrow streets and tea-rooms, the Mods and Rockers would engage in one- or two-day-long pitched battles. This led to lurid newspaper headlines which in turn fuelled further battles and led to yet another exercise – in a long history – of grown-ups questioning whether young people were out of control.

That the members of the Small Faces – as well as Ron Wood and eventually Rod Stewart – would be Mods was probably inevitable. Their urban, working-class backgrounds, their love of soul music and their aspirational desire were all reflected in the Mod ethic. When he was asked what he thought of Mod, Marriott agreed that they were part of it. 'It was just a case of, all me mates were Mods and I was a Mod ... we were just part of the movement.'[5] Ronnie Lane held the same view. 'That was all that was happening at the time. I didn't want to be a greasy Rocker, did I?'[6]

★

Following the pop music explosion that took place between 1955 and the early Sixties, there was no real form to anything that was happening on the music scene in Britain. Despite their aspirations to be in a band, the teenage Small Faces were more likely to be consumers of pop music than to be spearheading any musical revolution. In fact, prior to the end of 1962, British groups were likely to be modelled after The Shadows, a musical group who also backed English Elvis mimic Cliff Richard. Most pop records were asinine, bland and aimed at teenage girls. Males who took a serious interest in music were more likely to be into the blues and rhythm and blues records which came into the country through American sailors and commercially astute record-shop owners. These records were studied and deconstructed by aspiring musicians, trying to find out how to make their guitars and amplifiers – newly bought on extended hire purchase agreements – sound like they were being played in Chess Records' studio in Chicago.

However, at the end of 1962, a quirky, besuited Northern group called The Beatles had their first hit, a lumpy singalong tune titled 'Love Me Do'. Before the rest of the London music scene – such as it was – had taken a glance northwards, The Beatles had had three Number 1s and were being pursued down the A1 by a stream of other bands.

Dave Phillips recalls that the changes in youth subcultures and the clothes they wore was allied to a change in the music that young people were listening to. 'The thing about music at that time was that English music was incredibly boring and tedious, and what you listened to was American music,' Phillips remembers. 'Right up until 1963 you listened to American music. It used to be terribly important. I used to get *Record Mirror* because it was very important to see what was going on in the American charts.'

Despite the increasing importance of music, access was still limited by income. 'I never had a record player,' Phillips remembers. 'Owning a record player was a big deal: you had to be quite wealthy to own a Dansette record player. If you came out of the lower-middle classes – let alone the working classes – you didn't have access to these things, or transistor radios. So your main exposure to music was juke-boxes in pubs or the rich kids who could afford to buy records and owned Dansettes. American R&B had a sound, had a power, and you'd get these English cover versions and they were just the pits, mostly. It used to be a big event when The Beatles would release an album.

'Another big event was *Top of the Pops* which was on Wednesday evenings, I think, at six o'clock, and everyone would gather around the television in the common room. For me the sound of R&B was the most exciting thing, just that harmonica sound. There were a lot of pub-rock bands, none of them of any distinction. They played in big pubs, working-class pubs, beer on the floor. I was very lucky to be a student at the time that I was, 'cos there was this real burgeoning of British music. I liked The Beatles, but I was more with the Stones than The Beatles 'cos of the image. The Beatles were just a little bit too clean, and the Stones had this dangerous edge to them as well as bands like them and The Yardbirds.'

The London music scene – such as it was – was based around clubs, most notably the Crawdaddy Club in Richmond run by Georgio Gomelsky. Gomelsky's club was a magnet to the many aspir-ing blues players from around the South-East, including Alexis Korner, Charlie Watts and other nascent Rolling Stones. A small, sweaty place, on a good night there would be up to three hundred frantic people dancing to rhythm and blues pumped out by earnest young musicians. Not yet close to breaking into Gomelsky's circle, Marriott's group, The Frantics, were having moderate success. He changed the name of the group to Steve Marriott & The Moments, and got them on the books of the Clayman Agency, who found them occa-sional gigs around London and a residency at the Thingandmejig Club in Reading.

In 1963, The Moments signed to Decca, one of the labels which had turned down The Beatles ('guitar groups are on the way out') and which in turn had snapped up the Rolling Stones. The Moments recorded a cover of The Kinks' 'You Really Got Me', but Decca turned the track down. However, World Artists, an American label, picked the single up and rush-released it in the US in an attempt to pre-empt the release of The Kinks' own version. The single disappeared without trace, and shortly after, The Moments kicked Marriott out and replaced him with another singer.

In the same way that a band without a drummer isn't really a band, a singer-songwriter without a record release is just another wannabe. That Marriott had released a record, even though he hadn't written it, even though it was released in a foreign country, and even though he didn't have a band, marked him as different from most of the other aspirant musicians littering London and the wider UK in 1963. Buoyed by this, Marriott began writing material which he tried to hawk around London's Denmark Street, also known as Tin Pan Alley, a short side street off Charing Cross Road whose brown-bricked buildings were filled with Britain's music publishers.

After an unsuccessful day spent cold-calling at each of the offices, Marriott called – not for the first time – on his Aunt Sheila (who worked for a music publisher) whose contacts got Marriott in to see a publisher named Franklin Boyd. Marriott duly appeared at Boyd's office and played him a composition of his own called 'Imaginary Love'. Boyd liked the song but loved Marriott's voice, and made arrangements with Decca Records for Marriott to record a single.

Recording under his own name, Marriott recorded a Kenny Lynch tune, 'Give Her My Regards', backed with his own 'Imaginary Love'. Again, the single vanished without trace, leaving Marriott with no recording deal, no acting work and no money. In order to eat and live, he had to take a day job, and wound up working on Saturdays at the J60 music shop in Manor Park.

It may seem odd that within the space of a year, Marriott was able to record and release two singles without having a contract to record more. However, it has always been common in the music business to have contracts with the notorious 'options' clause – the recording company will either record and release one single, with an option to record and release more singles and perhaps an LP if the initial single is a success. However, the 'option' is always on the record companies' side – if an artist is a success, s/he does not have the option to go to another company; equally, if the record is not a success, the artist does not have the option to stay with the company. However, the record company can drop the artist whenever they want, usually as soon as the first single isn't successful. This means that for the artist, life is precarious and is premised upon having early success.

It wasn't until the late Sixties and Seventies that artists became successful enough to wield any sort of power over the record companies. And even at that time that power was only wielded by the biggest-selling artists. New acts were still in the same precarious position and the financial nature of the music business – with recording and promotion costs being so high – meant that initial success was a necessity, if only to demonstrate to the company that it was possible for them to recoup their costs.

The Pioneers – featuring Ronnie Lane and Kenney Jones – were still pootling along without much success, playing when and where they could. Lane had made a few changes – he stopped being lead vocalist and shuffled the line-up, with various members joining and leaving. Both Lane and Jones had day-jobs working at Selmer's, the amplifier manufacturer, with Jones installing the amplifiers and Lane testing them.

'There was a little soundproof room with a Fender Stratocaster and a Fender bass, and I was supposed to test the amps,' said Lane. 'During that time I really learned to play, mainly during the lunch break. I used to really dig Booker T & The MGs and fancied myself as a bass player.'[7] However, Lane had a problem – he had persuaded his father to buy him a guitar on hire purchase, and he wasn't that keen on Ronnie dropping guitar and playing bass. Ronnie eventually talked him round.

So one Saturday in 1963 Ronnie Lane set off with Kenney Jones to the local music store in Manor Park to find a bass guitar. They recognised the shop assistant as a 'Face' from the local music scene.

'I recognised his face straight away,' said Jones. 'He was already playing regularly with other bands from the area. But that wasn't where I knew him from ... it was like I dreamt I knew him.'[8]

Lane and Marriott got on instantly, and were soon talking about then relatively unknown American rhythm and blues artists like Booker T and Bobby Bland. Marriott cemented their friendship by selling Lane a Harmony bass guitar at well below the asking price. Lane, in turn, invited Marriott to sit in with The Pioneers at their one regular gig, the Earl of Derby pub in Grange Road, Bermondsey, off Tower Bridge Road. It was to prove an eventful night.

'We started drinking whiskies,' said Lane. 'There was this false sense of bravado about how much the pair of us could put back and in the end we got totally pissed.'[9]

Marriott tried to take over the microphone, then began to perform Jerry Lee Lewis impersonations on the piano, hammering at it wildly until it fell apart. The band were fired from the gig and barred from the pub. The Pioneers were not best pleased with Lane, who had brought this apparent lunatic into their lives and had got them fired from their only regular music work.

Lane too had had enough. 'I said to Kenney, "D'you fancy coming with this geezer, because I'm going with him?"'[10]

Marriott, Lane and Jones's next move was to find themselves a keyboard player. That the burgeoning Small Faces chose to have a keyboard player at all reflected a change in the way that new British bands saw themselves in the early Sixties. The main influence on English groups in the late Fifties had been – after Elvis, of course – Buddy Holly, whose geeky look made unappealing Brits think that anyone could be a star; whose compact songs provided a good formula for writing; and whose band line-up of two guitars, bass and drums was the model to follow. It was from Holly that The Beatles took their lead.

However, with the influx to Britain of rhythm and blues records, most of which featured either organ or at least piano, British groups began to prominently feature a keyboard player. As the members of the Small Faces were all fans of Booker T & The MGs, it was not surprising that they would follow the Booker T model. Booker T & The MGs were the house band for Stax records, from the Southern United States, and while their own records were instrumental, they provided the backing for many Stax hits, as well as writing hits for artists such as Otis Redding and Sam and Dave. Their line-up was guitar, bass, Hammond organ and drums. It was this prototype that newer British acts looked to.

Their search for an organ player was quickly over. Marriott remembered a Hammond player who sometimes came into the J60 Music Shop, Jimmy Langwith. Langwith was another East Ender, born in April 1945, and he lived at home in the pub his parents Bill and Cis ran, the Ruskin Arms in Manor Park. Langwith had started playing guitar but had switched to piano, and he was also involved in acting in both film and television, though for all professional appearances he was known as Jimmy Winston. His keyboard skills were limited, and Marriott would teach him his parts, but – as is often the case when bands are starting up – Langwith had other, more estimable virtues: he had transport, a van paid for by his brother based, according to Kenney Jones, on a tenuous agreement that he would receive five per cent of their earnings for life; due to his parents' pub, he had somewhere to rehearse; and he showed commitment to the cause by immediately going to buy a Leslie speaker cabinet for his Hammond organ.

'The van was an old ex-police meatwagon,' remembered Jones. 'All the equipment was on H[ire] P[urchase] – whatever happened I always had to find two pounds ten a month for my drums.'[11]

After very few rehearsals, the band began to play live. Jones and Lane had been fired from their jobs at Selmer's, and Marriott was terminally unemployable, and some form of paid employment, preferably musical, was urgently required. 'We just used to travel up and down the M1 looking for gigs and then play for nothing,' remembered Jones. Marriott had previously made contact with Maurice King, manager of the Walker Brothers, and arranged rehearsal time at the Starlight Rooms in Paddington which King owned. King had expressed an interest in managing the group, an interest which waned when he saw them rehearse. The band withdrew to the Ruskin Arms, playing gigs whenever they could get them, in places like Sheffield where they played the Peter Stringfellow owned Mojo club where Joe Cocker was making his name.

'It was damn fantastic,' said Marriott, 'extremely wild and full of Mods.' And more importantly, they got paid. After much pestering, Jimmy Langwith's parents relented and allowed them to play the Ruskin Arms. In the audience was an agent who worked for the Leicester Square Cavern Club. He thought the band had something, and booked them for a one-off gig on a Saturday night.

The other major problem for any new group is a name. One of the girls who hung around with them came up with the answer – the band were not very tall and they were 'faces' (the Mod term of admiration for another Mod) and there you go – the Small Faces. Thus named, Ronnie Lane painted a poster advertising the gig featuring a Mod in a Parka (a large, usually green raincoat, bought from army surplus stores and worn by some Mods as a means of keeping their suits clean when riding on scooters) with 'Small Faces' written on the back. With The Who – a band who were rebranding themselves in order to catch the new trend – playing regularly at the Marquee in Wardour Street, the poster helped to pull in any marauding Mods in the West End. The gig sold out and the Small Faces were offered the next four Saturday nights.

According to Marriott, the Small Faces set-list was limited. 'We had about six numbers ... and we played two hours with that,' he remembered. 'But we actually did have a following, we couldn't believe it ourselves.'[12] Lane, too, was less than effusive about the early Small Faces shows, describing them as 'a chaotic lesson in bullshitting an audience ... But we had such a lot of front, Steve did, that we got away with it.'[13]

★

With the burgeoning Mod scene, and with the music business's obsession with finding a bandwagon and clinging on to it for dear life, it didn't take long for the industry to start sniffing around. Pete Meadon, one of London's top 'faces', who was managing The Who along with Kit Lambert, heard about this band who were packing in the crowds down the road from where his own charges were playing. Meadon went down to see them and was impressed enough with the Small Faces and their following to offer them a management deal. Unfortunately he was too late.

By 1961/62, Rod Stewart was beginning to pay attention to the rhythm and blues explosion that was accompanying the emerging Mod movement. While the Mods had taken over the Beatnik haunts in Soho, Stewart was now starting to insinuate himself with the new crowd. In 1963, an old school friend asked Stewart to join his band The Dimensions as singer and harmonica player. However, this didn't last as The Dimensions had acquired a new singer who came complete with a reliable source of gigs. Early in 1964, Stewart was making his way home from yet another night out and sitting on a platform on Twickenham Station entertaining himself by blowing his harmonica.

'I was going back to London as was John but we were on different platforms,' remembered Stewart. 'John was on the right platform because I was probably drunk.'[14]

Long John Baldry recalled the meeting as almost mythic. 'What seemed to be a pile of old coats and scarves etc. was playing this harmonica riff,' he remembered. 'I thought, "That sounds pretty good, sounds pretty authentic, sounds just like Howling Wolf." Then this nose appeared from the top of all these clothes.'[15] Baldry was impressed enough to offer Stewart a guest spot with the band he sang with, Cyril Davies's R&B All Stars. However, Davies collapsed and died in January 1964 aged 32. Baldry kept the band going as the Hoochie Coochie Men and Stewart was contracted as second vocalist with the group, on a wage of £35 per week. For Stewart – who was still living with his mother and father in Holloway – this was a small fortune, and certainly more money than he'd ever earned doing a 'proper' job.

It was with the Hoochie Coochie Men that Stewart began to learn to perform. Unlike Marriott, who'd had training as an actor and therefore knew many of the principles of stagecraft, Stewart was having to learn on the job.

'Long John Baldry taught me so much stagecraft,' remembered Stewart. 'The first thing he ever told me was, "Never stand at the microphone with your legs together – it doesn't make you look confident."'[16] Stewart stayed with the Hoochie Coochie Men for nine months, making his first trip to the recording studio to sing on a Baldry B-side, 'Up Above My Head'. Stewart's contribution to the recording wasn't credited. Stewart also took the chance to start a solo career when a Decca talent scout spotted him singing with Baldry's band. However, the eventual single – a cover of Sonny Boy Williamson's 'Good Morning Little Schoolgirl' – vanished when The Yardbirds released their version at the same time, despite Stewart's appearance on the hit TV show *Ready, Steady, Go!*

The Hoochie Coochie Men had trouble gaining that elusive hit single and split in 1964. For six months Stewart sang with the Soul Agents, a spectacularly unsuccessful Southampton-based group, but when Baldry offered him the chance to sing with his new group Steampacket, Stewart all but bit his hand off. Steampacket was a British R&B proto-supergroup, put together around Hammond organ star Brian Auger by former Rolling Stones manager and by then all-round R&B entrepreneur Giorgio Gomelsky. It featured the group that had been Brian Auger's Trinity – Auger, Rick Brown on bass and Micky Waller on drums along with Baldry, Stewart and Julie Driscoll, a Yardbirds fan initially recruited to give the group a glamour quotient. Guitarist Vic Briggs made up the numbers.

Steampacket started out on the club circuit, but eventually supported the Rolling Stones and the Walker Brothers on a month's tour which climaxed at the London Palladium. Their special draw was in providing an entire soul and R&B revue when they topped the bill. The sight of the seven band members crammed on to a small stage, the powerful sound made by Auger's Hammond almost overwhelming everything else, and with Stewart occasionally stepping forward to take his vocal lead, already kitted out with his classic Mod three-button suit, bouffant haircut and the latest, shuffling dance steps, seemingly defying the sweaty, booze and speed-fuelled mayhem around him, marked Stewart out as a future star. It also gained Steampacket large audiences all over the UK and regular appearances on *Ready, Steady, Go!*, ITV's premier music and youth culture show which was required viewing for all Mods.

Despite Steampacket's apparent success, two albums' worth of material recorded by them was not even released due to contractual wrangling. In the meantime, Stewart was continuing to pursue a solo career. He signed to EMI's Columbia label where he made two singles, 'The Day Will Come' and a cover of Sam Cooke's 'Shake'. Neither charted, but Stewart described the recording as 'a crossing of the water'.[17] The transition from blues to soul, though increasingly common among British R&B artists at the time, was a seminal turning point for Stewart. By the summer of 1966, with the Small Faces riding high in the charts, Steampacket were contracted to play in an extended residency in St Tropez. The available money meant that the group couldn't afford to keep all three singers (Baldry, Driscoll and Stewart) and Stewart departed. However, this may also have been due to the constant rows between Stewart, Baldry and Auger. Baldry didn't stay long with the depleted Steampacket, and the group fell apart – though Julie Driscoll remained – but they went on to have a hit as Julie Driscoll, Brian Auger & The Trinity with Bob Dylan's 'This Wheel's On Fire' in 1968.

Straight from Steampacket, Stewart fell neatly into Shotgun Express, a group being put together by Peter Green and Mick Fleetwood who would go on to form Fleetwood Mac. Though they received praise for their live performances, their only single, 'I Could

Feel The Whole World Turn Around', flopped and the band fell apart. His deal with EMI having fallen through, Stewart found himself at the end of 1966 with no band and no record deal. But the London music scene was – as ever – very small, and a talent like Stewart's hadn't gone unnoticed. And so, as is the way with these things, at the very end of 1966 in yet another part of London, a highly rated guitarist called Jeff Beck was looking to raise himself from the gloom of leaving the highly successful Yardbirds by putting his own band together. Conversations took place, steps were taken, and a certain Roderick Stewart was approached to become the band's singer.

Despite appearances to the contrary, The Birds were proving a great success, though not on a national stage. 'We were the biggest thing since sliced bread in Salisbury,' claimed Ron Wood. 'We used to get mobbed, with girls actually wanting a piece of your hair – they'd actually rip it out or rip your clothes.' Though this side of being in a band seemed glamorous, there was a downside to touring. Bands would be packed into an old van, usually unheated, along with all their equipment which could come crashing down on them at any time. Hours were spent on Britain's nascent motorway system just sitting and waiting. The cramped conditions in the back of the van meant that there was little room to manoeuvre, and little to do except play cards and wait for a stop at a roadside café where bacon sandwiches and mugs of tea were all that was on offer.

The van very quickly took on the atmosphere of a teenage boy's bedroom, reeking of sweat, stale beer and cigarettes, with old newspapers and magazines littering the floor. The boredom was endemic, the only release being the gig. The physical constriction usually resulted in band members either fighting with each other or bonding, and usually both. But somehow, there were always compensations.

'We were also pretty big in the West Country, up in Derby, Altrincham in Cheshire,' remembered Wood. 'We were fucking big in Cheshire!'[18]

However, local success meant nothing if they couldn't get a record released or any national coverage. To this end, Leo de Klerk – the band's manager and the owner of a string of nightclubs – paid for the band to record an acetate vinyl record of 'You're On My Mind', a Ronnie Wood song. Acetates were made by recording directly from the master tape on to cheap vinyl which disintegrated a little more each time it was played. However, that first acetate meant that The Birds had actually recorded something properly, and had the plastic to prove it. De Klerk hawked the acetate around record and TV companies and managed to secure the band a spot on *Ready, Steady, Go!* in their weekly 'Battle of the Bands'.

The first prize was £1000 worth of instruments and equipment, and in June 1964 the band dutifully trooped off to the Associated-Rediffusion Television Studios in Wembley to take what they thought would be their big break. Things didn't go according to plan, however, and The Birds finished fifth out of the six competing acts. The flaw in The Birds' plan was obvious: though playing raw, highly charged R&B made them an attractive draw on the live circuit (high-powered R&B suiting a club atmosphere, filled with young Mods on amphetamines looking for something to dance to), the broader, national market expected a less threatening form. Even the Rolling Stones realised this and had tamed their wilder side (musically) for public consumption. However The Birds were beginning to get some attention – in August 1964 they appeared on the BBC's *ABC of Britain* and continued to play their (seemingly endless) club dates. By October they had secured a residency at the prestigious 100 Club in London's Oxford Street.

Along with their growing live reputation, the acetate had also been working its little plastic socks off – Decca Records' Dick Rowe heard the recording and passed The Birds on to his assistant Franklin Boyd who signed them. He put The Birds into Decca's studios in October where they re-recorded 'You're On My Mind'. However, the experience was not all good for the band, who were not used to the confines and discipline required to record. The release of the record – a huge moment in any young band's life – was another anti-climax, and the record only sold well in places that already loved The Birds' live act.

Unfortunately, having a hit in West Drayton, Salisbury and Cheshire doesn't really put a band on the map as much as it puts a map on the band. But at least The Birds had a record released, and once a band has a record released, then they are a proper band, not just playing aimless gigs but playing to support a product, something the music industry takes very seriously as record companies make no money from gigs. In addition, it meant that other musicians would take them seriously. The record release also meant that BBC Radio would begin to take them seriously, offering them two auditions for recording spots. Neither were successful.

In early 1965 The Birds recorded their second single for Decca, released in April of that year. As is often the case with bands trying to have a hit – any kind of a hit – it was a cover, in this case of a Holland/Dozier/Holland song, 'Leaving Here'. Again, the record failed to impress upon the charts, though the promotional round for the record did gain the band a spot on ITV's *Thank Your Lucky Stars* where they were lowered to the stage on wires and pulled off in the same manner. It was not the most dignified appearance for a band who took themselves seriously as musicians. And, more importantly, it did nothing to break them nationally.

A bigger problem was about to hit The Birds. As part of the folk breakthrough in America and tied explicitly to the 'British Invasion' of the US in 1964/65, a new group had emerged from America's West Coast – The Byrds. They had released a Beatle-ified version of Bob Dylan's 'Mr Tambourine Man' into Britain and were coming over to tour in support of it. The Birds' first inkling came when their fans complained that rather than receiving 'Leaving Here', they instead got the 12-string Rickenbacker-saturated, laid-back jangle of 'Mr Tambourine Man'. The Byrds' publicity machine had gone into overdrive with their arrival, and the publicity adversely affected The Birds' progress.

October 1965 saw the British Birds back in the studio for Decca. The result, the single 'No Good Without You Baby' – another cover version – was released to no acclaim whatsoever and duly flopped. There was never a shortage of gigs, as good live acts could still make money, especially for promoters and club owners. But if a band wanted to make serious progress, they needed a chart hit. Who wants to sit in the back of a van for the rest of their lives, stopping only to churn out the same old tunes? Certainly not Ronnie Wood.

Back in the studio for Decca again in March 1966, the band struggling with each other and their manager over money squabbles, they recorded a final tune for Decca called 'What Hit Me'. Though conceived as a single it came to nothing, not even released by Decca, who unceremoniously dropped them. The group continued to gig, and the problems over money with de Klerk grew. The band were now being courted by new management, and despite de Klerk getting them a new record deal with Robert Stigwood's Reaction label, the band went with the new managers. Unfortunately the management were the Richardson brothers, Charlie and Eddie, who were to South-East London what the Krays were to the rest of London. The group were suddenly in hock to proper, serious, grown-up gangsters.

The Birds started recording for Reaction in June 1966, but despite the group being happy with the songs, Stigwood was not and kept them in and out of the studio recording and re-recording. As it happened, Stigwood's attention was elsewhere as he was simultaneously grooming Cream, the 'supergroup' featuring Eric Clapton, Jack Bruce and Ginger Baker. Stigwood renamed the group 'Birds Birds' and tried to market them as a gangster group including an ill-advised photo session with the group dressed in Thirties Chicago period costumes. The group were not happy. Eventually, in September 1966, Reaction released a 'Birds Birds' single, 'Say Those Magic Words'. It went nowhere. It became obvious that Reaction in general, and Stigwood in particular, had no real interest in the group, not least because Stigwood was now trying to get a finger in Brian Epstein's NEMS pie, with The Beatles as his ultimate – and in the end fruitless – goal. As the group continued to argue among themselves, the Richardsons' reputation as gangsters grew and, despite recording more tracks for Reaction, by the end of 1966 The Birds were in grave trouble.

Elsewhere in London, Jeff Beck, free of the Yardbirds, was trying to set up his own band. He already had a singer, one Rod Stewart. Ron Wood, who knew Beck of old, gave Beck a call and asked him for a job. The Birds were gibleted, basted and roasted.

# THREE

# THE STONEDEST MEN IN TOWN

In the British music business, Don Arden was generally considered to be hard. Not hard in the sense that he was a difficult person to deal with (though this was also true), but in the sense that it was thought that he could – and would – beat the crap out of anyone who crossed him. A large man, gruff but well spoken, Arden had dropped out of school aged thirteen in order to pursue a career in showbusiness and spent the subsequent years honing that career as a stand-up comic and singer. By the age of sixteen he was entertaining troops before being conscripted himself. When the Second World War ended he made his way back into vaudeville, spending the Fifties traipsing the boards and adding Master of Ceremonies to his repertoire. His lack of major success – due in no small way to his backstage aggression – led him to branch out into promoting shows.

Arden had compered Gene Vincent's 1959 British tour, and when Vincent decided to move to the UK, Arden became his manager. Vincent was something of a liability, his own vicious temper when allied with alcohol well known, and Arden's relationship with him became increasingly fraught. By 1965, the pair had split, though by this time Arden was a successful promoter, involved with a number of groups including The Animals, the Move and the Nashville Teens. Arden also employed Peter Grant, later to become Led Zeppelin's manager and a disciple of Arden's reputed policy of proffering violence first and questions later.

The promotion business was suffering something of a slump, however, as Arden's policy of promoting American rock 'n' rollers was proving increasingly unpopular following the rise of The Beatles, Gerry & The Pacemakers and other beat groups which were springing up everywhere. American rock 'n' rollers were no longer required – indeed, why would they be, when Britain was producing music that was as successful in America as it was in the UK? Arden needed a British group who would become a success and make his name. It was at this point that the Small Faces came to his attention.

The Small Faces' needs were much more basic. 'We thought, "We'll go with whoever offers the most dough,"' remembered Marriott.[1] Arden came to see the group and was impressed enough by them to invite them to his office which was above John Stephen's clothes shop in Carnaby Street. This was a significant plus-point for the clothes-mad Small Faces. To add a little spice to the meeting, on the night in question Marriott and Lane were themselves a sight to behold, having been severely beaten up the night before as a result of a Mod turf war in which they had no part (other than the beating).

Though they were afraid that their battered appearance might put Arden off, he was instead impressed by their apparent 'hardness' allied to their East End charm. They signed to Contemporary Music, Arden's company, in June 1965. The deal they signed with Arden was ambiguous at best.

'Don said, "You can have a straight wage or a percentage deal,"' remembered Kenney Jones. 'We went outside in a huddle and said, "We ain't stupid, we want a wage and a percentage." We went back in and told him ... he agreed to give us twenty pounds a week, plus a percentage of the records and a shopping account in every clothes shop in Carnaby Street.'[2]

While twenty pounds a week was a lot of money to the four young men, the clothing accounts were a licence for the clothes shops to print money. 'Any money we got ... went on clothes,' said Marriott.[3] The following year it was estimated that the Small Faces spent some £12,000 on clothes (at 1966 prices).

'We were like old women at a jumble sale,' remembered Lane. 'Half the stuff we got we never even wore.'[4] 'Because you had an account in every single shop,' remembered Jones, 'and you had no money in your pocket, you'd go in and go, "I'll have that shirt, that jacket, no, I'll have two of them shirts, no, I'll have one in every colour."'[5]

Having sorted the boys out, Arden immediately commissioned Ian Samwell to write them a hit. Samwell was well known in music industry circles, having written 'Move It', Cliff Richard's initial Top Ten hit. Samwell, along with associate Brian Potter, took the riff from Solomon Burke's 'Everybody Needs Someone To Love' and turned it into 'What'cha Gonna Do About It', a solid block of British rhythm and blues. 'We had a couple of meetings with Samwell,' remembered Kenney Jones. 'We went into IBC Studios with him, and Glyn Johns was the engineer.'[6] Glyn Johns, who went on to become a major figure in the development of British rock groups and of the Small Faces and Faces in particular, had had an ambiguous entry into the music business. 'I had no knowledge of recording or interest in it. I was in a band, tinkered around like most teenagers. Somebody knew somebody who knew somebody who managed a recording studio, IBC studios in Portland Place, and I got an interview and that was it,' recalled Johns.[7]

The Small Faces appear not to have been too worried about being forced to record someone else's song. 'We loved "What'cha Gonna Do About It",' remembered Marriott.[8] 'What'cha Gonna Do About It' is R&B in the great tradition of all garage music, easy to play – built on three basic guitar chords – with plenty of room for vocal and instrumental riffing. It was to become a mainstay of young British bands, a song that practically anyone could play, but a song that was always identified with the Small Faces.

While the Small Faces were figuring their way through the recording process, Don Arden was busy setting up a distribution deal with Decca Records which saw the band release 'What'cha Gonna Do About It' in August 1965. The single rose to reach Number 14 in the British charts, a more than respectable performance for a debut single. Though Decca did little to market the record, appearances on BBC TV's *Crackerjack*, followed by an appearance on *Ready, Steady, Go!*, helped the single up the charts. But there was more to the hit-making process than immediately met the eye.

Don Arden felt that there was nothing wrong with giving the record a bit of a helping hand. And for Arden, the helping hand came in the form of a certain amount of chart manipulation. Arden would pay two individuals to boost sales of Contemporary Music artists' records from record shops. In addition, he would pay other figures associated with the various pop charts to boost the chart position of various records. And, finally, he paid other figures at Radio Caroline (then the top pirate radio station in the UK and the most popular pop station, given that BBC Radio 1 was two years away from being launched) to boost plays of the records.

'I knew that for certain sums, any record I was associated with could be elevated to the charts,' remembered Arden. 'I paid out anything from £150 to £500 a week to people who manipulated the charts and who in turn shared the cash with people organising other charts so as to ensure they tallied ... Of course, the Small Faces had no idea what went on.'[9]

That the Small Faces weren't aware of the scam is no surprise. Apart from the fact that they were new to the business side of pop music, it wasn't particularly in their manager's interest that the band should know what was going on. A single, simple off-hand comment to a journalist could have blown the whole thing wide open. And though Arden's involvement with the chart-riggers lasted two years, the practice itself – in one form or another – didn't begin with him, and (happily for all concerned – except, perhaps, the record-buying public) continued throughout the decades that followed.

Arden's view of showbusiness was that despite his liking for somewhat shady practices, acts had to work for their success. To this end, the Small Faces were sent out on the road to play an incessant run of one-nighters. Groups in the Sixties played in every town and in every type of venue. As late as 1964/65, even a major group such as The Beatles would play venues such as Lewisham Odeon, a cinema in South London.[10] Despite the current notion of the longevity of artists from the Sixties, the vast majority of acts fell foul of the 'here today, gone tomorrow' nature of showbusiness. Pop music's transition from 'throwaway' music to a culturally accepted art-form was still in midprocess, and pop acts were as likely to be seen as much as a novelty act as anything else. Managers – and Arden was no exception – thought that pop acts had to be milked for all they were worth as quickly as possible.

'If I've ever exploited anybody it's for their own benefit,' said Arden at the time. 'It's because they want to be exploited. I never exploit anybody who doesn't want to be exploited. There's no point to it. You could never be successful in exploiting an artist or a group of artists who don't want to be exploited.'[11] But as the Small Faces' debut single went up the charts, the media interest and the screaming fans increased. The model for fan behaviour had been set by the screaming girls at Beatles concerts in the early Sixties, and the Small Faces' fans were no different. And, given their relatively easy path to fame, it is no surprise that the adoration went to the Small Faces' heads.

'At first it was great for your ego,' said Jones. 'For about six months I had a big head, we all did for a while. But we did get fed up with it.'[12] Ronnie Lane agreed. 'It was exciting, man. There were chicks around and I was a pop star.'[13] But, as bands before them had found, there was a downside. 'It was quite violent,' Lane recalled. 'They really wanted to get hold of you.'[14]

Jones, too, began to see the other face of pop stardom. 'We tried to play the best we could live and ignore the screams,' he remembered. 'We really enjoyed playing with each other and sometimes the screams and the girls jumping on stage was a real drag.'[15]

Their early success and endless gigging notwithstanding, the band weren't happy as a unit. Organ-player Jimmy Winston, originally conscripted because of his access to an organ, a rehearsal space and transport, wasn't gelling with the other Small Faces. His limited playing ability along with his sometimes acerbic outbursts were starting to wear the others down.

'Jimmy went off his rocker every now and then,' remembered Marriott.[16] Ronnie Lane concurred. 'He was a bighead ... he had no talent as such,' Lane said later.[17]

Kenney Jones felt the same. 'He was only learning and he was wholeheartedly into it, but he was useless.'[18] But, as ever, there was more to it than a lack of playing ability. '[He was] a complete distraction from Steve,' remembered Jones. 'All those guitar poses and he was taller. It just wasn't happening.'[19]

Marriott, as frontman of the group, felt Winston's posturing the most. 'We did *Thank Your Lucky Stars* with "What'cha Gonna Do About It",' remembered Marriott. 'It came to that guitar part which I was proud of because it was my first solo on record, and I'd go and do it and suddenly Jimmy would go apeshit in the corner, waving and jumping about so the cameras would be on him.'[20]

There was a band meeting with manager Arden and steps were taken. 'We were a bit unkind to him,' remembered Jones. 'No-one would talk to him and he couldn't understand why he wasn't in the group any more. He came along to the gig and we had a new organist.'[21] The gig was at the Lyceum Ballroom in the Strand in London; the new organist was Ian McLagan.

Ian McLagan was born on 12 May 1945 in Hounslow, West London, to Alec and Susan. Obsessed with music from an early age due to listening to the scratchy sounds of early rock 'n' roll which came from his older brother Mike's Dansette record player, he decided that he had to have a guitar. When the skiffle craze hit Britain in 1956/57, McLagan tried to join in, forming his own band with his friends, but his limited ability on guitar quickly became apparent. Though largely self-taught, he had already had some piano lessons and so wasn't afraid of a keyboard. Playing rhythm and blues piano – at a basic level – isn't too difficult, but it was only when McLagan heard Booker T & The MGs for the first time that he knew what instrument he really wanted to play: the Hammond organ.

When McLagan left school he enrolled at Twickenham Art School, where he formed a new band, The Muleskinners. He also bought himself a proper keyboard, 'an annoying Hohner Cembalet electric piano. I was starting to get somewhere on the piano,' remembered McLagan, 'and anyway, there weren't many piano players in bands, and I thought there'd be less competition.'[22]

McLagan started hustling gigs for The Muleskinners and managed to get himself the job of Social Director of the Student Union, in charge of booking groups for end-of-term dances. It was in this position that he managed to book the Rolling Stones and book his own band as the opening act. McLagan was a regular at the blues nights at Georgio Gomelsky's Crawdaddy Club and the blues club at Eel Pie Island. Eventually McLagan managed to get – through sheer persistence – a support slot on a Rolling Stones tour. Regular club gigs followed, and McLagan switched from his 'annoying' electric piano to a Hammond L100 which, despite its phenomenal sound, had its own drawbacks – it was very, very heavy, making it difficult to carry from house to van to gig and back again.

The Muleskinners also got the chance to back authentic blues players such as Howlin' Wolf and Sonny Boy Williamson. As bizarre as it sounds now, these bluesmen weren't allowed to bring their own backing musicians with them when they toured Britain due to agreements drawn up between the American and British Musicians' Unions. It seemed that the unions were terrified that Howlin' Wolf performing with his own group would put good, solid British musicians out of work. The obvious stupidity of the policy aside, what it did do was to give young, hungry British players the chance to play with some of the greatest bluesmen and women from the USA. They always jumped at the chance.

McLagan was eventually asked to join a band called Boz & The Boz People. McLagan was sure that he wanted to make a go of it as a musician, and he was unconvinced that the other Muleskinners were so inclined, especially as they were already planning their post-college careers. McLagan therefore jumped ship and joined Boz and the gang, where he learned to smoke dope and found out about the rigours of constant touring.

As well as their own gigs, Boz played back-up to Kenny Lynch and even opened on the ill-fated Byrds tour of 1965. But eventually there were too many bad gigs and broken-down vans for McLagan, who quit the group one Saturday night on the access ramp to the M1 in North London. He was unemployed for less than forty-eight hours. On the Monday morning he got a call from Don Arden asking him to come for an interview, but not saying for what position. McLagan knew about the Small Faces and liked them – he'd seen them on TV – and he also knew that Arden managed them, but he had no idea what was awaiting him.

'There were eight by ten [pictures] of the artists he managed on the wall,' recalled McLagan. 'The Animals, the Nashville Teens, Small Faces and the Clayton Squares ... I thought it had to be the Clayton Squares.'[23]

When McLagan finally got to see Arden, having been kept waiting all day, Arden asked him one question, 'What are you earning at the moment?' McLagan was generous in his self-assessment. 'With a straight face I said, "Twenty pounds",' says McLagan. Arden told him he was on a month's probation at thirty pounds a week, with an even split with 'the lads' if all went well. 'Which lads?' asked McLagan. 'The Small Faces, of course,' replied Arden.[24]

Once introduced, McLagan fitted instantly into the Small Faces. 'I couldn't believe it,' recalled Marriott. 'Here's a guy, standing right in front of us, who was already one of the boys. The chemistry between us was perfect, although he was a bit shy at the time. His humour was perfect, his charisma was perfect – all I could do was hug him, because it was just like he was the missing part.'[25]

Though not a Mod at the time, it took little time to get McLagan appropriately togged out using the clothing accounts in the shops in Carnaby Street. And then McLagan was ready for his first appearance with the Small Faces at the Lyceum Ballroom in London. Lack of rehearsal was no problem for McLagan, who was merely required to mime to the Small Faces' second single, 'I Got Mine'.

The single had been recorded with Jimmy Winston and was released in November 1965. Written by Marriott and Lane, the single was performed by the Small Faces in a film, *Dateline Diamonds*, which was due to be released at the same time as the single, thereby helping to promote the single (and the film). Unfortunately, film-making being what it is, due to editing problems the film wasn't released until April 1966, long after the single had vanished from the charts. Decca took out a half-page advert in the *NME* to try and promote the record, and it received good reviews in the press.

'The reviews for that single were incredible,' said Marriott, 'saying the Small Faces are here to last, they've proved ... how talented they are.'[26] However, critical acclaim isn't everything, and despite extensive live performances and increasing TV appearances (including *Ready, Steady, Go!*), the single failed to chart.

Though December saw the Small Faces come sixth in the *NME*'s Annual Popularity Poll – no mean feat for a band which hadn't existed eight months previously – the Small Faces clearly had a problem. Popularity polls and good reviews were no substitute for record sales, and Don Arden wasn't prepared to risk another Marriott/Lane song as a single. He asked another professional songwriting team, Kenny Lynch and Mort Schuman, to come up with a hit for the Small Faces. They came back with a song called 'Sha La La La Lee'. Schuman sat at a piano and played the song to the group, who weren't exactly happy with the tune. It sounded like, 'a good little Saturday night dance record', according to Ronnie Lane,[27] but Lynch's production of the record was less to their liking.

'He [Lynch] wrote it and produced it and ended up bleedin' singing on it,' recalled Marriott. 'That's all he was there for, to sell his songs.'[28]

Kenney Jones remembered that it took the group four hours to record the song's introduction correctly. 'I thought "Sha La La La Lee" was a bit of an iffy number,' Jones said later. 'It was Don Arden's thing really. He said we couldn't afford another flop so we went with Kenny Lynch.'[29]

Ronnie Lane was even more damning. 'It wasn't what we were really good at, which was playing Black R&B,' he said. 'I think the rot began to set in around that time.'[30]

On Boxing Day, 1965, before the single's release, it was decided that the Small Faces should live together in a house paid for by Arden. However the house, in Westmoreland Terrace in Pimlico, was rarely occupied by the Small Faces. Kenney Jones never occupied it at all, preferring to stay with his parents in Stepney.

'I couldn't stand the late nights,' recalled Jones. 'I would get to Pimlico in the mornings in time to join in whatever was happening. Usually it was nothing and a complete waste of time because none of the others would get up until four or sometimes six in the evening.'[31] Eclectically furnished from random, local furniture shops, the house boasted an orange, revolving chair in the shape of an egg, an oak stereo unit and Mexican-style rugs and the permanent odour of mara-juana among other odds and ends.

'We were the stonedest men in town,' remembered McLagan. 'We'd get stoned, go to sleep stoned, wake up stoned.'[32] Along with the house came a series of housekeepers and a chauffeur-driven Jaguar Mk 10. The house did attract some famous guests – 'mentals like Marianne Faithfull', remembered Marriott[33] – but their excessive touring commit-ments meant that they were more usually in the back of a van or car somewhere on a motorway or off in Europe. The only real sign of their residency was the gaggle of fans who would hang around outside until they were moved on to the end of the street by irate neighbours, though the times they were at home were not uneventful.

'One night, sitting at home, and the living room door opens,' remembered McLagan, 'and it's a policeman. He says, "Do you want to lose all this?" and I'm holding a joint in my hands ... and I said, "No," and he says, "Well, if you leave the van door open and the front door open they're gonna steal your equipment." "Right, thanks,"' replied Ronnie Lane, just pleased not to be arrested.[34]

The failure of 'I Got Mine' did little to stop the Small Faces becoming the new pin-up boys of British pop. Appealing more to the younger siblings of those who were into the Stones and The Beatles, the audiences at their performances became increasingly hysterical. At the end of January 1966, Decca released 'Sha La La La Lee' and once more Arden's instinct to find (and pay for) a hit for a group paid off. The single reached Number 3 in the charts, leading to further appearances on TV, radio, even more gigs, and endless pictures of them in teenage girls' magazines including a bizarre appearance in their own comic strip in *Valentine*. Compared to their earlier adulation, the success of 'Sha La La La Lee' saw things really get out of hand.

'We became pop stars, which we never really wanted to be,' said Marriott. 'Not if you had integrity at all and smoked a little hash. To see all these young girls getting hurt in a crush and not being able to hear ourselves sing or play, we just wanted to go home.'[35]

And just when they thought it couldn't, it got worse. 'When they stopped screaming and we could hear ourselves play,' remembered Ronnie Lane, 'we weren't that good.'[36] Des Sadlier also remembered that the Small Faces changed after 'Sha La La La Lee'.

'We all used to love the Small Faces, 'cos they were like us,' he recalled. 'But that "Sha La La La" thing came out, and it was a good record, but they turned into a teeny-bop thing. It wasn't their fault, but suddenly they were a girl thing, and it felt as though they'd been stolen from us.' But the Small Faces were still the British band of choice for discerning Mods, despite the commercial success of the other pretenders to the Mod throne, The Who.

'I liked the Small Faces' style,' recalls Dick Hebdige. 'After "Sha-La-La-La-Lee", it was suddenly all over the place. I tried to get a barber in Shepherds Bush to give me a Small Faces haircut, but he did the bog-standard barber's massacre that tended to be the order of the day unless you knew where to go or threatened the stylist with physical violence. I remember backcombing round a centre parting and sneaking a few squirts of my mum's hair lacquer but it never looked right. I in turn massacred "Sha-La-La-La-Lee" a number of times while vocalising for my band, "Cacophony". The Small Faces were definitely a Mod band though. None of the "pop" bands (including, say, The Action and even The Who) ever really competed with black American or Jamaican acts like Marvin Gaye, Otis Redding, Martha & The Vandellas, Sonny Boy Williamson, Prince Buster et al, either for me or the guys I looked up to. There was a hint of today's "toy boy" bands about them all, and it was difficult to get as worked up as I had a few years earlier by bands like the Pretty Things, the Downliner Sect and the early Rolling Stones by a risible outfit like the aptly named "Dave Dee, Dozy, Beaky, Mick and Titch".'

'The Small Faces were Mods,' recalled Jonno Pavitt, a South-East London Mod. 'The Who weren't Mods. They certainly looked like them. But they didn't behave like them. And The Who always seemed to be in it to be rock stars. The Small Faces always seemed to be in the business 'cos they was just having as good a laugh as we all wished we could have. And being from London was never a bad thing. Everyone else wasn't from London. The Who were from London but the wrong parts of London. And when you did start listening to the Small Faces they were just so damn hip. They used lyrics that no-one else was using, I suppose. And then they stopped, just at the right time. And you can't really say that about The Who, can you?'

Pavitt puts the Small Faces' success with the Mod audience down to their sense of style and their lack of pretence. 'There are no ugly "Faces",' he says. 'There's also the "David Watts, he is the captain of our team" stuff. Every young man wants to look good and will base himself on looking like another young man. And it's never going to be the ugly guy. So there's got to be a certain amount of good looks about it. And they were called the Small Faces 'cos they were four guys who could all have been "faces" if they weren't already. So they already had the good looks and charm, and never underestimate a small role model for a small fella – there's a lot of us out here.'

★

The success of 'Sha La La La Lee' meant that the Small Faces needed to find yet another hit record to follow it up. Again Arden was prepared to let Marriott and Lane offer a song, and again their offer was accepted. 'Hey, Girl,' a cross between the R&B they loved and the simple pop of 'Sha La La La Lee', was recorded along with their debut LP, with Glyn Johns engineering. Rather than employing the more advanced recording techniques which were being utilised in 1965 and 1966 elsewhere in London (not least at EMI's Abbey Road Studios where The Beatles were re-inventing the process of making records), the Small Faces recorded more or less as 'live'. The album was consequently a reflection of the band's live performances, and was fairly rushed for a mid-Sixties recording, the object being to get an LP in the shops to capitalise on the Small Faces' popularity. And there was no attempt to make a coherent LP, another trend in the mid-Sixties.

'We weren't worried about albums,' remembered Marriott. 'In those days, albums were done in three days, as was the first one. We wrote about ninety per cent of that album without a thought for how commercial it was going to be. It was all singles, singles, singles.'[37]

Kenney Jones remembered the process of recording with some fondness. 'That was a very natural album,' he said. 'We weren't slick musicians but we were very inventive. It's got a great feel to it and it's a shame that as we progressed and became better musicians, we lost the riskiness that was so evident on that album. We just didn't care. Like Steve said it was just crash, bang, wallop.'[38]

But the recording process was also exciting for the young musicians after months of being unable to hear themselves play live because of screaming fans. 'We were more excited about hearing ourselves back, hearing what we sounded like,' Jones recalled. 'The studio was a welcome relief. We could jam together and we were a band. When we went out on the road, we could only play for twenty minutes but in the studio we could jam and from that came songs.'[39]

Glyn Johns' memories of the album are slightly less fond. 'Marriott had more energy and he was more blinkered. He was determined to do what he wanted to do with his music. He may well have been influenced by Booker T but he took that, like a little terrier, and hurled it around the room a few times. Marriott was a bolshy little bugger. I never really liked him very much. I got on all right with him, but he was cocky. He was obviously very insecure and he had a huge ego but he wouldn't have been the artist he was without it. Ronnie was a lot less aggressive. He was a milder individual although … he had an unpleasant side to him but Ronnie and Kenney were the two I got close to. The only time I spent with Marriott was when I was working. I never hung out with him.'[40] But for the fans, Marriott was a hero.

'In the early years, Marriott just looked good,' recalled Jonno Pavitt. 'If you look at him and his voice and you look at anyone else at the time … I don't think anybody else actually looked as though they were doing it for real. And then when you did go and see him he had exactly the same voice, he could play a guitar, and he had absolutely no pretension when he was up there. There was no leaping about, he was sweating 'cos he was playing, he wasn't sweating 'cos he was "performing". You got the feeling that if he was doing it in his bedroom with a tennis racquet he'd be exactly the same way. Ronnie Lane was exactly the same.'

The twelve songs on the LP featured seven originals, three songs written by Kenny Lynch and partners, Samwell/Potter's 'What'cha Gonna Do About It' and a cover of Sam Cooke's 'Shake' which opened the album. What the LP didn't feature was the single 'Hey Girl' which was released on the same day. As bizarre as it sounds today, this was a common marketing strategy in the Sixties. Albums were expensive to buy, and single sales significantly outstripped sales of albums. Until The Beatles began to take the LP seriously as a form in itself, albums were seen by the music business as a way of cashing in on successful singles. It was not uncommon for a group to release more than one LP in any given year – from 1963 until 1966 The Beatles released two LPs a year, plus at least four singles which usually didn't feature on the LPs, a prodigious output matched (and outstripped) only by the Beach Boys before their 1965 release *Pet Sounds*. The pressure to produce singles (even for inclusion on an LP) was wearing for the Small Faces who had never thought of themselves as a 'pop' group as such.

'We had all these big hit successful singles … that we had to play live,' remembered Jones. 'As we only played for about twenty minutes they were using up an entire set and this started to interfere with what we really wanted to play, which was more of the album-orientated stuff, and this was getting confined to rehearsals. It would really piss us off when we went to see bands we considered rock or blues bands – people like Georgie Fame, The Yardbirds – because that was how we saw ourselves. Not a pop band.'[41]

Released on 6 May 1966, the album – imaginatively titled *Small Faces* – was something of a critical and commercial success. It reached Number 3 in the LP charts, and was acknowledged as one of the more exciting releases of the year. However, there was no respite for the Small Faces and they were back out on the road, enduring a heavy schedule of live performances and TV and radio appearances until, in June 1966, Marriott collapsed from low blood pressure and was ordered to rest. At the same time Glyn Johns, worried by Ronnie Lane's failing appearance, ordered Lane to stay at Johns' flat until he recovered. But before long the gruelling schedule recommenced, this time augmented with recording sessions for a second LP.

As is often the case with budding songwriters, critical and commercial success – and the accompanying pressure to repeat that success – forced Marriott and Lane to greater heights. While in a recording session for the new album, Don Arden showed up looking to hear the track that would be their next single. Both Lane and

Marriott were working out songs that they considered to be suitable, but Arden was less than impressed.

'Plonk [Ronnie Lane] said, "Play him that tune you were working out,"' remembered Marriott. 'Don was knocked out and gave us two bits of paper and we wrote the lyrics in half an hour ... this song wasn't even on the agenda.'[42] The song was 'All Or Nothing' and was to go on to be their only Number 1 single. '"All Or Nothing" was getting us to where we wanted to be musically,' said Jones later. 'It wasn't as poppy but it was still commercial.'[43]

In July the Small Faces had finished eighth in the NME popularity poll. On 5 August, 'All Or Nothing' was released. The single climbed steadily until it reached the Number 1 spot in September, apparently tying for first place with The Beatles' 'Yellow Submarine'. For the Small Faces it was an enormous achievement, and a major victory for the four working-class kids from East London.

★

But the future of the Small Faces – and of the British music business in general – was presaged more by one event that occurred on the day of the release of 'All Or Nothing' and another that occurred twenty-four days later: 5 August saw the release of The Beatles' LP Revolver and 29 August saw The Beatles play their final gig at Candlestick Park, San Francisco.

Revolver was an album unlike any other – except for one: the Beach Boys' Pet Sounds. Studio technology and recording techniques had advanced dramatically in the years between 1964 and 1966. Artists like The Beatles and Brian Wilson of the Beach Boys had changed the way that they approached the making of an album so that it wasn't so much a collection of songs, but a musical form in itself, to be approached as a whole. This meant extended periods in the recording studio, trying out new ideas and sounds and approaches to songwriting. These were artists demanding to be taken seriously not just as pop stars, or artistes in the showbusiness sense, but as artists in the cultural sense. That The Beatles stopped touring (as Brian Wilson had done some time before, not least because his intake of drugs had made him too paranoid to get on an aeroplane) just added to this demand.

No longer were pop groups making silly little pop songs for silly teenage girls, they were writing serious music for serious people. *Revolver*, from its intricate cover (all the better to look at when stoned) to its musical arrangements that were sometimes sparse ('Taxman'), sometimes dynamic ('Got To Get You Into My Life'), sometimes psychedelic ('Tomorrow Never Knows', the album's cataclysmic final track), was talking to a new generation of artists and audience.

And, charting these developments from the marijuana haze of their house in Westmoreland Terrace, the Small Faces were acutely aware that they were – for the moment – outside of that loop.

# FOUR

# THE INDUSTRY OF HUMAN HAPPINESS

The summer of 1966 was memorable in London for more than just music. On a rare, endlessly sunny day in June, the England football team won the World Cup, beating West Germany 4–2 in the final at Wembley. And – to make it even better – the footballers, Bobby Moore, Geoff Hurst et al., looked and acted like pop stars. Suddenly the whole world was looking at London and everyone wanted to take credit – Prime Minister Harold Wilson was moved to say of England's victory that 'We only win the World Cup under a Labour government.'

Not only did London produce the best music, the best fashion and the best magazines in the world – now, along with Glasgow

Celtic's 2–1 victory over Inter Milan in the European Cup Final in Lisbon the following May, Britain had the best sportsmen as well. As a legacy of the welfare state which had given young people an education and the time to develop their art, the whole of Britain now seemed to be the centre of a global cultural revolution.

★

Following the success of their LP and single, the adulation facing the Small Faces was ratcheted up a few more notches. The gigs became even more frequent, the screaming louder, and the boys in the band were beginning to ask questions about their wages.

'We were playing every night of the week and we were still only getting £20 a week,' remembered Jones. 'So we complained and he gave us £60 a week. We were doing things like double gigs where we'd earn £600, sometimes a grand, which was an awful lot of money in those days.'[1] As is always the case, the music business in 1966 was a very small place and word quickly spread that the Small Faces were increasingly unhappy with their management. Other management companies began to sniff around, and Don Arden, feeling that his reputation might be impugned (and that he might actually lose the quite profitable Small Faces) took matters in hand. When an employee of Robert Stigwood's management company made a tentative approach to the Small Faces, Don Arden took immediate action.

'I had to stop these overtures – and quickly,' remembered Arden. 'I contacted two well-muscled friends and hired two more equally huge toughs. And we went along to nail this impresario to his chair with fright. There was a large ornate ashtray on his desk. I picked it up and smashed it down with such force that the desk cracked – giving a good impression of a man wild with rage. My friends and I had carefully rehearsed our next move. I pretended to go berserk, lifted the impresario bodily from his chair, dragged him on to the balcony and held him so he was looking down to the pavement four floors below. I asked my friends if I should drop him or forgive him. In unison they shouted: "Drop him." He went rigid with shock and I thought he might have a heart attack. Immediately, I dragged him back into the room and warned him never to interfere with my groups again.'[2]

Despite their disagreements with Arden, the Small Faces did respect him. 'He took us from a little band, unknown, with a small reputation, into a very big, important band,' remembered Kenney Jones.[3] 'A lot of people say about managers that all they can do is collect the money from the record company or arrange an interview,' recalled McLagan, 'but to build an act ... He was old school, he was a hustler.'[4]

Another time Ronnie Lane thought he would approach Arden about money, only to be introduced to 'Mad Tom', one of Arden's 'assistants'. It was agreed that the discussion could probably wait. And Arden could be wilier than merely threatening violence. When the group's parents demanded a meeting with Arden to discuss money, Arden was unequivocal.

'He sat them all down,' remembered McLagan, 'and said, "People in show business spend money ... And they've spent theirs." Our parents were horrified, and were inclined to believe him ... As if that wasn't bad enough, he went on to tell them we were all on drugs, which explained how such vast amounts of money had been spent in such a short time.'[5] The parents were obviously worried about their children, and it took some serious explaining from the group to pacify them. 'That was the last straw for us,' remembered McLagan. 'We knew that if we were ever going to sort out our finances we'd have to get away from "Uncle Don".'[6]

On the back of the Number 1 spot of 'All Or Nothing', Arden announced that the group were going to tour the USA in December. But the tour never came off, due – according to Arden – to a previous

McLagan drug conviction resulting in his being refused a visa. McLagan thinks this was just a red herring, and argues that 'He [Arden] was scared that we would meet with American agents or managers and find out how much money we should have been getting.'[7]

Glyn Johns saw the failure to tour the USA as the major factor in the ultimate demise of the group. 'If they had gone to America they would have absolutely cleaned up,' he argued. 'When English bands went to America … and made it, immediately their standing in Great Britain was tripled. That never happened with the Small Faces.'[8] Instead, the group found themselves booked on an October package tour of the UK featuring The Hollies and the Nashville Teens. A row about billing saw that tour fall apart. The band withdrew to the studio to record their second LP, and were being harassed to come up with a follow-up single to 'All Or Nothing' by Arden, who in turn was being harassed by Decca. In order to keep them all quiet, the Small Faces sent Arden a demo of 'My Mind's Eye'. Inexplicably, Decca got hold of the demo.

'We were driving home or to some gig up North,' remembered Marriott, 'and it just came on, "Here's the latest single by the Small Faces." Everyone was, "WHAT?"'[9]

Though the single, released in November 1966, reached Number 4 in the charts, it was a further nail in the coffin for the relationship between the Small Faces and Arden. Having already appointed an independent lawyer to look into their financial relationship with Arden, it lasted only until Christmas, when Don Arden and the Small Faces parted company. The parting didn't just mean they had to sign to a new management company; it also meant the Small Faces had to leave the Pimlico house that Arden had paid for. In one swift move, the band found themselves homeless, not just musically but literally, so that in double-quick time they had to get themselves four separate apartments.

Arden sold the group's contract for a reputed £12,000 to the Harold Davison group, part of the Lew Grade Organisation. Short of cash, the group needed to get some gigs and raise some money. Tito Burns, Davison's booking agent, placed the Small Faces on a package tour that included Roy Orbison. It didn't go well, and with other contracts flying about and lawyers doing their thing, the Small Faces booked themselves into Olympic Studios and started writing. Marriott and Lane had already come across the man who was running the label they really wanted to sign to, and they were just waiting to get the deal sorted. Eventually, their lawyers capitalised on a few legal technicalities, and they managed to extricate themselves from the Harold Davison group and sign with the label of their choice, Immediate Records, which was run by Andrew Loog Oldham.

★

By 1966 Oldham was – despite his relative youth (he was born in 1944) – a major and charismatic figure on the British pop scene. A slight though compelling figure, his sharp features were offset by his immaculate dress-sense, and he considered himself as much a celebrity as his artists. He had started off working for Mary Quant; he had done some time with Don Arden's management company; in 1964 he had stolen the management of the Rolling Stones from under Georgio Gomelsky's nose and had made them famous, promoting them under the slogan 'Would you let your daughter go out with a Rolling Stone?'; and in 1965, on the point of losing the Rolling Stones, he had started his own management/agency/record label, Immediate. Under the motto 'Happy to be a Part of the Industry of Human Happiness', Oldham's idea was to bring together a stable of artists who would write, produce and play on each other's records, something like Berry Gordy's Tamla Motown set-up in Detroit.

In addition, Oldham fancied himself as a record producer, a view not shared by Ian McLagan. 'This guy is not an engineer,' remembered McLagan. 'He's an idiot. He has no idea about sound. He couldn't produce a burp after a glass of beer.'[10]

That aside, Oldham felt that the music business was run by old men who didn't understand what the new groups wanted or needed; it was Oldham's assertion, based on the success of independent record labels in the USA such as Motown, Chess and Stax, that he could provide it. There would be no-one standing over groups in the studio with a stop-watch, clocking the time that was spent there; there was to be total support for the artists on the label. In the heady days of 1966 and '67, with pop music being taken seriously for the first time, this was a seductive mixture for any group, let alone one that felt like they had been incorrectly pigeonholed as a lightweight pop act.

But Oldham was also a shrewd businessman, and didn't care who knew it. 'I promote talent,' said Oldham. 'I take something and put it into a shape. I just try and make something presentable to the public, make it commercial. Anything that has an image to it, I get involved in. I'm a terrible user and a thief. I mean I'm not original. Every record is, "Oh yeah, let's steal a bit outta that." Five per cent of the people who are in the music business are in it for the right reason. They should be in it for money.'[11]

McLagan wasn't quite so convinced by Oldham's brashness. 'I didn't like him from the start,' he remembered. 'A big mistake was that we signed our contract with him over a joint. I think it's rule three in showbusiness – sign when you're sober. He was a creep.'[12]

Oldham's first success came when he licensed a hit record from the USA, the McCoys' 'Hang On Sloopy', which was followed up by Chris Farlowe's 'Out Of Time'. It was into this atmosphere that the Small Faces threw themselves in 1966. But, as ever, things weren't easy. Their first single with their new management and label was not released on Immediate. Decca, feeling the loss of their erstwhile charges, released 'I Can't Make It' in March 1967. Banned by the BBC due to its apparently suggestive lyric, and under-promoted by Decca, the record charted briefly at Number 26 before dropping out. Following the mediocre tour with Roy Orbison, the band played the *NME* Poll-Winners concert at Wembley before heading off to Scandinavia for a short tour.

Their return was marked by the release of another single, 'Patterns', on 26 May. Decca were doing their level best to make as much money as they could from the now departed Small Faces, and the band were livid. They went to the press to ask their fans not to buy the record, and they refused even to lift a finger to promote it themselves. The record flopped. The decks now apparently cleared, the band and Immediate were readied for the release of their debut single for their new label. 'Here Comes The Nice' was released on 2 June, and as it made its way up the charts, Decca announced that they were going to release an LP by the Small Faces. The group were touring Holland when the LP was released on 2 June. Titled *From the Beginning*, the album was a collection of unreleased, previously discarded material, demos and a couple of hit singles, thrown together for expediency rather than any artistic reason. Even so, the album did reasonably well, rising to Number 17 on the chart.

The artistic freedom and the limitless time in the studio offered by Immediate had had an effect on the quality of Marriott and Lane's songwriting and recording practices.

'After Decca Records it was heaven,' remembered Lane. 'Everything was laid on, we could have as much studio time as we wanted.'[13]

Glyn Johns remembers: 'I wasn't there when they wrote but I don't remember a lot of songs being started on a session. I think one [of Marriott and Lane] might come in with an idea and it would be built on from there. But sometimes they would come in with an entire song.'[14]

As with many pop writing partnerships, the Marriott/Lane combination wasn't based on a straightforward words/music relationship. 'We'd get the ideas individually and present them to each other,' remembered Lane. 'We didn't write a lot of stuff together from beginning to end, we more or less finished off stuff rather than actually wrote it together. In many ways it was just me helping Steve to write songs: a bigger percentage of the ideas came from him than me … When we got together something used to happen, whether it fell out of my head or his. We'd come up with something to knock each other out, I suppose, and once the ball got rolling, it would sort of finish itself.'[15]

'They were fairly equal, I think, in everything they did,' remembered Jones. 'One made a suggestion and the other would support it, strongly, or would come up with [another] suggestion – it was inspiring each other.'[16]

In common with many groups in the mid-Sixties, the Small Faces were now beginning to appreciate the possibilities offered by modern recording. 'Here Comes The Nice' was a marijuana-amphetamine-tinted paean to drugs.

'The "nice" was the dealer,' remembered McLagan. 'Steve had this expression, "It's nice to be nice". Steve would be getting a nice buzz on and would turn around, in a crowded room, and go, "nice".'[17] The song starts dreamily before kicking into a much harder chorus before reaching a bridge based on a floaty Hammond organ, but the lyric gives the game away with its references to speed. The single was released the day after The Beatles' *Sgt Pepper* and the subsequent furore in the media over The Beatles' drug taking. Consequently the BBC were too busy banning 'Lucy In The Sky With Diamonds' and 'She's Leaving

Home' even to notice what Marriott and the lads were saying. Thus spared an airplay ban, the song rose to Number 12 in the charts.

★

Since 1965, when the Small Faces had first emerged as a group, and 1967 and their signing to Immediate, pop music both in Britain and America – the main producers and consumers of the form – had changed dramatically. A series of apparently unrelated strands began to coagulate around the London music scene, all of which were to have a highly influential effect on pop music. As musicians spent more and more time in the recording studio, and thereby became increasingly confident and conversant with modern recording techniques, the vast possibilities of the recording process became increasingly apparent.

By 1965, the influence of American folk music – and of Bob Dylan and the breaking San Francisco LSD culture in particular – was seeping into British music. Apart from the plethora of Dylan covers – from the American group The Byrds through to Manfred Mann – Dylan was seen by British musicians as something of a genius. This was partly due to the simplicity of his songwriting added to the intricacy of his lyric-writing, but also because folk music had artistic credibility and an apparent authenticity lacking in ordinary, everyday, throwaway pop music. Folk music was studied by musical scholars – there were even recordings of folk songs in America's National Archive. When, in 1965, Dylan ditched his acoustic guitar for an electric model and got himself a backing band, he was allying himself to pop music in general. In addition, his pronouncement that Smokey Robinson was the greatest poet in popular music gave an intellectual credibility not just to black music – blues was already recognised as a musical form, with R&B and soul not far behind – but to the pop song generally.

This all came to a head in Dylan's 1965 single 'Like A Rolling Stone', a seven-minute slab of rage which all but vanquished the idea of the 'three-minute pop song' which had been the norm until that point. Equally, the gauntlet was resolutely thrown down in the same year by Brian Wilson of the Beach Boys. Wilson – who had psychological and drug-induced problems a-plenty – had stopped touring with the pop-surf band the Beach Boys and instead spent his days holed up in the Capitol Records recording studio in Los Angeles where he had been working on a series of masterpieces throughout 1965 and 1966. The first fruit of this was the LP *Pet Sounds*, released in 1965. Each song was intricately arranged, building from a base not just of pop musicians (i.e. guitar, bass and drums) but with a full orchestra. In what became perceived as a 'battle', The Beatles picked up the gauntlet and in response produced *Revolver*, released in 1966.

Utilising all the tricks they could muster in the limited confines of EMI's Abbey Road studios, they had too fashioned a masterpiece not just of pop, but of electronic music, the final track – 'Tomorrow Never Knows' – sounding unlike anything ever produced by a pop group, a myriad of strange sounds and disembodied voices suspended over a hypnotic bass and drum beat. The next offering from Brian Wilson and the Beach Boys, though merely a single – 'Good Vibrations' – was three minutes of pop genius, a mini-symphony which took six months to record. It was with 'Good Vibrations' ringing in their ears that The Beatles, having retired from live performance, withdrew to Abbey Road in late 1966. Rumours of what was going on in Abbey Road filtered through the British music business, and it was in February 1967 that the first results emerged. 'Strawberry Fields Forever'/'Penny Lane' sent shockwaves through the other British groups and marked The Beatles out not just for commercial greatness, but for artistic distinction.

The Beatles continued to work through the spring of 1967, and it was on 1 June that they released the results of their efforts. *Sgt Pepper's Lonely Hearts Club Band* wasn't just an event for pop music fans: it was a cultural event, described – perhaps just a little over-exuberantly – by critic and cultural commentator Kenneth Tynan as 'a decisive moment in the history of Western civilisation'. Though the unifying idea underlying the album was a little weak – The Beatles pretending to be another, different band – it was, nonetheless, the first 'concept' album in pop music, an undertaking anxious to be seen as an entire work rather than a collection of songs. But even this work retained its essential Englishness. Throughout 1966 and 1967, the new drug (LSD) culture had adapted itself in a very English way. Little drops of whimsy permeated everything about British pop culture in those years, from The Kinks' 'Dedicated Follower Of Fashion', 'Sunny Afternoon' and 'Waterloo Sunset', through The Beatles' 'Yellow Submarine', 'Penny Lane' and 'When I'm 64'. The fashion through 1966/67 was for Victorian paisley patterns and dress, from cod-Victorian names (the hip clothes shop 'Granny Takes A Trip' and even *Sgt Pepper* itself) to the wearing of Victorian British army red tunics.

Most British groups had taken drugs since the earliest days of the British Beat boom in 1963/64. The drug of choice was amphetamine (also known as 'speed'), not necessarily for recreational use (though this is undeniable) but simply so that the groups could get through the punishing schedules they were forced to endure.

'Amphetamine was a working drug,' remembered manager Simon Napier-Bell. 'Marijuana slowed you down, booze could make you fall off the stage, hard drugs wrecked your life, but amphetamine kept you going all night and gave you the edge you needed.'[18]

Audiences also took speed, usually in the form of tablets, the most popular being 'Purple Hearts' and 'French Blues'. Later, especially after 1965, many British groups began to smoke marijuana as a way of coming down after gigs and in a more recreational way. In addition, marijuana had the effect – especially on musicians – of making the smoker think that it increased their creativity.

The Small Faces were no exceptions to this, and took amphetamine and marijuana in vast quantities throughout the early part of their careers. However, in late 1965/early 1966 a new drug began to emerge in the fashionable parts of London. Lysergic Acid Diethylamide (LSD, also known as 'Acid') was developed by the Sandoz Laboratories in Switzerland in the Forties, and its startling effects when imbibed were quickly noticed by the authorities who attempted to find a use for it first in psychiatry, and later in the military.

By the late Fifties, the drug had filtered through to 'ordinary' people, who took it because they felt it had a 'psychedelic' or mind-opening effect upon them. Users claimed that it allowed them to experience music, art and everyday events in a new way, as if they were seeing the world for the first time with their personal, preconceived filters removed. Writers and intellectuals were impressed with the drug, and just as Aldous Huxley had advocated the use of mescalin among artists as a means to expand their horizons (though he thought the drug would be wasted on ordinary people) the recreational use of LSD was catching on. By late 1965, the drug had made its way to Britain, where it was taken by the fashionable set in London. And since musicians were now considered to be among the fashionable set, it wasn't long before they too were taking it regularly. The Beatles' own use of the drug is well documented, but the Small Faces also took to the drug, especially Marriott and Lane.

'After [the] first night,' remembered McLagan, 'we dropped acid more and more, usually at night, so that it would have pretty much worn off by the next day.'[19] LSD wasn't criminalised in the UK until early 1967. It was therefore through a shimmering haze of LSD that the fashionable set saw the summer of 1967, *Sgt Pepper*, the Small Faces and all.

In April 1966, *Time* magazine had published an article on 'Swinging London', despite the fact that London had swung only sporadically since the autumn of 1965. The piece was followed by similar articles in *Life* and the *Saturday Evening Post*. That these articles were a year late was itself unremarkable – the notoriously insular American media couldn't be expected to pick up on events so far away, so the fact that they had written about London at all was something of an achievement. What was remarkable however is that they incited a vast influx of teenage American tourists into the capital, and, as if on cue, London began to swing again. And, gliding on LSD and marijuana, it swung right into 1967. But politics were starting to impinge on the general dreaminess.

'In 1967 you get the anti-Vietnam war movement,' recalls Dave Phillips. 'There was the most violent demonstration in October 1967, the first violent demonstration of the war, where there were pitched battles in Grosvenor Square. We were charged by police horses and we were throwing things at them, so this was going on, but at the same time you had this bizarre "flower-power" stuff emerging. I went to the first event which was at the Round House in Chalk Farm, London. I just remember there was a big crowd, Pink Floyd were playing a lot, there were bubbles going off, and Paul McCartney was rumoured to be in attendance dressed as an Arab. Then there was a huge "Love-In" at Ally Pally [Alexandra Palace in London] which I remember primarily being characterised by this huge list of bands that were supposed to be appearing, most of whom didn't show up or came on late, and then trying to get back home from Ally Pally.'

London developed its own version of the American, West Coast 'hippies' which was premised on rumours which were filtering across the Atlantic. 'The hippies went from being a small movement, very much 'art college' London, a few underground papers – *International Times*,' remembers Phillips. 'It got very rapidly taken over by the music industry, so you had all these bands suddenly transmogrified into psychedelic forms of themselves. There was a lot of rebranding of bands and I think that's when we all first became aware that music was an industry. But we all thought that we were making history and inventing things for the first time which is the arrogance of youth. We used to listen to pirate radio – because the BBC was very cautious about playing this kind of music – Radio London and Radio Caroline, which wasn't as good as Radio London, and there was John Peel and his *Perfumed Garden* show. I went and interviewed John Peel because I wrote an article about the 'demise of pirate radio' for *Oz* magazine.'

But London was also 'swinging' for other reasons than LSD and pop stars: 1964 had seen the election of a Labour government for the first time since 1951. Where the Conservative government had been seen as staid and, well, conservative, the new Labour government were seen to be considerably more progressive and liberal under the leadership of Harold Wilson, who at 48 was considered to be young and radical (he had been to grammar school and appeared to have some kind of Northern accent which, genuine or otherwise, lent him extra credibility with Middle England if not the younger voters). He had become the leader of the Labour Party as late as 1963 following the sudden death of Hugh Gaitskell. Despite Wilson's promise that the new government would provide economic and social progress premised on what he called 'the white heat of the technological revolution', the new government quickly found themselves embroiled in a series of economic crises which would worsen as the decade went on. The Conservatives reacted to their defeat by dismissing their leader – Alec Douglas-Hume – and replacing him with the younger Edward (Ted) Heath. Wilson and Heath were to become the dominant British political figures for the next ten years, both mentioned in George Harrison's ascerbic 'Taxman' which featured on *Revolver*.

Amidst this mix of changing culture, changing drugs and changing politics, the Small Faces were still caught between two record labels. Because of the rushed release of the Decca *From the Beginning* LP, Immediate rushed out their own Small Faces album. Again titled *Small Faces*, the LP was released on 23 June and rose to Number 12 in the charts.

While everyone was still picking through the bones of their contractual problems, the Small Faces ensconced themselves once more in the studio. The resulting single, 'Itchycoo Park', marked a dramatic shift in the Small Faces' approach to recording.

'The record came in bits and pieces,' recalls Kenney Jones. 'Glyn Johns did much to pull it together. He didn't produce it, he was engineer, but he had lots of ideas. Whether we listened to him or not was another matter.'

With a more laid-back sound, which owed much to the plethora of folk, marijuana and hippy influenced records of the time, 'Itchycoo Park' was notable for its extensive use of a sound effect called 'phasing'. Phasing is caused when two tape machines with exactly the same recording on them are played together on to a third machine, but with a slight delay – .05 of a second – between the machines; hence the name 'phasing' – the tape machines are out of phase with each other. What's recorded onto the third machine sounds like it is being heard through a tin can which is being slowly opened and closed.

Phasing had already been used in classical and electronic music, and the Small Faces were not the first pop group to use this effect – The Beatles had used it more sparingly when recording certain instruments during the Sgt Pepper sessions at Abbey Road. The Small Faces' success with the effect came when they applied it to a whole track as they did on the bridges of 'Itchycoo Park'.

Glyn Johns doesn't take credit for introducing phasing to the Small Faces. 'My assistant was a guy called George Chiantz who was an extremely bright fellow. He was very technically minded and he figured out how to use phasing by using three tape machines. When I arrived he said, "Look what I've worked out this morning, I've finally managed to make it work," and he showed me what he had done. I thought it was absolutely fantastic. The band arrived for the session and we cut 'Itchycoo Park'. Then I said, "You know what we should do? I've got to show you this," and that's how it came about. I can't take any credit for it.'[20]

But tape effects alone do not a great record make, and 'Itchycoo Park' was more than mere phasing. It touched a moment in August 1967, and combined all the elements prevalent in the music which coloured the 'Summer of Love' – excellent production, a dreamy tune and a dreamier lyric.

The original idea for the song was Ronnie Lane's. '"Itchycoo Park" was a rip-off of a hymn called "God Be In My Head",' he recalled. 'It was set out in the form of a dialogue between an innocent, normal person and someone who was very hip, someone who had already been "there".'[21] With all the talk in the media about drugs and drug use, and with journalists now obsessively analysing song lyrics for any possible reference to drugs, it was no surprise when journalists picked up on the words to 'Itchycoo Park'. Phrases referring to 'blowing my mind', then a common phrase among hippies and users of psychedelics, were simply asking for trouble, though astonishingly none arose and the single made its way up the chart, peaking at Number 3 in the UK. More importantly, it also made it to Number 16 in the US, the band's only American chart hit.

Despite its theme, 'Itchycoo Park' itself wasn't some mythic, hippy enclave in East London. '"Itchycoo Park" wasn't really a park,' remembered Kenney Jones, 'it was an area in Ilford which was a bombsite, an area of wasteland all wild and overgrown that ran down to the railway lines, which was full of stinging nettles.'[22] In common with many English psychedelic songs of the period, 'Itchycoo Park' drew on the group's childhood, a common theme from a pop culture then bedazzled with LSD. The use of childlike images was common, the drug often taking the user into a childlike state, and the chorus, 'It's all too beautiful', reiterated another theme commonly stated by users of the drug. With their new, flared trousers, longer hair and floppy hats, the Small Faces may have been looking at themselves and the world anew through the shimmer of LSD, but they still somehow seemed to project the image of four lads from the East End of London on the make. However, the press were starting to characterise the Small Faces as something of a novelty act – chirpy cockney popsters who were able to put together a good 'turn', something not helped by the group's cartoon cockney manner-isms. It would come back to haunt them.

Since signing with Immediate, the Small Faces had been working with the other groups on the label. Marriott and Lane were writing for some of the other artists and in addition were producing them, while Jones and McLagan were playing with other groups. Marriott and Lane wrote and produced for singer Billy Nicholls, and, along with some-time Stones pianist Nicky Hopkins and John Paul Jones (later of Led Zeppelin), the Small Faces played on Nicholls' debut LP. In addi-tion, Marriott guested on 'In Another Land', a track from *Their Satanic*

*Majesties Request,* the Rolling Stones LP that was supposed to be their answer to *Sgt Pepper.*

'That came about due to us using the same studios,' remembered Marriott. 'I'd been in there from the night before working on our own stuff and Bill Wyman came over and said, "Do you want to have a play on this?" It was simple. Everyone used to do it. If there was someone in next door that you liked, and you were coming in, you would think, "What can they do on this or that?" Brian Jones wasn't there … so I filled in for him. I was apparently considered as a possible replacement because Brian was on his way out … Later I talked to Keith [Richards] about it, but back then Mick wouldn't have it. I don't think Mick took us seriously.'[23]

At the end of August 1967, the Small Faces travelled to West Germany to play a TV special with other Immediate artists, Twice As Much and PP Arnold. Arnold was a singer, a former Ikette (Ike and Tina Turner's backing singers), who had arrived in Britain for a tour and, having been introduced to Mick Jagger by Glyn Johns, had been persuaded by Jagger to stay in London. She signed to Immediate where she met the Small Faces, whom she asked to write some material for her. Marriott had been working on a song for another vocalist, Jenny Rylands, called 'Tin Soldier', and he offered it to Arnold. 'I had tried every goddamn trick in the book to lay her [Rylands],' remembered Marriott, 'so I wrote this song and she married me. We played it to PP and she completely flipped, so much so that I thought "I'm gonna keep it, it's got to be too good to give away." So we wrote her another song called "(If You Think You're) Groovy".'[24]

'Tin Soldier' was a move away from the more hippy sound of 'Itchycoo Park', back towards the R&B and soul roots of the Small Faces. Featuring PP Arnold on backing vocals, the song was another step forward for the Small Faces, constructed as it was to have a major dynamic shift from the start of the song to the end. A major work of British R&B, 'Tin Soldier' showcased Marriott's startling voice and the group's maturing musicianship. Released in December 1967, the song rose to a very respectable Number 9 in the charts.

In the meantime, warning signs that the days of Swinging London were drawing to a close were coming thick and fast by the end of 1967. The Labour government, following a spiral of economic crises which they largely mismanaged, were forced to devalue the pound from $2.80 down to $2.40. Harold Wilson went on television the following day to explain the situation to a bemused nation, claiming – ultimately incorrectly – that, 'This does not mean that the pound in your pocket … had been devalued.'[25] Economic reality was slowly beginning to seep into the otherwise pervasive frivolity of Swinging London.

★

Things had also got a little sticky for another member of the Small Faces. In November 1967, with a free few days, Ian McLagan decided to dash off to Greece for a short holiday with his then girlfriend (and subsequent wife) Sandy. When they arrived at Heathrow, McLagan was whisked away from Immigration into a small side-room. He was carrying a small lump of cannabis which was found by Customs and Excise officers after a perfunctory search, and he was duly arrested. McLagan was eventually fined £50 for possession of cannabis after the police dropped an earlier charge of attempting to smuggle the drug. Kenney Jones remembered that it was a problem that would haunt McLagan for some time. '[It] wouldn't be resolved until years later after we had formed The Faces and even then we had to play some places without him.'[26]

At the time of his arrest, McLagan had phoned Andrew Loog Oldham. 'A couple of hours later,' said McLagan, 'Andrew, on a rescue mission and smelling an opportunity to cash in on the free publicity, turned up at the police station wearing his customary shades and a stoned smile. He paid my bail ... and I was in the Roller puffing on a joint before we left the police station car park.'[27]

# FIVE

# HAPPY DAYS
# TOY TOWN

The Small Faces started 1968 with a 15-day tour of Australia and New Zealand along with The Who and Paul Jones, formerly the vocalist with Manfred Mann. The tour didn't go well, with the Australian press hostile to them in general and to McLagan in particular as his drug arrest was still fresh news. The tedium of being on the road in a foreign country hit the Small Faces hard. Whereas The Who had been touring the USA extensively, the Small Faces had been spending a lot of time in the studio. It was Keith Moon who was to teach them about the effects of boredom on pop groups – as a result of which a number of hotel rooms were destroyed. This carnage accompanied the groups to New Zealand, and the Small Faces were especially glad when the tour was over.

Back in London, it was decided that the group should hire house-boats and take themselves off to the Thames Waterway in order to finish writing their next album with no distractions. Since *Sgt Pepper*, groups had been trying to create albums as entire pieces of work with a unifying concept. Part of the reason for the Small Faces' seclusion was that they had no real concept for the LP, and the boat trip was somehow supposed to give them inspiration. In the end, the only theme that they could construct came from a stoned night spent looking up at the sky.

'It [the theme] is a kind of mystical journey,' said Ronnie Lane at the time. 'There's this kid who kind of falls in love with the moon, and all of a sudden he observes the moon being eaten away by time. And of course, when it's gone, he's all down; and then the thing is that, all of a sudden – boosh! – it comes back again, like life itself. And I thought that was something to pick up on, really, because you can often get brought down by something and you're just being stupidly impatient usually.'[1] Despite the fact that the theme seems weaker even than the theme of *Sgt Pepper*, it was this that Side Two of the LP was to address. Side One, on the other hand, was to contain new but unrelated songs.

As work continued on the LP, Immediate released a single, partly as a preview of the forthcoming album and partly just to keep the Small Faces in the charts, in the press and on the radio. 'Lazy Sunday' was probably meant to be another slab of English psychedelia in much the same way that The Kinks' 'Sunny Afternoon' had been in 1966. However, Marriott's 'Artful Dodger' vocal, combined with the tune, gave the feel of Lionel Bart's musical *Oliver!* rather than anything more musically substantial. The music-hall feel and the slightly odd sound effects (chirping birds and a flushing toilet among others) felt a bit out of time by May 1968.

Marriott defended his singing on 'Lazy Sunday' in a *Record Mirror* interview. 'I've been intending to make a record singing in a cockney accent for a long time ... In fact, about three years ago I was having an argument with one of The Hollies and I was saying to him, "You don't sing in your own natural voice." And he was saying the same thing to me. The thing is, it's your own voice when you're singing – but it's not your normal voice. It's not the voice you use for talking. But you don't really notice this when you're singing. So after this argument I decided to make a record singing in my own voice. That was three years ago and we've just got round to doing it.'[2]

The song was Marriott's idea, based on experiences he'd had when the band had returned from the ill-fated Australian trip. 'He was having a lot of trouble,' remembered Ronnie Lane. 'He was living in this residential part along Chiswick Walk, and a terrible European middle-class family lived next door, and, of course, there were records playing all night long and things like that, and his dogs were shitting all over the place and he didn't clear it up – there was a real running battle with them. He got it off his chest by writing "Lazy Sunday".'[3]

When Marriott brought the song to the studio, it still needed some work. 'It was slow,' remembered McLagan, 'and we just got bored with it – it wasn't going right. We'd been working over and over it, and in the end we started taking the piss out of it – all that "roodeedoodeedoo" and stuff – and speeded it up. We recorded it and we all thought it was fantastic.'[4]

The single was a hit, rising to Number 2 in the chart. However, Marriott and the rest of the Small Faces soon realised that, as with 'Itchycoo Park', there could be a critical downside to the success of the record.

'Things like that were cut for albums,' remembered Marriott, 'and a keen record company executive would see that they would be a very big single and would release them that way. In fact, it did our morale a lot of harm, because we wanted them to be album tracks: to say it's a funny song or it's a gimmicky song, but it's one fact of an album. We were in Rome when Andrew [Oldham] said "Lazy Sunday" was going to be the single and I had a terrible argument on the phone with him about it. I really fought it. When it's put out as a single and it's a hit, there were loads of drawbacks. You're supposed to do it every night on stage, and in countries where they've never heard of you and you get one record out like "Itchycoo Park" in the States – it was a big hit and they thought that's what we did. The Small Faces on stage were a completely different band to those records: just a loud rock 'n' roll band. I sang "Lazy Sunday" like that because it was creasing everyone up in the box, but to take that kind of joke out of context can be a screw-up. The joke backfires on you.'[5]

But this dispute between the Small Faces and Immediate illustrates the difference between musicians who consider themselves artists, and the record companies, whose sole mission it is to make money. It is any record company's obligation to release the songs that are most likely to be hits, in order to make the most money that they can, for the record company, the publishing company and the artist.

Artists' income is dependent on three sources: record sales, publishing revenue and gigs. The money from gigs belongs entirely to the artist (and the artist's agent, who books the gigs). Record sales provide the musicians on the record with income. The majority of the money for artists comes from the publishing of the music, a system that rewards those who write the music. The music publishing rewards the songwriters, both in the number of records sold, but also in the number of times the record is performed, essentially – for pop music – on the radio and television. So the songwriter/s in any pop group will always be the most wealthy.

The way that the money is split is – in some ways – odd. For record sales, each track on a single is worth exactly the same money. That is to say that sales of any single garners the B-side exactly the same revenue as the A-side, no matter whether it's ever played. For radio or television performances of a song, the money is solely paid on the song that is performed. And for albums, each song on each album that is sold is worth exactly the same. This is why in the early days of rock and pop music, many producers found it worth their while to force their artists to record a song that the producer had written, just so that it could be released on the B-side of a hit single, thereby claiming for the producer half the proceeds of the hit.

Record companies argue that they invest heavily in recording and paying the artists; they must make a return on their investment. It may not suit the artist's self-impression to release so-called 'joke' records like 'Lazy Sunday', but it obviously suited Immediate and especially Andrew Oldham, who knew a hit record when he heard it. The fact that it got to Number 2 in the charts was justification enough for any record company; the fact that it presented the Small Faces with problems with the critics was of little consequence to the record company.

★

The Small Faces continued recording through early 1968. Problems knitting together the 'concept' side of the LP led Marriott and Lane to recruit the services of the eccentric English actor 'Professor' Stanley Unwin. Unwin, who developed his own particularly garbled form of English which he called 'Unwinese', was a comedy 'turn' – in a vaudevillian sense – who was very successful during the Sixties and Seventies.

Carol Chaffer, a television executive who worked with Unwin on the cult Eighties TV show *The Tube*, described Unwin as 'a pleasure to work with, a charming man who would slip into "Unwinese" in normal conversation, which could be a little disconcerting but was very funny'. Unwin was chosen to link the songs on the album, telling the story of 'Happiness Stan'. The actor spent time in the studio with the group, picking up on their verbal mannerisms and incorporating them into his final script.

'It made us laugh,' remembered Marriott. 'Anything that made us laugh we liked. God knows how it worked but it did and I'm very proud of it. We gave [Unwin] a glossary of hip terms to throw in with the cockneyisms.'[6]

'I can remember the sessions at Trident and I can remember sessions at IBC,' says Glyn Johns of the epic recording task. 'I know we did Stanley Unwin's bit at Olympic. I don't remember it taking a long time. It might have been done over a long period of time because it was a concept album and they had to figure out how to put it all together.'[7]

With the album finally recorded, mixed and ordered, the band's attention turned to the LP's cover and the name of the album. Following the release of *With the Beatles* in 1964, LP cover design had become a growth industry, with covers becoming increasingly intricate to the point where The Beatles' *Sgt Pepper* cover was commissioned from British pop artist Peter Blake, like any other work of art commissioned by the aristocracy of old. Ronnie Lane was taken with the idea that the LP cover should be a tobacco tin, and Andrew Oldham got in touch with tobacco manufacturer Ogden's, who sent the Small Faces books showing pictures of their old tobacco tins.

'We were rummaging through them,' remembered McLagan, 'when Steve noticed a rectangular label for "Ogdens' Nut Brown Flake" and fell about laughing. "There it is," he screamed. "*Ogden's Nut GONE Flake!*"'[8] The band adopted the title for the album, the Ogden's label for the cover, and Oldham came up with the idea that having a circular LP sleeve would get them extra publicity. The round sleeve was an elaborate five circle affair, each circle attached to the other along a short section. Pleasing to the eye, the sleeve wasn't always entirely practical.

*Ogden's Nut Gone Flake* begins with the phasing-soaked, pulsating instrumental title track, a lazy, dreaming sparkling ode to LSD not unlike the instrumentals coming out of San Francisco during late 1966 and early '67, especially Country Joe & The Fish's first LP, *Electric Music for Mind and Body*, which filtered into the UK through John Peel's *Perfumed Garden* radio show.

Marriott/Lane's 'Afterglow' begins with an almost crooneresque introduction before exploding into a full-blown rock/soul ballad that builds to a crashing chorus drenched with growling Hammond organ, Marriott screaming his way through the chorus. Jones's final drum fill is quickly faded before the introduction to McLagan's 'Long Agos And Worlds Apart'. McLagan's offering, while based around a basic R&B musical premise, sounds like it could have been recorded by early Pink Floyd, but in the hands of the four Mods from the East End, it retains a working-class charm that the Floyd could never hope to achieve, even through to the meandering reprise.

The next track, 'Rene', was – according to Marriott – based on a real person they knew when they were young. Another musical nod towards music hall, Marriott and Lane sing in their best 'Artful Dodger' voices, an almost mocking caricature of the voices of East London telling a fairly common story of East London – the mother with a number of kids of a number of colours with a number of fathers. In the postwar years, the East End of London still had docks, and still had dockers, which in turn meant that there would be a number of sailors from all over the world fresh off the cargo ships and looking for company.

'Song Of A Baker' sounds like it was carved out of Jimi Hendrix's cover of The Troggs' 'Wild Thing' with its big, expansive chords and words designed to remind the listener (who would obviously be on acid) of expanses of space. The track owes much to Hendrix's style, with the guitar solo sounding as though Hendrix himself was playing it. Having said that, Marriott's playing style was never that far away from Hendrix, who may well have picked up a few tricks from Marriott as Hendrix was noted for his ability to pick up on inventive guitar playing. 'Lazy Sunday' winds up Side One of the LP. Already a hit, it was a perfect piece of English psychedelia in the style of 'Sunny Afternoon' or 'Penny Lane'.

The standard for English psychedelia was set by Pink Floyd, who applied a very English, middle-class approach to the process of making music. Part of the problem for British groups was that the information coming out of San Francisco in the mid-Sixties was hazy. In Britain they were aware that something was happening, but due to the lack of record releases in Britain at that time, there was limited aural information. So Pink Floyd adapted what they knew – essentially R&B and English folk music. It developed into a pecu- liarly English form of psychedelia, with melodies and harmonies based around English folk metres, but played on electric instru- ments, with the new effects available to musicians. In addition, Pink Floyd were aware of developments in classical electronic music – serial music and the sound collages developed by Stockhausen among others.

All of this went into the mix and emerged all at once on Pink Floyd's debut LP *Piper at the Gates of Dawn*, recorded at Abbey Road studios while The Beatles were recording *Sgt Pepper*. The same mix was applied by the groups who aspired to the psychedelic, with vary- ing degrees of success – the Rolling Stones failed disastrously with *Their Satanic Majesties Request*, while others such as Jethro Tull were more successful. The Beatles, though obviously the most successful, forged their own path through psychedelia. But it was from this base that the Small Faces approached Side Two of *Ogden's*.

Side Two begins with Stanley Unwin's narration, followed by Marriott and Lane's 'Happiness Stan', a typical piece of British psychedelia, part whimsy, part heavy rock song. After further narration from Unwin, Marriott and McLagan's heavy R&B number 'Rollin' Over' follows, featuring another bleeding-throat soul vocal from Marriott. 'The Hungry Intruder' – another Marriott and McLagan collaboration – follows before 'The Journey', credited to the whole group, both steeped in the same psychedelic whimsy. 'Mad John', credited to Marriott and Lane, is part folk, part English music hall, while the next track, 'Happy Days Toy Town', written by Marriott, Lane and McLagan, is pure English music hall couched in an R&B style, Marriott namechecking the breakfast cereal All-Bran. The 'concept' part of the album completed, the LP finishes with 'Tin Soldier', a British R&B classic, Marriott's soulful vocal giving the lie to the psychedelic nonsense which precedes it.

Released in May 1968, the LP went straight to Number 1. The previously muttering press went wild for the album. In the *NME*, Keith Altham described the record as 'a landmark for the group … and almost certain to put the group in the same smash album bracket as the Beach Boys, the Stones, the Jimi Hendrix Experience'. *Melody Maker* and *Disc* made the LP album of the month, and in the pages of *Melody Maker* came the praise that the Small Faces had craved for so long.

'In case you hadn't noticed,' wrote Bob Dawbarn, 'the Small Faces are no longer a teenybopper group … they have, in fact, developed into one of the most rewarding groups on the British scene, continually trying new things yet retaining contact with the public. Between them they have also developed into a real force as songwriters … the whole album is pop of a very high order.'

Even the album's cover won a prestigious award from the Council of Industrial Design, among others. 'We cleaned up every award in the book for it,' remembered Marriott, 'and Andrew [Oldham] collected them. We caught him on the stairs of Immediate's office, his arms full of bits of plastic – "Best Artwork", "Best Design", "Best Album". We said, "Where the fuck did you get all those?" His face just went crimson.'[9] It was as good as it was going to get for the Small Faces.

★

From May and into the summer, the Western world was thrown into political turmoil. The month of May 1968 saw students in France instigate an ultimately futile though very influential general strike. The summer saw major student protests in London and across America. In Prague, Czechoslovakia, the Communist regime was turned over to Alexander Dubcek, who liberalised the regime offering 'socialism with a human face'. The USSR allowed the experiment to continue until August when troops from the USSR, Poland and East Germany invaded Czechoslovakia and ended the reforms. Dubcek was replaced the following year.

'I went to the LSE in the mid-Sixties, so I went through all the happenings at the LSE in the late Sixties,' remembers Dave Phillips. 'The first sit-in was in opposition to Walter Adams who'd come as the director in 1966, and who'd formerly been Principal of University College Salisbury in Rhodesia. The first political march was a protest against UDI.'

Rhodesia – a British colony – was dominated by its white, minority population. Under the leadership of Ian Smith, the white minority was determined not to succumb to the British policy of decolonisation which resulted in elections from which the black majority populations would gain power. After unsuccessful negotiations between Smith and Harold Wilson, Smith's government announced that Rhodesia (now Zimbabwe) would unilaterally declare independence (UDI) from Britain in November 1965.

'That was probably the issue that got me into politics,' remembers Phillips. 'CND had gone through a bit of a slump in the mid-Sixties. Then I got into student politics and then Trotskyism and then the International Socialists.' Radical left-wing politics held a huge appeal for intellectuals in the mid-Sixties. 'The mainstream Left were – and in some ways still are – the most boring set of people,' says Phillips. 'They're not into fun – well, it's a "petty-bourgeois" pleasure, hedonism is not on the agenda, which is why they've been so unsuccessful: how are you going to appeal to young people?

'The Sixties were a real time of hope, that things could be changed and that you could have a role in changing them,' recalls Phillips. 'There was a huge ferment of publications and the music sounded just as radical and it felt fantastic. Then it fell apart for a whole variety of reasons. I've never seen it replicated and all the accounts that I've seen of the Sixties don't begin to come to terms with the mix. What you often hear about the Sixties was that they were about psychedelia and drugs or about the history of rock music and you don't get the downside – there was terrific elitism in the Sixties, women were treated like shit in the Sixties, all that's talked about is these rock musicians who are treated like medieval princes with their own courts. It wasn't "joined up", there was no coherence and there was a lot going on.

'If you look at the British experience as against the rest of the world there were lots of differences. If you look at German politics there was the SDS who were modelling themselves on a radical version of the Hitler Youth. They were organised and military and had tactics for charging through the police. As for the Japanese, they were doing hari-kari politics really, they were just extraordinary. Meanwhile in Britain we were doing *Dixon of Dock Green!*'

One of the issues raised by Phillips, the role and status of women in society, was slowly beginning to be addressed within the nascent 'women's movement'. However, if women were given any role in this brave new world it was, as Lucy O'Brien writes, that they 'assisted the revolution by doing the washing up, rolling the roll-ups, making coffee and taking the Pill.'[10]

As Britain was slowly becoming radicalised, the Rolling Stones recovered from their disastrous year in 1967 by releasing 'Jumping Jack Flash' and then disappeared into the studio to record 'Sympathy For The Devil' with French film-maker Jean-Luc Godard; The Beatles returned from India bored with being hippies, telling the world that LSD didn't have all the answers and ready to record the epic mish-mash that was *The White Album*; Manchester United Football Club, with Georgie Best ('El Beatle' himself) and Bobby Charlton, won the European Cup.

And in the record stores, shop assistants were having trouble stopping copies of *Ogden's Nut Gone Flake* from rolling off the shelves. The copies that made their way into people's homes had an award-winning cover that fell apart after being opened just a few times. Pop music was going back to basics, and despite very good sales, *Ogden's* seemed to have dated very quickly. While the optimism of 1965 and '66 had funnelled into the laid-back, LSD-laced grooviness of 1967, the effects of the devaluation of the pound were finally setting in with prices of imported goods rising rapidly.

The year 1968 was rapidly becoming the hangover after the party. Dave Phillips remembers that despite the efforts of the musicians, there was some mistrust between the radicals and the music business. 'I think at the time in the Sixties it was very difficult to connect between the politics and the music,' he recalls. 'It was just that so many people were supporting radical causes, like the anti-Vietnam war campaign, and at the same time they were listening to the music so they made those connections. The problem for politics was to join them together. It took them a very long time. I don't think it joined in a major way at all until "Rock Against Racism" in the late Seventies because the leading figures in the Left didn't listen to the music and were very suspicious of the culture and were very suspicious of the sexuality and the sexual freedom which was all a diversion – diverting the working class from its "historic mission", so it was not to be welcomed at all.'

The way that politics and music did join was more mundane. 'The way it was lived was that you went to talk about politics down at the bar and the jukebox would be pounding out the Four Tops, Tamla Motown, Jefferson Airplane, and that was the soundtrack to the politics. The other thing was that we were very sniffy about the political pretensions of musicians. We thought that they were pretty out of touch, 'cos they lived like princes. Maybe they were princes – there weren't many women around, and they had retinues of hangers-on, they were wealthy, and they had minimal contact with those of us who were trying to sell copies of *Socialist Worker* outside Mount Pleasant Sorting Office [a major post office establishment in London].

'So we were quite critical of that kind of world, and the attempts of people like Jagger to give a political element to their work in something like 'Street Fighting Man' always seemed to me to be a bit phoney, a bit unreal, I felt it was better that they stuck to writing about the sheer emotional hell of being young, they did that better, not to try and link it to social commentary. Whenever there were attempts to make musical social criticism it always seemed pretty naff to me. I suppose the only person who came near it was Dylan.'

Though the Small Faces had never held any political pretensions, perhaps because unlike many other groups they were genuinely just working-class lads on the make, given the ferment in both the music business in particular and the world at large, the Small Faces would have to decide very quickly what they were going to do next. The success of *Ogden's* aside, the band were starting to appear out of touch with the world.

It seemed – especially to Kenney Jones – that the next thing to do was to take *Ogden's* out on tour, but there were obvious problems. Jones's idea was to take Stanley Unwin and a brass section out on the road, but the limited live performance technology of 1968 meant that the intricate arrangements, plus the studio effects, were practically impossible to reproduce live. In addition, the band had spent the best part of a year in the studio. Their last major shows had been with The Who in early 1968, and that had shown the Small Faces how their own live performance had, if anything, deteriorated since the glory days of 1965/66.

'Our recording had gone on leaps and bounds,' remembered Marriott, 'and we were all very interested in the techniques and art of recording. We let down a lot of people who wanted to hear *Ogden's* on stage. We were still very raucous and sort of smashing away, and in the end the audiences became disinterested in our stage perform-ances, I think. It was our own fault because we should've had the guts to tackle it … we just stuck to the formula that had been successful for us for a long time, which is always the kiss of death.'[11]

Ronnie Lane agreed that live performance had lost any appeal. 'You couldn't take it seriously,' he remembered. 'It's like playing in a pub and everyone's talking – only everyone was screaming. After a while we got very half-hearted about it … the screaming did stop eventually, but by that time we'd gone through it, really, the match was spent … In the end the recording and the live work got so totally divorced from each other that if you bought a record and we were playing and you'd go to see us, it wasn't necessarily so that we'd play what you'd just bought on the record. We more or less treated the two things as totally separate entities. We got into a very weird attitude about the stage things.'[12]

Part of the reason for this separation (which afflicted more bands than just the Small Faces) was that recording techniques had improved way beyond anyone's ability to reproduce them live. Plus, in the late Sixties, LP sales actually started to outstrip the sales of singles, so record companies were beginning to see the 7" pop single as a mere device to promote an album, and encouraged artists to spend increasing amounts of time recording. In this environment, live performance was just another way of promoting LPs (and record companies made no money directly from concerts), and there was the increasing dichotomy between record companies trying to put artists out on the road to promote records they couldn't play live.

But, perhaps, more importantly, rock music – as it was now being called – was moving away from studio trickery. Groups like Cream and the Jeff Beck Group were playing a more basic, blues-based music, using the new amplifiers that were louder than anything anyone had heard before. There were long articles written in the music press regarding guitar players' technique, and an almost intel-lectual affectation was applied to the hitherto ignored processes of playing in and as a group. If the release of *Sgt Pepper* had been a cultural event, its legacy was a cerebral approach to the appreciation of popular music which bordered on the obsessive.

After a brief tour of Ireland in July 1968, the Small Faces went back into Olympic Studios to start recording again. They cut two tracks – 'Wham Bam Thank You Mam' and 'The Universal', which Marriott had recorded in his garden on a portable tape machine. A more wistful, regretful song than those on *Ogden's*, 'The Universal' was released as a single by Immediate, but could only manage to reach Number 16 in the charts. The recording sessions weren't overly successful either; while recording 'Wham Bam Thank You Mam', McLagan lost patience with Steve Marriott's aggressive approach and walked out. He was replaced on the track by Nicky Hopkins and eventually returned. It didn't matter; it was becoming apparent that the Small Faces were starting to unravel.

In September 1968, the Small Faces toured Britain with Canned Heat, a group from America who played supercharged R&B. The Small Faces' disillusionment with all aspects of touring again came to the fore. As Ian McLagan remembers, it was 'the cold shower we all needed'.[13] Canned Heat impressed the Small Faces and McLagan in particular.

'Canned Heat never stopped playing. On stage, in the dressing rooms, in the corridor, in the bus, they played constantly because they loved it,' remembered McLagan.[14] In November the Small Faces found themselves on yet another package tour with The Who, along with Joe Cocker, Arthur Brown, and The Mindbenders. It just reminded them how limited their live performances were. And more importantly, Steve Marriott was not a happy boy.

Increasingly in rock music, a sole personality would be singled out as the driving force behind a group, especially a guitarist. Eric Clapton had been through the process, as had Pete Townshend of The Who, and Paul Jones of Manfred Mann. While it is true that there are dominant personalities within groups, a group's success is generally premised on the balance of personalities within the group. And by late 1968, Steve Marriott was beginning to have ideas larger than the Small Faces, who he saw as holding him back. After suggesting that Peter Frampton be brought into the Small Faces so that Marriott could concentrate on singing and playing rhythm guitar, Marriott invited

Frampton to sit in with the Small Faces one night but – according to McLagan – 'it didn't feel like the Small Faces any more'.[15]

The last night of 1968 saw the Small Faces playing at Alexandra Palace. Marriott invited Alexis Korner to jam with them live on stage at the end of the show. When Korner eventually joined them, Marriott walked off. The subsequent confrontation which took place in the dressing room was brief: Marriott told the other Small Faces that he was going to get a band together with Frampton and that, as far as Marriott was concerned, the Small Faces were over.

But none of them could simply walk away – there was a short tour of Germany and some English gigs already booked, and facing a future with no money, all of the Small Faces agreed to fulfil the contract. The atmosphere on the tour was a little strained, to say the least, with Marriott's attention already elsewhere and the remaining Small Faces staring down the barrel of unemployment. The German tour came and went, the English gigs also, and the Small Faces came to an unceremonious end in Devizes.

There was nowhere left to run.

# SIX

# THIN

While the Small Faces were busy scaling the heights, Rod Stewart had also been on an adventure of his own. Faced with the end of his tenure with Steampacket and disheartened by any solo success, he was open to anything that would get him an income. Unknown to him, his immediate future was to lie in the hands of one of London's leading guitarists with one of London's leading groups, Jeff Beck of The Yardbirds.

Jeff Beck was a laconic figure on the London music scene in the mid-Sixties. Recognised as one of the top session guitarists in the country, he had joined The Yardbirds when Eric Clapton decided that they were too commercial for his purist tastes and had quit. Having brought Jimmy Page into The Yardbirds, Beck then fell out of the group, unable to cope with the hectic schedule of touring. For Beck, as for many guitarists in the mid-Sixties, the arrival of Jimi Hendrix in London in 1966 had proved both a blessing and a curse – Hendrix was clearly a far better guitar player than anyone else in London, yet his playing opened up possibilities for the electric guitar which most players hadn't considered.

Once Beck had got over his initial, shocked admiration for Hendrix's outrageous playing style, he set about constructing something which might be able to compete with Hendrix's astonishing ability. The first signs appeared when Beck conscripted Jimmy Page, Keith Moon and session bassist John Paul Jones for a session ostensibly under The Yardbirds' label. The result, 'Beck's Bolero', was a chunk of proto-heavy metal which was never released under The Yardbirds' name. It was shortly after this recording that Beck left the group and signed with producer Mickie Most, then responsible for hits from groups like The Animals and Herman's Hermits. Beck fully expected that Most would make him a star.

He then set about assembling a group who could play like he wanted to play. His first recruit he met at one of the London rock scene's favourite hang-outs, the Cromwellian.

'There was one guy there ploughing into some food and getting drunk on his own,' remembered Beck. 'He didn't even look at me, so I went over to see what was happening. He was really drunk. So I asked him whether he was still playing with Steampacket [actually Shotgun Express] …

'He said, "No, I'm not gonna stay with them."

'So I said, "If you ever want to put a band together …"

'He said, "You're joking."

'I said, "No."

'He said, "You ring me tomorrow. I'll leave Steampacket."

'So I rang him and that was it.'[1]

The hungry drunk in the Cromwellian was Rod Stewart. With a singer on board, Beck held rehearsals in a place near Goodge Street in

London, and went through players including Jet Harris, a former Shadow. The next recruit was – following a phone call – Ronnie Wood. But Wood wasn't to play guitar – Beck wanted him to play bass. Rod Stewart and Ronnie Wood had already come across each other on the London session scene, and Wood had played on a session that Stewart had done for Immediate. 'I know where I first met him,' remembered Wood. 'In the Intrepid Fox in Wardour Street. He had a black eye. And he came up to me and said, "Hello, face. How are ya?"'[2]

Beck enlisted an old friend, drummer Ray Cook, and the Jeff Beck Group was underway. Well, almost underway – Ron Wood didn't own a bass guitar, so he took steps to acquire one. 'I got it from Sound City on Wardour Street, right by the big Durex sign,' remembered Wood. 'I chose a Fender Jazz because it was nearest the door.'[3]

Mickie Most's first act was to get Beck to record the Tin Pan Alley written 'Hi Ho Silver Lining'. Beck hated it and it duly became his greatest hit. 'I didn't like the song,' Beck remembered. 'It was ghastly, stupid. But it's still a mega-success all around England: they play it at the end of discos, turn it off halfway through and everyone sings along.'[4]

Prior to the record's release, the band were booked to play on the ill-fated Roy Orbison/Small Faces package tour in late 1967. They lasted one night, the first night of the tour, at the Finsbury Park Astoria. 'We all walked on stage in our band uniform,' remembered Stewart. 'We all had white jackets and Jeff had a different one because he was the leader of the group. We got through one number and the electric went off. Somebody had pulled the plug. We immediately blamed the Small Faces ... Beck decided this was the end of the show, he wasn't going to stand any more and walked off stage. I remember I wasn't too pleased because I looked down and saw I hadn't done my flies up. We'd been on stage for one and a half minutes and the curtain came down and nearly knocked Woody over ... I caught him and he knocked into me and we sort of did a dance off the stage.'[5]

The press attacked Beck for the poor showing and Beck responded by replacing the drummer with Micky Waller, whom Stewart had played with in Steampacket. Waller didn't last long, replaced first by Rod Coombes and subsequently Aynsley Dunbar. The group began to pick up a reputation, playing alongside such acts as Cream and John Mayall's Bluesbreakers. April 1967 saw the release of Beck's second single, 'Tallyman', which charted at Number 30. Again, Mickie Most wanted Beck to sing the song, while Beck wanted Stewart to take over the vocals, and the compromise of both of them singing was reached. However, Most later asserted that 'Beck didn't want us to record Stewart in case he became more popular.'[6]

Beck's version was that 'Rod didn't have a name and I did, and Mickie Most just said, "Okay, well, I've got to go where the money is."'[7]

The summer of 1967 also saw the rise of the outdoor festival in Britain, and the Jeff Beck Group did their fair share, playing the Reading Festival and the Seventh National Jazz & Blues Festival at the Royal Windsor Racecourse. By the time they played Windsor, Dunbar had decided to start his own group, so yet again Beck recalled Micky Waller.

The group continued to play a series of one-off gigs, developing their reputation for playing the loudest, dirtiest blues in town. However, their stage presence didn't match up to their volume, with Rod Stewart not yet confident enough to command a stage (or an audience), partly because he was – even after all those years – still learning his trade, and he had an understandable nervousness about taking over on stage from Beck who, after all, was the star and the name of the group. Another problem facing the Jeff Beck Group was the success of Cream, who were working in the same musical area.

Cream, who featured another former Yardbird, Eric Clapton, had achieved critical acclaim coupled with sparkling live performances and large record sales.

It was the lack of a hit record that was holding the Jeff Beck Group back, and Mickie Most took a further step to alleviate this by making Beck record 'Love Is Blue' with full orchestra and choir. The song reached Number 23 on the chart, but it neither reflected the Jeff Beck Group in reality or aspiration. Both Beck and the rest of the group were not happy. Beck's response was another change of personnel, and this time it was Ronnie Wood who left. It was to be the start of a serial sacking and reinstatement policy towards Wood, who reacted by taking up an offer from his old friend Kim Gardner to join his group The Creation. Wood flitted between the two groups for most of 1968 but when Jeff Beck asked Wood to join him on a tour of the States it was a simple choice – regular, well-paid work in America with Beck, or pointless gigging around Britain. Wood threw his lot in with Beck.

The Jeff Beck Group continued to tour through 1967 and into 1968, playing throughout Europe. While Europe was in semi-revolutionary turmoil in May 1968, the Jeff Beck Group were in EMI's Abbey Road studios recording their first LP. Their recording time was limited, so they basically had to bash out the tracks as quickly as they could. And, as often happens in creative situations, the limitations forced the group to be more inventive. While recording the LP, they were also acting as backing group for another of Most's artists, Donovan. Although Beck was signed with Columbia Records in Britain, Most couldn't get the LP released immediately. It was at this point that Peter Grant, who was a partner in Most's management company, took a hold of the group's faltering career. He booked them to play at the new Fillmore East venue in New York, as support to the

Grateful Dead. The gig went well despite Stewart being too tense to sing the opening songs – even though the audience couldn't see him.

'We played two numbers in a segue to open,' remembered Beck. 'Rod came out from behind the amps – he sang from offstage – in a mackintosh and a hat, ready to go home. I said, "I think you can take 'em off – they liked it."'[7]

Rod Stewart's account differs slightly and points to the tensions that would eventually destroy the group. '[Beck] had got himself a name as a guitar player, because they were all into guitar players – they still are – and no-one was going to listen in this country, we didn't think ... I didn't feel I was very wanted, from the audience standpoint: I used to think, "Well, they've only come along to listen to Jeff, so I might as well just sing along," and that's when that big thing happened about me hiding behind the amplifiers. I really did ... the first night at the Fillmore and my first night ever in America, and I was so nervous that my voice gave out on the first line, which was "Let me love you", off the *Truth* album. And that's when I hid behind the amplifiers.'[8]

The performance at the Fillmore East made the Jeff Beck Group's reputation in the US. The press reviews were ecstatic and resulted in a deal for Beck with Epic records. Their US tour extended through to August, playing ever larger venues, and all this despite their not having an album to promote. By the time the LP was released in late August 1968, the group were on their way back to London. It reached Number 15 in the American charts on the strength of their previous performances.

It was on that tour that Stewart began to take steps to improve his stage act. The bigger venues in America – where the Jeff Beck Group played to venues that held upwards of 2,000 people at a time – meant that there was more room to move about. In many ways performers find it easier to play to a large crowd in a large venue – it's easier to play in front of 2,000 people than to play in front of twenty, simply because a large crowd becomes impersonal, a swaying mass, whereas twenty people are few enough to remain individuals. In addition, a larger stage means that the impetus is on the performers simply to fill the space, so gestures become magnified and performers are forced to become larger than life. These were the lessons learned by Stewart on that American tour, and he developed a style inspired by Al Jolson, an early musical hero of Stewart's.

'It's very hard to analyse how you develop a style,' said Stewart. 'You try and think of someone you'd copy, but I can't think of anyone.'[9] Part of the reason for this was that there was no recognisable way for rock musicians to perform in the late Sixties. The vast majority of rock acts basically stood on the stage and played. In some ways, especially with the blues purists, all theatricality was frowned upon, which conveniently ignored the fact that the original bluesmen and women had seen themselves as performers first and foremost, and were prepared to be as theatrical as an audience demanded in order to get paid.

The rock acts with the most identifiable stage acts were The Who, who used to smash their instruments at the end of the show, and the prancing, preening Mick Jagger. By the mid-Seventies, there was a format to rock shows, and an expectation from audiences of how rock acts should perform. In the late Sixties that format was still being developed.

★

Back in London, and with the LP still to be released in Britain, the Jeff Beck Group set off on yet another British tour to build on their extensive success in America. When the album was eventually released in October, the group were back in America.

The *Truth* LP was greeted by good reviews in all the music press except the *NME*. But with virtually no airplay – apart from the ubiquitous John Peel, now on BBC Radio 1 – and with the group themselves out of the country and unable to support the record, the album stiffed. Nonetheless, the group returned to Britain to play gigs in December and January before heading back to the States in February for yet another tour. When the time came for the Jeff Beck Group to return to the States, they did so without Ronnie Wood. Beck had decided to replace both Wood and drummer Mickey Waller with Douglas Blake, an unknown bass player from New Zealand, and Tony Newman.

Stranded in London, Wood went to visit Ronnie Lane, who was jamming with the remaining Small Faces following Steve Marriott's departure. Wood had barely begun to think about his future before he got a call from America. Jeff Beck's new bass player had left the band, which in turn had resulted in gigs being cancelled, and since the tour was scheduled to last a while longer, Beck had to find a new bass player fast or risk the wrath of the promoters' lawyers suing for lost income. Wood flew out on the first available flight, but all was obviously not well.

'Ronnie was well pissed off with it,' remembered Stewart. 'You could tell he was just using the group as a filler while he looked for another band.'[10]

This tour wasn't as successful as the previous tour had been, as they were essentially playing the same material. Beck realised that he would have to do something about it, and the group cancelled the end of the tour to return to England to record a second LP.

'We did *Beck-Ola* in about two weeks,' remembered Beck. 'The whole album was pretty well dreamt up on the spot.'[11] Writing was always a problem for Beck, and Stewart and Wood were relied on to come up with tracks for the album.

'We used to write the songs in Ronnie's mum's council house,' remembered Stewart. 'We used to sit 'round and have two bars of the heating on ... Mrs Wood used to come in and say, "Don't waste the electricity – turn that other bar off!" That's where we wrote "The Plynth" – in Ronnie's mum's council house.'[12] Ronnie Wood remembered the writing process as being more theft than invention: 'Rod and I would say, "Oh well, take that bit where The Temptations do this and Booker T does that."'[13]

'The Plynth' itself is a sparkling early result of Stewart and Wood's writing partnership. Starting with a music-hall piano clip, and built around a huge, elegantly simple blues riff, it traverses themes which recur in Stewart's writing – the traditional blues themes of loneliness (and a lack of sex) and how the narrator's life has been squandered, trapped in a situation he cannot control. Though these are themes from the Southern states of the USA, somehow Stewart manages to locate them for a British audience, for all his attempts to sound like Sam Cooke. The lyric calls up images of cold rooms and abject misery before it lapses into self-pity. The rest of the LP suffered from the rush to finish it. Various delays put back the release date for the album, and the group headed off to America for yet more concerts. Once in the States, things between the band members began to be strained. The LP wasn't due to be released until June, and May found the group in the States trying to promote something that wasn't available.

The relationship between Beck and Stewart was never great and deteriorated further in America. According to Ron Wood, Beck and Stewart 'had more of a thing of not talking to each other. I got on so well with Rod that I joined in the fun as well, but I wouldn't let it go too far because I respected Jeff's ... purist approach to being a great manipulator of his guitar.'[14] Added to this, Beck was constantly irritated that Americans presumed that Stewart was 'Jeff Beck'.

Wood remembered that the band's management also fuelled the tension. 'They treated me and Rod and the rest of the guys like second-class citizens, both musically and financially. Jeff stayed at the Hilton while me and Rod crammed into one room at the Gorham Hotel. We were so desperate at times that we'd go down to the Automat to steal eggs. That's how we lived.'[15]

By June 1969, Stewart, Wood and Beck were avoiding conflict by avoiding each other, but newer members of the group were not so content, effectively striking matches in a gas-filled room. Nicky Hopkins, who had joined the group to play keyboards, complained about the financial and managerial arrangements for the group; Tony Newman – yet another drummer – also complained about the financial arrangements. The group became suspicious that they were being ripped off by both the management and Beck, and when Beck bought himself a £1,000 'Hot Rod' in Boston they were convinced. But Beck himself had no idea what was going on.

'None of the guys got their money,' he remembered. 'Of course, I got the blame for it. We were getting ripped off ... fleeced.'[16] Hopkins' complaints eventually resulted in his leaving the group in June. A break in the American tour schedule in May and June gave Rod Stewart the time to return to London, where he had another project to engage his attention.

Stewart hadn't been idle since joining the Jeff Beck Group. His ambition remained to have a solo deal, and it was his performances with Beck that had persuaded Mercury Records' Lou Reizner to offer him £1,000 and a car to record an LP. Despite the fact that Stewart had never been in control of a recording session, he claimed that Reizner's credit as producer was overstated.

'I wouldn't exactly say he produced the album,' remembered Stewart. 'He sat there and made sure we were all in tune.'[17] Stewart stuck with musicians that he knew well – Mickey Waller on drums, Ron Wood played bass and guitar, Martin Quittenton played acoustic guitar and the Small Faces' Ian McLagan played keyboards.

The album, *An Old Raincoat Won't Ever Let You Down*, featured four self-penned compositions as well as covers of Ewan McColl's 'Dirty Old Town', the traditional 'Man Of Constant Sorrow', Mike D'Abo's 'Handbags And Gladrags', and the Stones' 'Street Fighting Man', a last-minute inclusion because – as Stewart remembered – it had less chords in it than the other option, 'The Girl Can't Help It'. Stewart's own compositions, 'Blind Prayer', 'I Wouldn't Ever Change A Thing', 'Cindy's Lament' and the title track, lacked the punch of his later collaborations with Quittenton and Wood, and the album itself was a bit of mix 'n' match, but its folky feel harked back to Stewart's early love of Bob Dylan et al. in the early Sixties.

In many ways, at a time when the Jeff Beck group were pushing the boundaries of R&B, Stewart was returning to something more reflective. The album was largely ignored in the UK, though the *NME* did note that, 'Rod "The Mod" Stewart commands a lot of respect among pop people for his unusual blues voice and this album does him full justice … a very worthy album which deserves to do well.' Released under the title *The Rod Stewart Album* in the States, it received critical acclaim.

An enthusiastic Greil Marcus, writing in *Rolling Stone*, found it, 'a superb album … Imagination pervades the music … unlike so many of the records of 1969, issued with a flood of hype and forgotten after a dozen playings, this one is for keeps. Many LPs are a lot flashier than this one, but damn few are better.' While sales of the LP were relatively poor both in the UK and the USA, it was an impressively promising debut and the packaging contained an example of Stewart's bloody-mindedness.

'Rod could be very silly,' remembered McLagan. 'He liked saying the word "thin" and he'd pronounce it thinly as well.'[18] Stewart had wanted to call the LP 'Thin', but Mercury Records thought better of it, the eventual titles being a compromise. But Stewart still managed to get the word 'thin' on to the album cover, printed in very small type in the bottom left corner.

In between recording his debut LP, the Small Faces persuaded Stewart and Wood to guest with them for a couple of gigs along with Art Wood, Ronnie's brother. They did it for the money, playing as Quiet Melon. Back in America with Jeff Beck, the new material from the *Beck-Ola* LP was wowing the audiences but the relations between the band members were increasingly attritional. On 13 July, at the Singer Bowl in Queens, New York, the band were playing as support to Vanilla Fudge along with Ten Years After. Led Zeppelin were also backstage, and when the Jeff Beck Group started to play 'Jailhouse Rock', they were joined on stage by a horde of drunken musicians.

'The stage was full of people,' remembered Rod Stewart. 'We were doing "Jailhouse Rock" and it was fucking incredible. I finished the whole thing by shoving a mike stand up John Bonham's ass and he got arrested, the cops pulled him off and I ran away … we were all pissed out of our heads. And Vanilla Fudge couldn't follow it.'[19] Vanilla Fudge indeed could not follow it, since the audience started to leave when the Jeff Beck Group et al. wandered off stage. But, more importantly, some time after the show the bassist and drummer from Vanilla Fudge, Tim Bogert and Carmine Appice, asked Beck if he wanted to form a band with them. Beck had been a long-time fan of the group, and was certainly up for it.

In the meantime, the Jeff Beck Group had an itinerary to complete, and spent the end of July playing shows in which the singer and the guitarist were openly hostile with each other on stage. Though they had been booked to play the Woodstock Festival, Beck cancelled the rest of the tour (including Woodstock) and everyone went home. In retrospect, it looks a little deranged to withdraw from what was to become the most famous gig in rock history; at the time it was just one gig too far for a group that was dead on its feet. It was time to go home.

# SEVEN

# FACE TO FACES

In the days following Steve Marriott's departure, the three remaining Small Faces were thoroughly depressed, not only with the lack of a viable future, but with the mechanics of the music business in general. The problem with pop success, they had discovered, was that if it all fell apart, the music business had little to offer. What the Small Faces did have was their contract with Immediate Records, and they still owed the record company an LP, and they should – in theory – have been paid an advance to record it. However, without a frontman, only half a songwriting partnership and no manager, it didn't seem likely that Immediate would stump up the cash. And to make matters worse, the financial position of Immediate itself was starting to look dubious.

Ronnie Lane – the original Small Face and now erstwhile band leader – booked the remaining Small Faces into a rehearsal room. Despite all their years of playing together, Lane, McLagan and Jones were directionless without Marriott. The days spent thumping out old tunes just reinforced their misery. The Small Faces' rehearsals came to an end without any forward movement. McLagan was approached by Pete Frampton [the singer/songwriter with whom Marriott was forming Humble Pie] to play keyboards with Humble Pie, but nothing came of the offer. The future looked bleak, and the band were forced to downgrade their lives, moving houses, fending off bailiffs, and seriously considering getting day jobs.

The group were also suffering the trauma of Marriott's departure. 'It's like you lose your best friend, your brother, your band member,' remembered McLagan. 'And it's times four, 'cos the whole band had to break up, didn't it? We'd had this magical mix of four people. It's very sad.'[1] It affected Ronnie Lane, too.

'When he [Marriott] went off to join Humble Pie I was staggered. I felt a huge personal loss because we had been very close,' he said later. 'Just after Steve left I was in a right state ... I wasn't even sure that I wanted to stay with Kenney and Ian ... we rehearsed, just the three of us mainly because we had nothing else to do. I changed my mind from day to day. It was like a love affair that is past its prime. You get into a nice, comfortable rut, and while things aren't really together, and you don't care too much about the girl, you hate the thought of someone else going out with her. That's how it was until suddenly I realised, we all did, that we did want to stick together.'[2] The Small Faces were in deep trouble. They needed a kick-start from outside.

As the Small Faces were contemplating a life outside of music, Ron Wood, having recently split from the Jeff Beck Group, was also at a loose end. Sitting around at home one day, hungover and flicking through the music press, he noticed an article about Marriott's decision to leave the Small Faces. Wood saw an opening, and he immedi-

*Above:* Getting on
with their neighbours –
the Small Faces at home
in Westmoreland
Terrace. Kenney Jones,
Ian McLagan, Ronnie
Lane, Steve Marriott

*Right:* Rolling Over –
the Small Faces near
the end, 1968

A mod on the make – Rod Stewart, 1964

Biding their time – The Jeff Beck Group.
Ron Wood, Jeff Beck, Micky Waller, Rod Stewart

Jeff Beck, Woody and Rod looking pensive

Introducing the Faces – clockwise from back: Kenney Jones,
Ian McLagan, Ron Wood, Ronnie Lane, Rod Stewart

Wearing it well – Woody and Rod on *Top of the Pops*

Getting down to business – the Faces blues it up

Thin – Rod goes it alone

Rod holds the mic while Ronnie holds the note...

... and the bottle

Mac lights up

ately tracked down Ronnie Lane's phone number. As Wood remembers it, the conversation was brief.

'What ya doin' man? You've got to keep the group together!' he told a startled Ronnie Lane. Though unconvinced – but with little else on offer – Lane invited him to new rehearsals. Basically poverty stricken, Lane convinced Ian Stewart, the Rolling Stones' road manager (better known as 'Stu') of their predicament, and Stu arranged for the remaining Small Faces to rehearse in the Stones' own rehearsal studio in Bermondsey.

Rehearsal rooms are dingy, depressing places at the best of times. Usually badly lit, with no windows (though perhaps – if you're lucky – a mirror on one wall), they are unventilated, hot and smoky and smell of stale beer, stale cigarettes and stale sweat. The floors and walls are covered with old carpets, speckled with cigarette burns and grown musty with age, to deaden the sound. Every available horizontal surface – the tops of amplifiers and keyboards – are crammed with beer bottles, overstuffed ashtrays and half-drunk cups of tea. In the studios, the group tend to rehearse in a circle, with the drummer facing the amplifiers, speakers and the rest of the band, so that s/he can hear what is going on. And because drum kits are quite loud on their own, the volume in the room is generally very, very loud. Bands tend to go into rehearsal studios in the late morning and stay until the early evening, which is largely what gives people at the lower end of the music business food chain that pallid appearance. The room the Faces used was no different, though it had one concession to humanity – their room had a window onto the adjoining room.

Stuck in the rehearsal room, the three remaining Small Faces, along with Wood, ran through the usual repertoire of blues covers – 'Mojo Working', 'Hoochie Coochie Man', 'Kansas City'. It was obvious from the outset that this was a line-up that worked: the tight groove of the rhythm section – Lane's bass and Jones' drums – had always neatly intersected with McLagan's Hammond organ and electric piano. The addition of Wood, free from the burden of playing bass with Jeff Beck and revelling in his new-found space to play his beloved bottleneck blues and funky blues riffs, gave the Small Faces a tougher, boozier sound. It didn't take them long to realise that they were nearly a great group – but only nearly.

The group needed a frontman, someone able to work a crowd, to outperform the rest of the group, to have the charisma to light up any size of room. And Wood, Lane, McLagan and Jones knew that they didn't have it. Though Lane and Wood were both able vocalists and McLagan could hold a tune, they had all been around the business long enough to know that this was never going to be enough. The Small Faces needed a frontman, and more: he had to be able to sing.

As interest in the daily rehearsals began to wane, the band began to spend more time in the King's Head, the pub down the road from the rehearsal studio. They were joined regularly by Rod Stewart, the other refugee from the Jeff Beck Group, who had begun to attend the rehearsals, not so much to watch the group as to go to the pub with them afterwards.

'Woody brought Rod down and he became part of the furniture, one of the lads,' remembered Kenney Jones. 'He used to sit on the amps, watching us.'[3] The landlord of the King's Head was very impressed with them – he was overheard describing them as 'nice boys – all shorts'. For once, he wasn't referring to their height, but their practice of drinking spirits in abundance. Back in the rehearsal room, Stewart would occasionally join the group for a tune or two, simply to keep his throat in good nick. But despite his distinctive voice, he was not immediately accepted.

Part of the problem was that following their experience with the unpredictable Marriott, the Faces were suspicious of anyone who wanted to be a frontman. And, for all his obvious talent, Stewart hadn't really been a dominant frontman before – in his previous groups he had at best shared front-of-stage with other singers or musicians. It was only in his time with the Jeff Beck Group that he was prepared to perform at the front of the stage. Notwithstanding his close friendship with Wood and increasingly close friendship with the other members of the group (and the fact that he was one of the few people who could match the Small Faces drink for drink), the band were not ready to leave themselves open to being used by another egomaniac.

The other part of the problem was that it didn't particularly seem to be in Rod Stewart's own interests to join another band. Having taken his opportunity to escape from the auspices of the Jeff Beck Group, Stewart already had his own solo recording deal with Mercury Records. Although he was interested in putting together a backing band of his own to promote his solo work, the Small Faces with Ron Wood on board were already clearly an entity in their own right. It was difficult to see how it would suit Stewart to jump straight in with another band. So the rehearsals and the visits to the King's Head continued.

The constant drinking and hanging around together, plus the shared love of soul music and R&B, added to the fact that they were all working-class London boys in an increasingly middle-class industry, cemented a bond between the five. It was no act of genius for the band to realise that something had to give or they would all soon be looking for day jobs. And in the world of day jobs outside the rehearsal room, life continued much as it always had. Though the educated middle classes were still digesting the events of 1968, for the working class in Britain everything was much as it had been since the Fifties. The sexual revolution hadn't happened to them; the social revolution had only happened to a few – The Beatles, David Bailey, Michael Caine among perhaps the most prominent. The rest of the working class were caught in the same trap – they left school early (the school-leaving age at the time was fifteen), they got a job and married early.

There were only limited opportunities to escape this fate: sports (with boxing and football being the principle prospect); education (which was limited to the absurdly gifted) and showbusiness, principally acting and music. And it was the music business which was – on the face of it – the easiest: anyone could learn to play the guitar, and once you had four chords, you had a song. Or, at least, you could copy someone else's song. So for the remaining Small Faces – and Stewart and Wood – there was a vast incentive to get it right. None of them wanted to end up in some dull factory marking time until marriage and the potential of a mortgage dried them out.

But there was no inevitability to the formation of The Faces – it took a simple but definitive act from the most pragmatic of the Small Faces, Kenney Jones, actually to transform the bond into a band. One day, as Stewart watched the Small Faces run through another clutch of R&B covers, Jones got up from his drum stool, marched over to where Stewart was sitting, and literally dragged him over to the microphone.

Long John Baldry says that Rod Stewart's appeal is his 'little boy lost' look. But behind that look lay a canny (and cunning) intellect, a natural gang leader with a withering sense of humour which he would direct at anyone outside of the gang. And even before he officially joined, through the long evenings spent in the King's Head, Stewart had adopted The Faces as his own. Kenney Jones' act of physically dragging Stewart to the microphone was just an admission that both parties had separate problems and that this was the most equitable way of resolving them. Nothing else was ever said: The Faces were born and the five found their way out of their working-class trap.

★

The British working class in the late Sixties were still easily identifiable – they mostly worked in factories, shipyards, steelworks and coal mines. They were highly trade unionised and were relatively well off, compared to their parents at least. But the welfare state which had been responsible for this general well-being was beginning to come under pressure. Chancellor Jim Callaghan's devaluation of the pound in late 1967 was followed by an international monetary crisis in March 1968, which was in turn followed by another international financial crisis in late 1968. These were the days of prices and incomes policies, and the trade unions – a partner in the so-called 'social contract' between government, unions and business – were becoming increasingly belligerent. Militant shop stewards were calling numerous unofficial strikes which in turn were – it was felt by government – damaging the economy. The Labour government's attempt to resolve the situation, a White Paper called *In Place of Strife* proposed by cabinet minister Barbara Castle, never made it through Parliament, largely because of splits within the Labour cabinet, which included many ministers sponsored by trade unions.

The year 1968 had seen an influx of East African Asians into the UK as they were expelled by Idi Amin's government in Uganda. In order to respond to this, the government introduced a Race Relations Bill which aimed to stem immigration, but not before both the Conservative Party in general and Enoch Powell in particular stoked the fires of racial tension. On 20 April, Powell gave a speech in Birmingham where he claimed that, 'As I look ahead I am filled with foreboding. Like the Roman, I seem to see the River Tiber foaming with much blood.'[4] Despite being dismissed from the Shadow Cabinet, he received over 100,000 letters in support.

The same year also saw the resurgence of nationalism in Northern Ireland. The Catholic community, drawing inspiration from the

American Civil Rights movement, formed a Civil Rights movement of their own in order to draw attention to their plight. October 1968 saw serious rioting in Derry, provoked by the province's police force, the RUC. By the summer of 1969 there was widespread violence within the province, comprising regular riots against the police and random acts of sabotage. Further riots and a chasming sectarian divide led Home Secretary Jim Callaghan to send the British Army into Belfast and Derry in order to separate the factions but implicitly to spare the Catholic community from the province's government. However, by this point the situation had been removed from the hands of the moderate Civil Rights movement: a group of militant Nationalists split from the 'Official' IRA. Calling themselves the 'Provisional' IRA, they set up the Provisional Army Council and with about 600 activists, began a campaign of urban terrorism. Northern Ireland was to provide an often tragic and always violent backdrop to the Britain of the Seventies.

By the end of the Sixties, many of the old working-class communities were being broken up as the new housing estates moved people out of the slum areas which had been the homes for the working class. Along with the break-up of those communities went a shift in the value systems which had sustained the working class. Though some of these changes were tangible – people were physically living in different places – some of them were less obvious: the breakdown of the extended family, the perceived embourgeoisement of traditional working-class areas, the push towards home ownership rather than renting from the local council, the so-called 'sexual revolution'. These changes were most keenly felt by working-class teenagers who were, for the first time since the war, starting to be subject to rising unemployment and the resulting uncertainty. Working-class youth subcultures began to respond to these changed circumstances.

By the late Sixties, British youth subcultures had started to frag-
ment. The Rockers and Teddy Boys of the late Fifties/early Sixties had
largely dissipated, and the Mod subculture that had spawned the
Small Faces had splintered, the Mods seeping into either Britain's own
version of hippy, or the harder, more extreme version of Mods that
were Skinheads. What young, white males were looking for was any
sort of reaffirmation of their identity, and this search for identity mani-
fested itself as Skinhead. Skinheads drew on two apparently incom-
patible sources for their lifestyle – black, West Indian immigrants, and
a mythical white, working-class idea of 'community'. Where traditional Mods had been upwardly aspirational, Skinheads were apparently happy to be part of the lumpen working class.

Ironically, the place where white, working-class males found the
affirmation of their culture and identity was among the West Indian
communities which were strewn around the country's cities. Black
West Indian culture was conservative, holding out against the pervasive and dominant white, British cultures within which West Indians
were living. This was partly to preserve their own culture, but was
also because West Indian immigrants were denied equal access to
British culture simply because of the colour of their skin.[5] The rituals,
language and style associated with West Indian culture provided a
model for the young Skinheads, whose only other apparent choice
was the 'hippy' model which was, of itself, conspicuously middle
class, based around university campuses, and which was rebelling in
favour of change.

It was change itself that the Skinheads were alienated by, and their
appearance itself was almost a caricature of working-class dress – the
workmen's jeans, the Ben Sherman shirts, and especially the boots.
However, Skinheads also picked up tips in style from young West
Indians – they shared a love of ska and reggae music, and the

Abercrombie coats and severely cropped hair were both redolent of the 'Rude Boy' look prevalent among young West Indian men. Skinheads were therefore attempting to resolve the tension 'between an experienced present (the mixed ghetto) and an imaginary past (the classic white slum)' by taking elements of style and culture from both.[6]

However, the supposed truce between the Skinheads and young West Indians was also constituted within the terms of creating an 'other'. Most ideas of community are premised around notions of who are 'us' and who are 'they', and are usually situated in a very real territory or locale. For the Skinheads the 'they' were hippies, 'queers' and Asians, all of whom were encroaching on traditional working-class territory (the council estates and remaining slums of Britain's cities), and all of whom were treated with disdain and often attacked at will. And the Skinheads weren't discerning in which group of Asians they attacked – whether they were from India, Pakistan, Bangladesh or Uganda, the Skinheads' gift to the English language was the phrase 'Paki-bashing'.

This new youth subculture was noticed by the music business, and Seventies Glam band Slade's earliest incarnation was as a 'Skinhead' band; however, the Skinheads' reputation for violence of a very real kind meant that Slade and the music business moved quickly to distance themselves from it. It didn't matter, though, as the process of development of Skinhead as a subculture meant that they didn't want or need their own bands, preferring instead to listen to the music which came out of Jamaica, itself a secret pleasure and thereby keeping the subculture in an outlaw world of its own.

Even football violence – which was starting to make its presence felt at stadiums around the country – was itself steeped in class, culture and territory. Football has been played – in one form or another – for hundreds (perhaps thousands) of years. The game has always been associated with the lower classes, despite the pivotal role played within the history of the game by the predominantly middle- and upper-class public (private) schools. Perhaps the most renowned early reference to football comes in Shakespeare's *King Lear*, when the Earl of Kent refers to a 'base football player'.

As Britain became increasingly industrialised during the end of the nineteenth century and early twentieth century, the limited time away from work enjoyed by the working classes meant that they would increasingly join in to watch the mass spectator sports that were available. Games were traditionally played at three o'clock on a Saturday afternoon as the working week was from Monday to Friday with a half day on Saturday (Sundays were for church). The working man (and it was almost entirely a male pursuit) would make his way from the factory to the football ground, and in massive numbers they did – crowds averaged in the region of 60–70,000 in the Thirties, and following the Second World War, the crowds remained undiminished.

However, towards the end of the Sixties – with other diversions for the leisure time of the working class and the rise in football fan violence – crowds began to tail off, though the numbers attending games were still high. Fans supported their local club; and from that, the football ground was a shared, local space, a space to be defended and held against the supporters of other clubs.

The rise in incomes for young people meant that young men could afford to travel around the country following their team. To this end, British Rail started laying on 'Football Specials', trains which would run from the major cities on a Saturday, packed with football supporters.

'They were the worst trains,' remembered Kevin McDonald, a Chelsea fan who frequented the notorious Shed at Chelsea. 'If there were any seats they were all ripped up, there were no lights and if there were we used to smash them anyway, and the whole train would stink of piss, beer and sweat. Standing in that for four hours up to Manchester or Leeds, no wonder everyone got off ready for a fight.'

The greatest achievement for visiting supporters was to take the home crowd's end – each set of supporters would have a part of the ground which was 'theirs', usually behind one of the goals. The opposition fans would then attempt to 'run' the home fans out of their 'end' by the simple process of charging them until they were either successful or repelled.

However, by the early Seventies Skinhead had passed into 'Suedehead', basically a grown-out version of itself. The hard-core Skinheads remained, but they were beginning to get a reputation for involvement in far-right politics, the National Front finding the Skinheads on the football terraces a rich recruiting ground.

By 1969, Britain seemed to be a gloomier place. In spite of public dissatisfaction with the Labour government, most pundits still thought Labour would win the 1970 General Election, though there was a feeling that Wilson's government had let the country down, perhaps premised on the economic crises in 1967/68. But it couldn't be said that the living standards had dropped – far more people owned their own homes, and ownership of cars, washing machines, fridges and TVs had risen steadily during the Sixties.

The government had also liberalised the laws on homosexuality, abortion and divorce, had abolished the death penalty for murder, had introduced a law which required employers to pay men and women equally for work of equal value, and had reduced the age of majority (the age at which people can legally get married, vote and enter into financial dealings) to eighteen. And yet for most people in the country, it felt as though Wilson's Labour Party hadn't increased national prosperity quickly enough.

'In truth, Britain only "swung" for most of its citizens through the columns of their tabloid newspaper,' wrote Roy Hattersley later. 'Topless models, open marriages and drunken orgies were what they read about. But it's doubtful if a majority of adult voters even supported the state's gradual withdrawal from the private lives of its citizens.'[7]

And perhaps as a punctuation mark to the decade, on 20 July 1969, Neil Armstrong stepped from the Lunar Module and stood on the moon, the scratchy pictures and sound received around the world on television. Though Armstrong's view of the earth needed full colour to be appreciated, the grey picture on most televisions did full justice to the moon itself. In the end it was just a big lump of dusty rock.

This feeling of disillusionment hung over Britain like a shroud in 1969 and 1970. Although they were better off than they had ever been, the British working classes were more confrontational. However, the music business – previously in the decade the keenest reflection of working-class culture along with sport (especially football) – was becoming increasingly bourgeois. An obsession with musicianship, along with a desire to see their music as a serious art form, led to a breed of musicians who saw themselves as artists first and entertainers later, if at all.

This was never something that The Faces were to be accused of. But despite a new singer and guitarist, the gloom did pervade The Faces to some extent: they had no manager, a dubious recording contract, and a significant debt problem. Jones, McLagan and Lane were now in constant battles with bailiffs – McLagan once throwing the contents of a bedpan over two unlucky debt collectors – and Ron Wood had no income whatsoever. Stewart alone had his small contract with Mercury Records to produce LPs, though it was difficult to see how this could benefit the rest of the group directly. Kenney Jones was deputised by the group to find them a manager, and he went to see songwriter and arranger Jimmy Horowitz, whom they'd met early in the Small Faces career, and Jones explained the group's problems. Horowitz put Jones on to the man he thought could do the job, an up and coming manager who'd worked with the Robert Stigwood Organisation, Billy Gaff.

Music business management had changed since the days of Don Arden's involvement with the Small Faces (though Arden was to go on to greater success with groups like Black Sabbath in the Seventies). Managers had to be music business savvy (rather than just showbusiness savvy), had to know how to deal with increasingly powerful record companies and with an increasingly intricate music business machine. But they also had to be able to deal with a group, to placate (in The Faces' case) five different egos and push them to a common goal. In many ways, the role of the manager was simply to act as a barrier between the business and the group, passing on the wishes of one to the other in the most acceptable way. Gaff's first job with the Robert Stigwood Organisation had been to work with Cream, the supergroup featuring Eric Clapton.

'I told Robert I wouldn't know where to start,' recalled Gaff.

'He replied, '"Have you ever looked after children?"'

'So I said, "Yes, my sister's got three."'

'Stigwood said, "Good, just think of it like that and you'll be fine!"'[8]

Given The Faces' depression and lack of money and increasing propensity to argue with each other, it was the only attitude to take. As Kenney Jones said, 'We needed a fucking referee!'

Horowitz arranged a meeting between Jones and Gaff at the Speakeasy where Jones laid out the many problems The Faces had.

'Gaff had this little leather hat on,' remembered Jones. 'He listened attentively to all this and says that he thinks he can sort everything out.'[9] Gaff had a meeting with the group's solicitor and got the remaining Small Faces out of their contract with Immediate. He then set about trying to get the group gigs and a new recording contract. However, no-one wanted to give The Faces a recording contract.

Polydor told Gaff that the band were nothing without Steve Marriott, and a similar response came from Track and Apple (The Beatles' label). Warner Brothers records didn't want to sign them either, but luckily for Gaff and The Faces, Joe Smith, the chief of the American arm of Warners, was in town, eager to sign British talent to the American label. He already knew of Stewart and Wood from their time with the Jeff Beck Group, and saw that they could build on their success in America. Gaff walked away from Warners with a £30,000 advance and a five-LP deal, plus the assurance that the records would be released in the UK by Warners UK. In addition, the group found a new agent for booking gigs. As Gaff was still attached to the Robert Stigwood Organisation, it seemed obvious that they should act as agents for The Faces, though Stigwood had an ulterior motive – Stewart, with his solo deal and growing reputation, was a good signing, whether with The Faces or alone.

The Faces were overjoyed, not least because the new deal would keep them off the dole. They celebrated the resumption of their careers by blowing some of the cash on cars in an attempt to match Rod Stewart, who owned a Marcos obtained as part of his solo deal with Mercury. Ron Wood bought a 1959 Jaguar XK150, Lane a silver Mercedes 190SL, McLagan a Triumph TR6 and Jones an MGA.

For a group that was essentially on its uppers, they travelled in style.

# EIGHT

# STARTING
# THE PARTY

The first dates booked for The Faces were in November, in Effretikon, near Zurich, Switzerland, just to get the group some live experience together. December saw the group ensconced in Olympic Studios in Barnes, London, to record their first LP. They had recorded some demos with Glyn Johns, who was by now one of the top producers in the country and had been working with The Beatles on the *Let It Be* sessions. Johns was happy to produce them, but asked for a two per cent royalty rate on each copy of the album sold. The band – led by the increasingly cash-conscious McLagan – refused, wanting instead to pay him a flat rate. Johns declined, not needing the obvious hassle of working with The Faces. The Faces therefore produced themselves, accompanied by engineer Martin Birch.

This was a brave decision for a group who hadn't recorded themselves before and had hardly played live. The record company allowed the group to get away with it because by the late Sixties, artists were increasingly taking control of the recording studio. The heavy touring schedule endured by most groups also meant that there was very little time to write songs on the road, the writing increasingly taking place in the studio.

Though each of The Faces had made records before, they hadn't made records together. They were yet to find their own sound, and without a producer to take them by the scruff of the neck and shake them into shape, there were always going to be musical problems. The results of their labours were released in March 1970 under the title *Small Faces*, though due to the cover – which showed the five Faces sitting in a row, Ron Wood in the centre holding a book titled *First Step – How to Play the Guitar* – the LP is better known as *First Steps*. The reason for the group being billed as 'Small Faces' was because the American label wanted to cash in on the Small Faces' 1967 success with 'Itchycoo Park', a decision which The Faces hated. They didn't want any association with their past, and steadfastly refused to play any Small Faces material, no matter how often audiences would call for it.

The album itself is a mixed bag. It opens with a cover of Bob Dylan's 'Wicked Messenger', obviously chosen by Stewart, laden with McLagan's Hammond organ and Wood's guitar. Already, though, the influence of Stewart and Wood's time with Jeff Beck are apparent – the sound is much heavier than anything the Small Faces had produced, but the folkier influences brought by Stewart and Ronnie Lane appear in hints. Next up is Ronnie Lane's 'Devotion', a more reflective track, arranged almost like a gospel song. 'Shake, Shudder', penned by Lane and Wood, is a straightforward rocker in the Beck style. 'Stone', penned and sung by Lane, is a piece of whimsy recalling American folk and bluegrass. 'Around The Plynth' is the most obvious steal from the Jeff Beck Group days, a direct copy of 'The Plynth' from *Beck-Ola* with no credit for Beck.

'Flying', written by Stewart, Wood and Lane, drifts in from nowhere, led by Wood's guitar and McLagan's Hammond. A precursor to the (rightfully) much-derided 'Sailing' some years later, it tells the same story of returning home to a longed-for lover. Wood's instrumental 'Pineapple And The Monkey' is a homage to Booker T & The MGs, and 'Nobody Knows', penned by Lane and Wood, is another ballad in the style that Rod Stewart would become so adept at belting out in later years. Jones and McLagan came up with the filler instrumental 'Looking Out The Window', followed by Stewart and McLagan's 'Three Button Hand Me Down' to close the LP. Obviously the most well-constructed self-penned song on the LP, 'Three Button Hand Me Down' gives the best foretaste of what The Faces might become. A basic R&B romp, lyrically premised around a tale of sartorial elegance but also around the need to remember your roots, belted out by Stewart, the track sounds like a band finally letting go and having a damn good time.

'"Three Button Hand Me Down" is my favourite Faces song,' says Jonno Pavitt. 'I just like the fact – it's probably a Mod thing – that this guy bases everything he does, and his whole outlook, on a suit. I can remember doing it myself, going out wearing a white shirt, white trousers, and white shoes, with a blue cravat, going to a club. Looking back now I think, "Jesus Christ, I probably looked like Terry Thomas." But at the time I would not have worn anything else that night. And people didn't take the piss 'cos if you wore it right ... Other people turned up wearing all sorts of stuff and we ripped into them. But if you put it all on in the right order ... But whatever article you have, it's your basis. If you base your whole life around owning a good suit, or having a tailor, that's got to mean something, I reckon. I have a tailor, and I love saying to people, "Do you want my tailor's number?" And if your dad had handed you your suit, you've got all your traditional working-class values there, haven't you. You've got the love of your dear old dad; and then the fact that you actually want to look good. And it doesn't actually matter if your bird don't like it 'cos she can bugger off – there's always another bird but it's a fucking great suit.'

As a whole, the LP sounds like it lacks direction. The sound is constant without being much more than a set of musicians playing and having the sound they make recorded. Only on 'Three Button Hand Me Down' do The Faces really gel as a group. The lack of a producer also shows in the length of the songs – the shortest is just over three minutes and the longest nearly six minutes. It is sometimes a problem with good musicians that they don't know when to stop playing, and with The Faces there was no-one in the studio to take control and force them to focus on the songs rather than their playing. But for a group who had only recently formed and who were finding their feet with each other both as players and writers, it is a more than competent effort. The album was tepidly received in the media, and both the LP and its associated single – 'Flying' backed with 'Three Button Hand Me Down' – made little impression.

'*First Step* was recorded on a very limited scale,' said Wood later. 'It was very disjointed because there were so many personalities to tie it all together, which is good in a way because we're still discovering things about each other.'[1]

With product to sell, the band went out on the road to promote the record. They had already played the Lyceum Ballroom in London on New Year's Eve, 1969, and by the time of the LP's release they were gigging extensively.

'We worked bloody hard in those days,' remembered Stewart. 'In the first six months I don't think we played to more than one hundred people at each concert. When we first started nobody wanted to listen to us and nobody was taking us very seriously, and we decided to go round the pub beforehand. Call it Dutch courage if you want, but that's what it was down to. We were just lacking confidence, and I think all the boys enjoyed a drink more than anything else.'[2]

This was reflected in their developing stage presence. While Stewart would take command of the stage, swinging his microphone stand around like a demented baton twirler, the rest of the group would talk to each other, cadge drinks from offstage, and generally try – and fail – to remain standing for the whole gig. More often than not they ended up in a heap in the middle of the stage, with Kenney Jones sitting behind them still playing while Wood and Lane learned to play while lying on their backs. At a time when other musicians playing live would be huddled over their instruments, each note the result of contorted concentration, the British public didn't know what to make of The Faces. And in early 1970, they didn't make much of them.

'When we all got together, one thing we had in common was that we liked to put on a show,' Stewart said later. 'We didn't say, "Why don't we go out and jump all over the stage, get drunk and fall about?" – it was a natural reaction to what was going on around us at the time. If you want to listen to the band sounding like the record, go home and listen to the record because you've got it there in stereo. But if you come and see us you've got to put up with our mistakes, our silliness and everything else that goes along with us, because we're visual, we were one of the first bands to be visual. People don't come along to see The Faces for the sound quality – I hope not, anyway, because we've been terrible some nights. They come along for the atmosphere.'[3]

They also had their first national TV exposure under their belts, appearing on the BBC's *Top of the Pops* to promote 'Flying', followed by an appearance on BBC2's late-night music programme *Disco 2*. But neither the endless gigs nor the TV appearances could save the single or LP, and it seemed that The Faces' first steps could be their last.

★

Britain in February 1970 was cold. So cold, in fact, that snow and ice caused blizzards on Dartmoor and closed Heathrow Airport. Eager to leave the cold, at the end of March 1970, The Faces were due to undertake a 28-date tour of North America, starting in Toronto, Canada. The lack of success in the UK didn't seem to restrain Rod Stewart's eagerness for the trip.

'Half the battle is already won,' he enthused. 'The Faces will go down fantastically well because everyone in the band has improved musically so much. It's Ronnie, Mac and Kenney's first trip to America and they're all going to get very homesick ... This is going to be a great two months. I really think that Marriott was holding their playing back. Since he left, they really seem to have come into their own.'[4] Whether it was sheer bravado or not, The Faces made their way to Canada. No-one in England noticed them leave.

The Faces first show in North America was in the Varsity Arena in Toronto. First on a bill which included Canned Heat and the MC5, they were justifiably nervous. In the event, they didn't have to be: the crowd absolutely loved them. They took their success to Boston, where they opened the Boston Tea Party for three nights supporting organist Lee Michaels. However, it seemed that The Faces hadn't managed to leave Britain's icy weather behind them.

'It was cold and windy,' remembered McLagan. '[We] hadn't realised how cold it could be in the North East. Rod and Woody must have had an inkling because they wore winter coats.'[5]

When they got to the venue, again impressed at the size of the place, The Faces and their roadcrew produced a football from somewhere and took on the headlining act plus their roadies. Hoofing the ball around the cavernous room, it wasn't long before the two teams were kicking lumps out of each other, stopping only when blood was on show. The Faces were already breaking new ground for band behaviour: the football match on arrival at a venue is nowadays an established touring tradition, simply as a way of a group letting off steam after hours spent en route. There was a further problem, which plagued their first night – McLagan's organ wouldn't work properly because of the difference in voltage between the USA and the UK. The problem was overcome by the second night, but again it mattered little: the audience adored The Faces, a fact reflected backstage after each show.

'The dressing room was packed with girls,' remembered McLagan. 'Rod and Woody already had a following … A crowd of them came back to the hotel and gave us all a seeing to over the next few nights. It was trousers off and away we went.'[6]

Similar scenes and adulation followed them to Detroit, a city The Faces made their own – originally booked for two nights in April, they were rebooked for three more nights the following month. Ian McLagan almost didn't make it at all – he got lost on the first afternoon in town with no money, no idea where his hotel was, and only a thin leather jacket to keep out the freezing temperatures. He wandered into a predominantly black populated district of the city, and was saved by some of the locals putting him in a cab and sending him on his way.

The Faces supported Savoy Brown, a British group who were huge in Detroit at that time. It made no difference to The Faces' reception. Stewart and the boys were beginning to get a reputation in the business as a band who were difficult to follow on stage, a reputation cemented in San Francisco where, supporting Lee Michaels again, they blew him away. Michaels was renowned for the vast volume generated by his Hammond organ and it was said that it was only that volume that drowned out the sound of the crowd calling for more from The Faces.

It was in San Francisco that The Faces also began to get a reputation for being at the centre of 'nasty accidents'. The group drunkenly piled into a car and tried to recreate the car chase from the movie *Bullitt*, zooming aimlessly around San Francisco's hills; and on another occasion, they were caught by the police bouncing up and down on the roof of their rented station wagon. Bizarrely, when Stewart explained to them that the car was rented, the police left them to it.

The relative sexual freedom The Faces encountered in the States was complemented by the band's propensity for destruction. Touring in a band is tedious at the best of times, each band member and the roadcrew living out of suitcases, with nothing to do but travel between shows, staying in hotels which, even if they are of a high standard, are essentially bland, boring, soulless cells. And more than that, the only consistent thing on the road is the other people in the group; all they have that is familiar is each other. So bands on the road become increasingly insular, jokes and key phrases become increasingly meaningless to anyone outside of the group, and arguments and rows take on increasing significance within the group.

The insular nature of touring bonds a group together, a shared experience which is inexplicable to anyone outside. It is an ironic but oft-repeated fact that despite the vast distances and different cities, countries and cultures that bands encounter on tour, for the band there is just each other, the hotel, the transportation (plane, coach or limousine) and the gig. The hotels in the USA were even more bland than those in Britain, generally built on the edge of town close to a freeway, with no bars or life of any description.

When The Faces returned from their shows, with fans and groupies in tow, they would continue the heavy drinking and drug-taking which had begun at the venue. As much a part of The Faces' experience as the show, 'The Party' as it was known by their fans, would start in the hotel bar, move to a swimming pool if the hotel had one, and end up in The Faces' bedrooms and the corridors outside.

'I'd get back to the hotel sometimes and just flop on the bed ... knowing exactly where I was, but no idea where that was and still drunk from the night before last!' remembered McLagan.[7]

Despite the major success, the American tour also started to create rifts within The Faces. The trouble had started before they set off: 'Rod and Ron were all cocky about going to America because they had been there before,' remembered Kenney Jones. 'They had their following, knew their way around, and became all flash by saying things like "Oh, we know this great place in New York that does boiled eggs" and all that. We were seen as Rod's and, to a lesser extent, Ronnie's band, which I could see was going to be a problem.'[8]

Part of this problem was, as Jones points out, that Stewart and Wood were already known in the States due to the previous success of the Jeff Beck Group, but in addition, Stewart's first solo LP had been well received while not selling massively, making him appealing to American journalists. For the American market, Stewart was obviously the man to watch, and American audiences found it difficult to tell the difference between Rod Stewart the solo artist and Rod Stewart the Face. It was a situation which would continually undermine the Faces. But there was also a closeness within the group which outsiders often couldn't understand.

'Rod could be a sarcastic bastard at times,' remembered McLagan.

'He'd pull a twisted grimace behind a victim's back and make a derisory sound like "Hmneigh" usually not heard or understood by the poor sucker, so that everybody would be in on the joke except the person being laughed at.'[9] The humour, which began with Stewart and Wood and spilled over to the other Faces, excluded everyone who wasn't a Face.

It wasn't always particularly funny – sometimes it could just be pointlessly cruel. 'Rod's mate Ewan came to the studio one day,' remembered McLagan. 'When Rod asked him if he'd like to play tambourine with us while we cut "Three Button Hand Me Down" he jumped at the chance ... he'd never been in a studio in his life, so he knew nothing about recording. Rod explained to him that he'd have to play in the corridor, outside the studio ... This was his big chance to be on a record, and it was a bloody shame really, since he had absolutely no sense of rhythm and his microphone wasn't even plugged in. We cut the track and walked out of the studio to see Ewan banging away and sweating like a real musician.' Stewart invited his friend back into the control room to listen back to the tambourine that wasn't there. The engineer turned the playback up as loud as was feasible, and Stewart enthused over the track as his friend strained to hear the missing tambourine.

The other Faces cracked up behind his back as he asked Stewart if the part was OK. 'It's really good, Ewan,' said Stewart. 'Yeah, you sound pretty good,' said Stewart. 'It's really useless, Ewan,' said Stewart as he slapped his friend across the back of the head, the other Faces shrieking with laughter.[10] 'Rod was the biggest piss-taker of all time,' remembered Jones.[11] 'We did share the same sense of humour,' said Stewart later. 'And the same women sometimes, on a dark night in Des Moines.'[12]

★

The Faces returned to England buoyed by their success in the States. Returning home was a disappointment, though. The problem they found was that Stateside success meant nothing in the UK. The music press still largely ignored them, and they found themselves playing back in small venues to a couple of hundred people at best. They even played a show at Dudley Zoo supporting Marc Bolan's Glam-rocking T Rex, where they were introduced by Edgar Broughton as 'drunken, East End yobbos'.

'We came back after a successful two months to nothing,' remembered Wood. 'We expected a flood of gigs but nothing happened. We had quite a job to do at home, it just hadn't taken off. I remember saying I'd rather go back to the States than bash people's heads against a brick wall … In the States we started fresh and new. I wanted the band to make it in England, but by the back door, not by hype! People were very critical of The Faces at the start, or else they just ignored us. We weren't given a chance in England.'[13]

Because during the Sixties British acts such as The Beatles and the Stones were successful both at home and overseas, British bands have traditionally been given a rough ride if they gained success overseas before they made it at home. It's almost as if bands were not allowed to leave Britain without having the blessing of British success.

'We had strict ideas about the States,' said Wood. 'We had a direct approach. We pretty much organised it so that the places we played were the most important.'[14] The other side of their successful trip to the States also accompanied them back to Britain.

'They all came back from that first trip to the States with the clap,' remembered McLagan's then wife, Sandy Sarjeant. 'Probably Kenney got away with it … It was a sign of things to come. They all came back really excited, raving about something called Thousand Island Dressing which they'd never seen before, as if having the clap didn't matter. So the trouble started straight away with all the wives and girlfriends. They spent more time trying to sort out domestic situations when they should have been trying to be a band.'[15]

In what seemed at the time a mere coincidence, while The Faces had been away it had been formally announced that The Beatles – the Crown Princes of British pop – had split. The split was widely attributed to the band's marriages – John Lennon to Yoko Ono and Paul McCartney to Linda Eastman. At the time, The Beatles' press officer, the languid Derek Taylor, was moved to say, 'I think that it would be easier for four men to get on with each other than for four men and four wives.'

In Britain, the summer of 1970 was golden. Well, not so much golden as the fuzzy shade of light grey that black and white televisions rendered Brazil's gold shirts. Though colour televisions were available, and though the television companies had been broadcasting in colour since the late Sixties, most households did not have the income to enable them to buy the more expensive sets. The 1970 World Cup in Mexico was the first overseas tournament to be shown live on European television, with England and Brazil strong favourites to win. All over the country, small boys coveted the Esso World Cup Coins, small discs of metal featuring pictures of players which were to be attached to an unwieldy cardboard cover.

In the event, England went out of the tournament to West Germany and the small boys found that if you sharpened the coins (which were pretty sharp already) on the pavement, they were pretty good weapons. But that Brazil team caught the imagination not just of Britain but of the whole footballing world – these exotically named geniuses, playing in bright sunshine, performing with the grace and power of ballet dancers, were literally and metaphorically thousands of miles away from the drabness of Britain. And over a few short hours one summer, a love affair developed between football lovers in the grim birthplace of the game and the players from South America who took the game to unmatched heights of artistry.

But for the football-loving Faces, the summer of 1970 wasn't about being huddled in front of a dodgy black and white TV listening to David Coleman's crackly commentary on Brazil and the 'beautiful game' – for The Faces were back in America. Their second tour there was again ecstatically received, and they flew directly from America to Scandinavia for more gigs culminating in an appearance at a 'Love and Peace Festival' in Germany in the face of a Force Ten gale before returning to Britain.

On a break between tours, Stewart returned to the recording studio, aided and abetted by Wood and occasionally Lane and Jones (though not on this occasion McLagan, who was on holiday), to record his second solo LP. The resulting album, *Gasoline Alley*, was well received in the press, the *NME* asserting that 'Already assured of a place among the Larger Than Life Personalities of Pop, Rod Stewart currently appears to be receiving some of the respect and attention his talent deserves … The whole is a triumph for all concerned.'

The album was also a commercial success in Britain and more importantly in the USA, where it reached Number 27 in the charts. The title track opens the album, returning to the perennial Stewart theme of returning home, the phrase itself the result of a casual remark by a girl backstage at the Fillmore East in New York who had said that she had to get home before her mother could accuse her of having been 'down gasoline alley'.

The following track, a cover of Bobby Womack's 'It's All Over Now' made famous by the Rolling Stones, was the first example of Stewart's ability to turn an ostensibly downbeat song into an upbeat, football terrace anthem, something at which he would become increasingly adept. Four cover versions followed, the first, Bob Dylan's 'Only A Hobo' given a suitably (for Stewart) reverential reading. It was followed – in a move that could only be described as barefaced cheek – by a cover of the Small Faces' 'My Way Of Giving', which Stewart transforms into a loose, funky workout. Next came Elton John and Bernie Taupin's 'Country Comfort' which sounds like nothing more than a precurser to the dreadful 'rock ballads' which were to haunt the Eighties.

'Cut Across Shorty' – made famous by Eddie Cochran – follows, given a sharper edge as the band try to force it into a folk style. Stewart's own 'Lady Day' is folky, though ultimately aimless, drifting away from any central point, and another Stewart original, 'Jo's Lament' owes its origins directly to Scots and Irish folk tunes, rather than the American tinged folk from which Stewart usually drew inspiration. When Stewart composed without Ron Wood his writing was simpler, more direct and wore his influences rather more obviously. Another cover, 'You're My Girl (I Don't Want to Discuss It)' finished the LP off – a tougher, rockier turn to the album, reminding the audience that Stewart had been in the Jeff Beck Group.

While the album was in some ways an improvement on *An Old Raincoat* ..., the high number of cover versions let it down. Though Stewart could (and does) argue that as a singer, interpretation of a song is as important as writing them, his burgeoning songwriting partnerships – with Ron Wood in particular – were strong enough that he could (and should) have made more of an effort. However, for many years it was Stewart's favourite among his own work, and in some ways it's easy to see why: the young man with the outgrown, spiky bouffant who stares confidently back from the inside cover, replete with red trousers, buckled shoes and a tartan scarf knotted around his neck had put together something he felt he could be proud of, and he had done it by himself, credited co-producer Lou Reizner having little input. Stewart could see where he was going, and the album's success in America was justification.

★

Between the release of *Gasoline Alley* and The Faces' next foray abroad, television screens around the world were dominated in September by probably the first 'terrorist spectacular'. From somewhere in the Middle East, Dawson's Field (an old Royal Air Force airstrip in the Jordanian desert) became the theatre upon which a bizarre drama was enacted. Three hijacked European passenger jets carrying a total of 255 passengers were held hostage by Palestinian terrorists demanding the release from prison of another of their group. The three planes were parked on the airstrip facing towards each other. The hijackers took all the passengers and crew off the planes and, for the benefit of the world's TV cameras, blew the three planes up. The hostages were released when the hijackers demands were met. Aircraft hijackings would become increasingly familiar events through the following years. And just as ordinary people were beginning to gain access to affordable flights overseas, the prospect of flying seemed decidedly less glamorous and significantly more dangerous.

Despite any simmering resentment within the group, the success of *Gasoline Alley* gave The Faces the opportunity to do what they liked best: by October 1970 The Faces were back in the USA for another 28-date tour. They headlined most shows but weren't at all fazed by second billing, and once again wowed audiences from New York to Los Angeles, where they set up yet another stronghold, selling out the Santa Monica Civic and ripping up the audience like a five-man musical commando unit, all swagger and groove. However, the rift first exposed in the previous tour began to widen when the band noticed that in the wake of the success of *Gasoline Alley*, some concert promoters were billing the band as 'Rod Stewart and The Faces'. It first came to the band's attention in Boston, but Stewart himself managed to placate the rest of The Faces by spending the evening's show hiding from the audience when he wasn't singing.

The Faces were re-bonded the following day when they were scheduled to play two shows in one day in the same venue in Rochester, New York State. It seemed a strange booking to The Faces, who thought they'd be lucky to fill the place once; and so it proved. The early show was little more than a rehearsal, while there were quite good ticket sales for the second. Between the shows, The Faces returned to their Holiday Inn hotel, where they started drinking hard. Billy Gaff, as their manager, had to get The Faces back to the gig. But the band were in session, and as men on a mission they weren't keen to leave. Gaff tried everything to get them into the cars and on their way. Eventually he was successful, having whined, bribed, cajoled and pleaded with them, and the band arrived at the venue the worse for wear but ready to go. They hadn't counted on the fact that the show was running an hour late because their first support act – Savoy Brown – had arrived late and their second support act – the Grease Band sans Joe Cocker – were ensconced on stage and refusing to get off, surrounding themselves on the stage with their roadies to ensure that no-one could force them off.

Gaff managed to negotiate a thirty-minute extension from the venue management, but that proved irrelevant. The Grease Band played until 1 a.m. when The Faces ran onto the stage to start their set. They ran through one number before the venue management – complete with a dozen or so security guards – cut the power mid-song, leaving only Jones' drums to be heard from the stage. Stewart flung his microphone stand into the backdrop, and the five Faces stormed off stage to join the developing mêlée. The crowd started chanting for The Faces' return until the management turned up the house lights in an attempt to get them to leave. The crowd's response was to hail the stage with small change. The police turned up and explained that unless everyone went home peacefully, the 'guy with the funny haircut who slung the mike would be charged with incitement to riot'.

The Faces quickly developed a plan: Stewart would try to disguise himself and they would leave, as quickly as possible and carrying as much booze as they could. Billy Gaff and the roadcrew could stay behind, sort out the mess and collect as much loose change as they could. As they ran from the stage door to the waiting car, they were met by a shower of bottles, cans and general rubbish thrown by the crowd who had gone out to meet them. The car sped off, back to the Holiday Inn, with the five Faces whooping and screaming with laughter inside.

'That's what we were, really,' remembered Ron Wood. 'The Marx Brothers on the road.'[16]

# NINE

# FEEL SO GOOD

The tour was just under half done and the band were in Milwaukee when they were told that the last sixteen dates were sold out in advance. For a band with no hit record anywhere and with limited (to say the least) success at home, this was a major achievement. In fact, a major achievement worthy of celebration. Worthy of celebration in their manager's hotel bedroom, it was decided, where Billy Gaff's bed was overturned, his trousers and all the lightbulbs stolen, and his bathroom flooded. Gaff was left naked, under his upturned mattress and in an inch of water. The Faces had really arrived.

But the group's baiting of Gaff wasn't always good-natured. Later that month, when they arrived in Detroit for a show that had been moved from the large East Town Theatre to the huge Olympic Stadium, the billing outside read, 'The Small Faces Featuring Rod Stewart'. The group sat silently, with Gaff, in their limousine, staring at the huge sign, until Ian McLagan cracked Gaff over the head with a bottle and told the driver to carry on.

'The band so deeply resented those marquee signs advertising Rod separately to The Faces,' remembered Peter Burton, the tour publicist for The Faces. 'They refused to be relegated to the backing band. Ronnie Wood was a charismatic performer in his own right, an awfully nice man, so he had his own space, somewhere to go. But Ronnie Lane felt marginalised as a writer as much as anything else. There was a lot of power play, whispering and jealousy adding to the tension and then the girlfriends started adding to it when they began flying in for certain dates.'[1]

But the tour had been another success, the venues vast, holding audiences ranging from 8,000 to 18,500. Their status and reputation in America were assured. 'The reason I started drinking Cognac is because of The Faces,' recalls photographer Robert Matheu. 'It's because I'd seen them wandering on stage with bottles in their hands. I'd heard that Bobby Womack had told them when they'd asked him, "How did Sam Cooke manage to get his voice to sound like that?" And Bobby was teasing them and said, "Well, he gargled with Cognac before he went on stage."

'Well, a year, a year and a half, later Bobby shows up and there's everyone, Ronnie Lane and Woody and Rod, and they're all in the dressing room with big snifters of Cognac, gargling, and he goes, "What are you boys doing?" And they go, "Well, it's what you told us that you boys do, and we've been doing it ever since then."'

★

They returned to England in November to record their second album and to promote a single, 'Had Me A Real Good Time', which they had recorded between gigs and which was supposed to act as a taster for the unrecorded LP.

The schizophrenic nature of The Faces' lives in late 1970 was laid out before them on their return to the UK: a week after selling out the massive Chicago Syndrome, The Faces were playing at the Wake Arms, Epping, to a couple of hundred people. In between the endless travel and debauchery, the group had spent the American tour working up songs for their next album. During the end of 1970 and early 1971 they went into the studio to record it. Again they were without a producer, something the British music press identified as arrogance, though the real reason probably had more to do with money (and not wanting to spend it). The Faces defended their decision to record without a producer.

'I think it's a valid point that a producer can act as a referee if there's indecision,' argued Wood, 'but a producer is only of value if he works the buttons himself.'[2] McLagan also defended their decision by adding, 'Producing is a musical thing and most producers didn't know or wouldn't know one note from another. We didn't really know the notes but we could play them.'[3]

The role of the record producer is full of vagaries. Producers can be all powerful, such as Phil Spector, defining the sound of a group, even down to the choice of songs. But producers can also be facilitators, such as George Martin with The Beatles, someone who can translate the ideas of musicians into actuality. And producers can fall into all categories between those two extremes, forcing the music into an identifiable sound while bringing on the ideas and performances of the musicians. The other thing producers bring – especially to the recording of an album – is discipline, both in the quality of the recorded music, but also the way in which it is recorded.

The Faces had been given six months to record their next album, a not unreasonable length of time given that in the early Seventies bands would write songs in the studio and pore laboriously over their recording. But The Faces were never really like that, and most of their songs were recorded practically live in the studio. Kenney Jones recalled that The Faces' recording sessions were often anarchic.

'Rod and I were very frustrated when it came to recording with The Faces,' he recalled. 'We had a bit of a drink and that's all. The others were already getting a bit out of hand on other things. Everybody in the band took a lot of other things, we were night owls, we used to live through the fucking night! Rod and I would have preferred to have gone in the studio at eleven or twelve in the morning, worked through the day, finished at eight and then gone out and partied. That's sensible and that's how you do things. But in those days, the earliest we could persuade the others to come in was about seven at night. Rod and I would get there at six just to loosen up and play a while and we would inevitably be waiting there 'til ten o'clock and in most cases midnight. In the end, we would think, "Fuck this." We couldn't handle it. It was The Faces' in-house behaviour that would let them down when it came to recording.'[4]

Although The Faces could have argued that by behaving as they did they were just being 'rock 'n' roll' at a time when music was taking itself too seriously, the resulting album simply wasn't good enough. Out of the six months given to the recording of the album, only two weeks were ever used. The results of their work were released in March 1971 as *Long Player*, its brown and blue art deco sleeve announcing the frail joke on the fact that it was a long play record.

The album opens with 'Bad 'N' Ruin', a Stewart/McLagan composition, driven by Kenney Jones' relentless Booker T & The MGs groove. Stewart draws on the old blues theme of returning home a failure. He also draws on his new-found American fame and lack of the same at home, claiming that he is now unrecognisable. But, being Rod the Mod, he doesn't set the tale in the American South but firmly in London, citing Cannon Street Station as the place to find him, the station being the arrival and departure point for the boat train to France. Stewart was at this point developing his songwriting style, drawing on his own experiences as a beatnik travelling Europe and applying it to the classic blues metaphor of the travelling loser returning home. 'Bad 'N' Ruin' is a very British blues, and ends on a very British note with Stewart crying that he's tired as the song peters out.

Ronnie Lane's 'Tell Everyone' follows, an affectionate paean to the everydayness of being in love, musically almost gospel in style. Stewart, Wood and Lane combined to write the next track, 'Sweet Lady Mary'. Almost a precursor to 'Maggie May', which Stewart would record and release in 1971, the acoustic guitar, Wood's slide and McLagan's organ, along with the slight, but definite, Celtic folk influence helped to develop (on a Faces recording) the sound that would lead to Stewart's solo success.

'Stewart had been through more bands than the other Faces,' argues Jonno Pavitt. 'In many ways he'd got a far bigger musical education to bring with him. He'd come in through a different way. In reality he was "Rod the Mod" for a very short time before he became whatever he was after that. Rod the gob, probably. The other Small Faces had done it all together, from when they were kids, really, so all the stuff that they did, all the psychedelic stuff that they got into, they all did it together, 'cos it was what they happened to be doing. I don't think they went looking for it. That's one of the things that's different about the Small Faces from The Faces – they never seemed to go looking for anything, they just seemed to be able to do it. There was no jumping on bandwagons, there was no pretence. I think that's the whole thing.'

Though Wood's slide guitar dominates the next track, Ronnie Lane's 'Richmond', the song is almost a pastiche – the bottleneck bluesy style of the song makes it sound like Lane wants to be in Virginia rather than West London. But the feeling of homesickness that pervades the song is infectious, reflecting another side of The Faces' American success.

The next track is a blistering cover – one of two on the album recorded live at Fillmore East, New York – of Paul McCartney's 'Maybe I'm Amazed'. The band had heard it first in a station wagon in Connecticut. 'Ronnie ... twiddled the knobs on the radio looking for a decent station,' remembered McLagan. 'He caught a song halfway through that sounded so soulful we had to turn it up to deafening to get the full effect. When the song ended I said, "That's the sort of record Paul McCartney should be making." But I was too clever for my own good, because minutes later the DJ told us it was his new single "Maybe I'm Amazed" from his first solo album.'[5]

The Faces' cover is a fairly straight copy of McCartney's version, with Ronnie Lane singing the quieter first verse before Stewart blasts out the second, Wood's guitar caressing the vocal melody, Jones' drumming insistent, driving the song without ever forcing it, Lane's bass holding it all together and McLagan's Wurlitzer electric piano and Hammond organ busy but adding an almost spiritual feel.

'Had Me A Real Good Time' is another Wood/Stewart/Lane track, a fairly straightforward steady good-time blues, seemingly written to order as a show-ending number. The song swaggers on its way, giving each Face a chance to shine, from Jones' steady groove, through Lane's bass runs, Wood's easy blues guitar and McLagan's frantic piano, and Stewart gets room to stretch his voice. However, the second half of the track seems to have been an afterthought, The Faces augmented with a Stax-style horn section and even a saxophone solo.

Wood and Lane teamed up to write 'On The Beach', which they recorded on a portable machine in Ronnie Lane's spare room at his new flat in Richmond. A murky blues, it has the brooding feel of the Rolling Stones' *Exile On Main Street* with none of the menace. Willie Broonzy's 'I Feel So Good' is the other live track on the album, The Faces faithfully reproducing the song while never really extending themselves, though as a singalong live song it was a major success. The final track is simply Ron Wood playing a two-minute, slide guitar version of the hymn 'Jerusalem' for which he claims a writing credit.

Overall, though the individual tracks are sometimes impressive, *Long Player* is disappointing. Some tracks are again too long, and the inclusion of live tracks on studio albums is always dubious, though it's easy to see why The Faces thought this would be a good idea – the essence of The Faces was in their live performances, which had led to their success thus far. But while 'Maybe I'm Amazed' works because of the sheer ferocity of the performance, 'I Feel So Good' just sounds like any half-decent R&B band with a good singer.

From the band's own perspective, *Long Player* was also disappointing: of the nine tracks on the album, only four were recorded in the six months allotted at Morgan Sound Studios, 'Bad 'N' Ruin' and 'Tell Everyone' being recorded at the Rolling Stones' Mobile Recording unit parked at Mick Jagger's house. And despite Wood's cheeky writing credit for 'Jerusalem', three of the nine tracks were cover versions.

The press weren't over-keen either. *Rolling Stone* took the album and The Faces to task, saying that, 'So intimidating is Stewart's presence apparently in what should, of course, but hasn't thus far been a mutually beneficial way, that the other chaps are all too eager to defer to Stewart's tastes. The present result being that instead of getting both Faces and Stewart albums, "Long Player" [is] nothing more than a grab bag of tit-bits good enough to tide us over until Stewart's third solo album.'

The *NME* were more generous, calling The Faces 'brash, noisy, alive, splendidly funky, direct, and on this album bursting at the seams with energy ... They deal in spirit; as a rock group they produce broken booze bottle music; all jagged edge up front, smooth below.'

It is a reflection of the times that the playing of individual Faces came in for close scrutiny in the music press, and Ron Wood's guitar playing in particular.

'Wood frequently fancying pleasant if disposable bottleneck laden variations on De Booze ...' sneered *Rolling Stone*. 'Ron Wood is probably one of the best guitarists for a beginner to copy,' jeered *Disk & Music Echo*. Writing at a time when the musicians and music critics were obsessed with musicianship, this is not surprising, even though it seems a little pedantic. More to the point, in the interviews The Faces gave to the British music press in support of the LP, the band found themselves having to describe the birth of the group and explain the break from the Small Faces despite the fact that *Long Player* was their second album and they were already a success in America.

'We had a terrible time trying to flog ourselves,' Ronnie Lane told the *NME*. 'All we had was the three of us.' In fact, by the release of *Long Player*, the *NME* was beginning to champion The Faces.

Although *Melody Maker* had dominated much of the late Sixties and early Seventies in terms of the British music press, the *New Musical Express* was taking them on and was slowly developing into the most important newspaper within the British music press. Up until 1970/71 it had essentially been a trade magazine, written for the music business – retailers, record companies and musicians. However, at the turn of the decade it had started to pay attention to its 'lay' readers – those who bought records, the fans. And the writers were beginning to change, with younger writers such as Charles Shaar Murray and Nick Logan being given the chance not just to interview musicians, but to go on the road with them and live the lifestyle. It was an opportunity that the writers jumped at and the musicians put up with. In addition to the music press, The Faces were beginning to gain other influential supporters. The Radio 1 DJ John Peel was an early admirer, playing Faces records when no-one else would.

'I was a very serious hippy when I met The Faces for the first time backstage at one of their concerts,' remembered Peel. 'I felt absolutely shocked – sober and precious as I was – when they stumbled out of their dressing room, loud, vulgar and very cockney. "Ahm, no thanks. No, really," I mumbled nervously when they called after me, something that sounded like "Come on, John – old sod, we'll have a drink." While they stormed down the hall and disappeared, I realised that The Faces were having a lot more fun in life than I had. Next time they invited me I went along. And the other times too. The Faces and their lead singer Rod Stewart changed my life. During one of their gigs I'm supposed to have danced with a bottle of Blue Nun [very sweet white wine] in my arm. And I'm a person who never dances. Never, never, never.'[6]

★

The Faces set out for yet another tour, this time in the UK to promote the *Long Player* album. The shows – honed by their raucous appearances in the States – were a greater success than any previously done in Britain. The band had developed something of a stage show, which involved a bar at the side of the stage from which roadies dressed as waiters would serve the band drinks throughout the show. In addition, out of sight of the audience, the waiters would have lines of cocaine cut, ready and waiting for whichever Face was in need. And just to make sure the audience were in the same state as the band, The Faces did away with the idea of a support act, giving bottles of wine to the audience in advance of the show.

'We'd get the roadies to dish out fuckin' great crates of the stuff,' remembered Wood, 'and then wait for about an hour and a half while the audience were soaking it all up and come on when they were completely pissed.'[7]

The bar and waiters on the stage would go further – on later American tours there would also be a mobile bar, taken from Face to Face by a dwarf in white tie and tails. 'None of The Faces remembers much, but that was just the beginning,' said Wood. 'Things got much worse on later tours.'[8]

Jonno Pavitt identifies the reasons why he thought that The Faces were beginning to gain greater audiences in Britain. 'Well, you grow up with them, don't you,' says Pavitt. 'Suddenly they turn from the guys who are into speed and looking good and getting women and playing music – the Small Faces – into the guys who are into drinking and getting women and playing music – The Faces. And it depends on where you are at the time. You can move into that. And, obviously, fashions change.'

★

Perhaps one reason for Britain's increasing acceptance of The Faces' outlandish behaviour was the increasing national dissatisfaction with life in the UK. Edward ('Ted') Heath's Conservative Party had been surprisingly elected into office in the General Election of 18 May 1970 – an election that saw 18-year-olds vote for the first time – forcing Wilson's Labour Party into opposition. The world of politics was very ideological in the early Seventies.

'Communism was still an active force,' remembers writer Lucy O'Brien. 'Marxism framed everybody's language and ideology, no matter whether you were pro- it or anti- it. It was just as much part of the political culture as debates about hanging. And Marxism fuelled trade unionism at the time.'

Dave Phillips says that the effects of the events of the late Sixties had been over-exaggerated. 'In retrospect, what seemed very tremendous and all-embracing as a cultural experience was actually confined to a very narrow elite. Part of the experience since the Sixties has been a "mass-ification" of that in terms of dress and music and media. Students were an elite – we were three per cent of that age group, we were a tiny group, terribly privileged, so there were some problems, not least a political credibility problem … we were these pampered voices of the Left. We were very pampered in real material terms, with the student grant – while it wasn't huge it was, in real material terms, worth a lot more than it would be now.'

Heath's government put into place their policies to reduce taxation, increase the size of the police force and deal with the trade unions. Though the effects of these policies would not kick in until later in 1971 and more severely in 1972, the government's announcement of the policies along with the government's unconcealed belligerence towards the trade unions changed the atmosphere in Britain. An Industrial Relations Bill was introduced which established a National Industrial Relations Court which could make collective industrial wage deals enforceable in law. The trade unions were not happy, and a series of one-day stoppages and unofficial disputes followed as the government attempted to hold down wage increases through the court. Strikes were held by local authority manual workers, dockers and the electrical power industry.

The winter of 1970 saw the power workers force the Government into declaring a State of Emergency, reducing power supplies leading to queues for candles and cooking gas. In the early Seventies, trade union power was almost absolute – if a particular group of workers were on strike, no other unionised workers would cross their picket line, and scenes of rowdy pickets and lines of policemen struggling with each other became common.

Watched on the same black and white televisions that the year before had brought Pele's Brazil to the nation, Britain couldn't have seemed grimmer. And as if to add insult to injury, as part of the government's policy to reduce taxation, the government took an axe to public spending. In what seemed to be a particularly stingy yet characteristic move, the new Minister for Education, a little-known politician named Margaret Thatcher, announced that in future the government would no longer be providing free milk for schoolchildren, thus gaining her notoriety as 'Margaret Thatcher milk-snatcher'.

Added to this, the situation in Northern Ireland was careering out of control. The tension between Catholics and Protestants had not diminished since the late Sixties, and the government's response (aside from ultimately futile political machinations) was to increase the British Army presence in the province. The warm welcome originally extended to the British Army by the Catholic community – who had seen the soldiers largely as their saviours – did not last. The British Army quickly became the focus of Republican ire, and the increasingly well-organised Provisional IRA orchestrated unrest in the Catholic strongholds in Belfast and Derry, though the local youths didn't need much incitement.

Young Catholic men, reacting to the years of oppression from the Protestant majority which had been ignored by successive Westminster governments, quickly learned the techniques of violent unrest – the screens of the black and white televisions all over Britain were filled with pictures of groups of young men, wearing handkerchiefs to cover the lower parts of their faces (partly to avoid recognition, partly in case the Army and police fired tear-gas), throwing at first rocks and later petrol bombs (milk bottles filled with petrol with a wedge of burning paper or rags stuck in the bottleneck) at the collected security forces.

But there were also other pictures of ordinary life in Northern Ireland, grainy film of soldiers in full battledress, carrying Armalite rifles, huddling in doorways of ordinary-looking houses, driving armoured personnel carriers down roads that could have been anywhere in Britain. For the people of mainland Britain, the pictures seemed strange and without context – Northern Ireland seemed a long way away, and the scenes of petrol bombs exploding under armoured cars were someone else's problem. Until, that is, February 1971, when the first British soldier was killed. While it still didn't seem to affect Britain directly, it brought Northern Ireland a little closer to home. And it would get even closer.

The dodgy black and white televisions also provided other diversions. Perennial favourites like *Til Death Us Do Part*, and *Steptoe and Son* pulled large audiences, while newer shows such as *Please, Sir!* and *Jason King* got the younger audience. Saturdays were given over to sport: *Grandstand* on BBC1, while ITV offered *World of Sport* presented by Dickie Davis, which featured wrestling. Saturday evenings were the domain of variety shows, fronted by variety performers such as Des O'Connor. Comedians Tommy Cooper and Morecambe and Wise also had large rating shows, not least because there were still only three television channels. Since most households owned a single television, the whole family would be forced to watch, at least until the children were old enough to go out by themselves. But this also meant that *Top of the Pops*, the BBC's chart show, was required viewing in households with teenagers.

'*Top of the Pops* always had the feeling of an "event",' remembered Lucy O'Brien. 'You'd come into school the next day and you'd say, "Did you see Suzi Quatro on *Top of the Pops*, wow, wasn't she amazing." It was so exciting when "Can The Can" went to Number 1, it was history in the making. The Seventies was the heyday of the single, really. And singles would stay around for weeks and weeks in the charts and climb really slowly up the charts. It was all a big event. Listening to the Top Forty on a Sunday night was a big event. And we'd all tune into it on a Tuesday lunchtime to find out what the Number 1 was. We'd all sit round the radio and it was all incredibly exciting. It was like waiting for the football results.'

In football, each May the four 'Home' nations would play the so-called 'Home Internationals', alternating home and away fixtures each year. The games would be played over a couple of weeks, some games played mid-week with highlights shown late at night, the dark pictures showing Northern Ireland and Wales battling to defeat the significantly stronger Scotland and England. The other games would be played on a Saturday afternoon, shown live on TV, and the highlight was always the England vs Scotland game. The Scots took the fixture personally, and took great pleasure whenever they beat the English. The Scottish national squad of the Seventies was packed with players who plied their trade in England and with the two Scottish giants, Celtic and Rangers, and were a force in European football, going on to qualify for the World Cup in both 1974 and 1978, something England couldn't achieve.

But it was another TV diversion, the sitcom *Dad's Army*, which perhaps spoke to the British condition in the early Seventies. Set in the fictional town of 'Walmington-on-Sea' during World War Two, the series was premised on the relationships between members of the Home Guard, the British civilian defence force. The middle-class Captain Mainwaring (bank manager), the aristocratic Sergeant Wilson (chief clerk) and the slightly deranged Corporal Jones (butcher) – 'They don't like it up 'em!' – reflected both a simpler time and the intricacies of the British class system. The actors who played the roles were themselves old enough to have fought in the war, and one of them – Clive Dunn who played Corporal Jones – had actually spent four years as a prisoner-of-war. As they undertook their weekly, incompetent fight against fascism (whose representatives were only very rarely seen) they gently worked through issues regarding the British class system in a changing world. While the series was obviously nostalgic – it was set, after all, during Britain's 'Finest Hour' – it was also a way of addressing a new world (the early Seventies) while trying to let go of the memory of the war.

The social life of the majority of the country was dominated by pubs and social clubs. The clubs would feature variety acts – a comedian, a singer or two – and the men would buy the drinks while women were often not allowed to go to the bar. The men would inevitably drink beer – lager, if it was consumed at all, was a woman's drink, sold by the half-pint – and when they got home, there would be a Watney's 'Party Seven', a seven-pint tin of beer operated with a tap powered by a small carbon-dioxide canister, to wash down the fish supper (basically fish and chips in the South of England, fish, chips and curry sauce in the North, and, maybe, haggis and chips in Scotland). There were Indian and Chinese takeaways, though these were not often frequented. Pizza and McDonald's were a generation away, the only concession to hamburger culture being the Wimpy chain, whose red-fronted restaurants peppered high streets up and down the country.

But behind the high streets, many of the bomb sites from the Second World War had still not been redeveloped. Certain parts of London – around the Elephant and Castle, for example – still had large areas fenced off with a mixture of corrugated iron and large wooden frames covered in chicken wire. They were used as rubbish dumps by adults, as playgrounds by children. And in each major city, the old docks, with their cranes and massive warehouses, stood idle.

Though the words 'Docklands Redevelopment' were to become a part of the vocabulary, it would not happen for another decade. In many ways it was also a time of innocence.

'There was all of that double-standard stuff where the boys could sleep around and the girls couldn't,' remembers artist and lecturer Sue Westergaard. 'On the other hand, when you talk to them now, the boys weren't all sleeping around, it was all just lies. Everyone was just boasting to each other and saying that they were doing all sorts of things and they weren't. We used to do things like we'd all go swimming, then we'd all go back to my house, I don't know how many girls and how many boys, and it seemed to be quite a regular thing. We'd all go up to my bedroom and you'd snog whatever boy you were sitting next to and then you'd swap round. And it didn't mean anything, no-one minded. It was just like practice.'

Lucy O'Brien also remembers life being difficult for young women. 'It was very repressive being a girl,' she recalls. 'I started going out with boys and it was really hard. You were either frigid or a slag, you couldn't win, you were one or the other. It made absolutely no sense to me. You just had to kiss a few boys and you were a slag. Maybe things are still like that in teenagerdom, I don't know. It felt like, as a girl, you weren't supposed to step out of line, talk too loud or be too big for fear of being thought too boyish or unfanciable, which was an absolutely terrible thing. There was a lot of peer pressure to have a boyfriend and to get engaged, it was the big thing. You'd probably have a bit of a job before you had children. It was alright if you didn't mind conforming and being a typical girl, but if you didn't want to be it was very bewildering.

'There was this aching about wanting to do things but there were no role models and just a feeling that you were going out on a limb if you expressed that. Just being in a band was quite unheard of until

Punk. I wanted to be more active in the world, and that was the thing; as a woman your role was quite passive. You got your drinks bought for you, your boyfriend went up to the bar, and you sat there – there was a lot of sitting and waiting as a girl. And it was considered really forward to go and buy a drink or ask a boy out or any of those things. It was very passive and I think for those of us who wanted to be active participants in our lives it was very frustrating.'

But, increasingly around the country, there was also violence. From the scenes on the picket lines, the pictures from Northern Ireland, and increasingly, on the football terraces, the general undertone of violence was swelling to become a cacophony. Public fears over violence came to a head with the release of Stanley Kubrick's film, *A Clockwork Orange*. Promoted with the lurid tag-line, 'Being the adventures of a young man whose principal interests are rape, ultra-violence and Beethoven!', the film was a highly stylised (and subsequently highly imitated) reading of Anthony Burgess's novel of the same name. Blamed by the newspapers for a rise in crime among young men, Kubrick had the film withdrawn, not accepting responsibility for any rise in violence but not wanting to be blamed for it.

But though Britain was making its own contribution to violence, there were also the seemingly endless stream of pictures from Vietnam, where the American government were sending thousands of young men to die. These were pictures of frightened young men, of bombers flattening jungle, and of terrified Vietnamese. Protests against the war had been taking place around the world – including Britain – since the late Sixties to no avail. The American government kept sending the soldiers and pictures kept coming back.

The year 1971 also saw a change in the currency. The old pound, shilling and pence (£.s.d., an acronym which amused many young people in the heady, acid-soaked days of 1967) were replaced with a decimal system. When *Long Player* was released, it was marked up at the stately price of '£2.15 new pence'. There were many grumbles about the new money and the way the old money was incorporated (the old sixpence became two and a half new pee, the old shilling became five new pee), but people eventually got used to it. With all the trouble people saw coming, a change in the money was the least of their problems.

'It was a really bleak time,' remembers sociologist Chris Sparks, who was fifteen at the time. '1970 to 1975 was shit the whole time. Everything was shit. The football was all shit; there was no subculture – it's the period between hippy and skinhead, and punk. I remember we were all totally cynical. It was comprehensive education. We all went to these big comprehensive schools which nobody understood. Everybody was fucked off.

'One of the things – I don't think we were aware of it at the time – my lot, we knew we'd all missed the Sixties. We'd been waiting 'til we were old enough to join in, we'd lived through it as children, we knew all the music and everything – we all had big brothers and sisters – and when we got there it was gone. It was all crap, and though we were all very young, we sort of knew it was crap, we knew that everything was crap, and we knew the music was crap too. That's why everybody liked The Who and the Stones 'cos they'd been good, we knew that when we were younger, we knew they had been good. When you went to their gigs all you ever wanted them to do was their old stuff, you didn't want them to do anything new 'cos it was boring.'

Sue Westergaard, who was at school at the time, remembers the sense of 'missing out' on the Sixties. "Cos I was a child in the Sixties I was too young [to do the Sixties],' she recalls. 'But I did want to wear a floppy hat and walk down the King's Road and I thought that other people were doing that. You believe the image, don't you. And then, by the Seventies, it's an acceptable thing to do that.'

It wasn't an entirely shared experience, though. Growing up in the Yorkshire town of Todmorden, Carol Chaffer remembered that she 'never felt like I'd missed out on "the Sixties", it felt completely the opposite to me because I had older sisters who were ten and eight years older than me, so I read all the Sixties magazines, *Honey* and *Petticoat* and those kind of things, and I loved all the fashions. I read about Tyrannosaurus Rex before they became T Rex, there was Luke Jarvis, "Man About Town", doing a fashion column and that's the point when I was about eight and I decided that I was going to move to London, because I never saw the Sixties as a "thing", an entity in itself, I always saw the Sixties as a postcode in London. I always saw those things as tied so I never expected to grow up and hit anything like that youth culture outside of London. I didn't really have much knowledge of life outside Todmorden. I'd been shopping to Manchester once or twice but outside of that, I didn't have much knowledge of other cities, I just thought that everything automatically happened in London.'

Chaffer was also aware of the limitations of working-class life in a Northern town in the Seventies. 'I always had wider horizons,' she remembers, 'and I don't know where that came from because its nothing within my family. I think it was those magazines in the Sixties. I just looked at them and I thought, "That looks like good fun, I'm gonna do that when I grow up." But a lot of my friends still live there. To them it was leave school at sixteen, get money and go down the pub at night. I was the only one of my friends to stay on to the sixth form.'

The early Seventies found Dick Hebdige forging a new path. 'I liked "Gasoline Alley" and for a brief period (somewhere between the Small Faces massacre and the skinhead crop) I sported a mullet in emulation of Rod Stewart. In late summer, 1969 I moved to

Birmingham to do English at university where, in the early Seventies I helped run a sound system for a mate, an ex art student from Bournemouth called Mike Horseman. The sound was called the Shoop and it happened every Thursday night over the Golden Eagle pub in Hill Street just off New Street near the Bull Ring.

The Shoop attracted a very large, loyal and for those days unprecedentedly heterogeneous crowd of art students, Irish Brummy townies, proto punks and hardcore dreadlocks from Handsworth. We played an eclectic mix of old R&B, rock, funk, ska and heavy dub reggae . Many of the townies were on Mandrax and other sleepers and one of my jobs was to help them to their feet when they collapsed on their girlfriends while dancing to what one of their number called "shaggy music" (i.e slow rockers and soul). The Shoop became a distribution point for imported and homegrown "Ganja" thanks in large part to the Handsworth contingent. The elderly ex-military doorman, whose son was in the CID, kept the local constabulary sweet and no doubt skimmed ample compensation off the top. The owner of the pub, alarmed by the presence of black people (at this point the city centre was largely out of bounds to young black folks especially to dreadlocked rastas) insisted that Mike play "no more than 5% black music", an injunction he judiciously ignored.

At Whitsun 1974 we held a mod revival Shoop to commemorate the tenth anniversary of the mod-rocker "seaside riots". Guest of honour was Duffy, an original mod and amphetamine casualty from Northfield who, discombobulated by a week without sleep on speed, had burned down a hotel in Brighton in 1964 when working as a bell-boy, thus serving as a possible prototype for the character in *Quadrophrenia*. Duffy was cockney-identified and used archaic Sixties London backwards and rhyming slang in order to inhabit permanently the no longer physically extant Soho/Brighton of both his youth and his arrested dreams. He was sound as a pound and had a heart of gold and I acknowledge him as a mucker and a mate in "Subculture". Incidentally, Horseman went on to manage the Special AKA and Dexy's Midnight Runners in the later Seventies.'

But it was the violence that framed the times. 'It did feel quite a violent time,' recalled Lucy O'Brien. 'Not just on the news, but generally. There was a culture of violence. At school there would be fights all the time, quite hard. And The Faces made absolute sense within that. Crude. I do think young people today are more sophisticated in the way that they relate to one another and their own culture.

'It was all about "bovver boots" to me. And kicking. Literally, you had the big boots and somehow that symbolised the whole thing, that at some point someone was going to give you a good kicking. Male or female. It really was part of the culture.'

# TEN

# EVERY PICTURE TELLS A STORY

It was against this backdrop that The Faces went on the road to promote *Long Player*. And it was in this context that the British public began to wake up to The Faces. The album got to Number 31 in the charts while in the States it did even better, reaching Number 29. The concerts were so successful that Billy Gaff extended the tour right up to July, when the band were due back in America.

In between these live dates, Rod Stewart had to record his third solo LP. Largely because of the restrictions on his time due to his commitments with The Faces, the album was recorded with more or less the same personnel who had featured on the previous records. The result, *Every Picture Tells a Story*, is the high watermark of

Stewart's early solo work. 'When I went in to make *Every Picture* I wanted to make it another *Gasoline Alley*,' recalled Stewart. 'If your last album's moderately accepted, you go in thinking, "If that was good and that's something that really pleases me, I'll try and do it again, but better." It didn't turn out like that.'[1]

Though the album retains Stewart's folk/soul influences, the spirit of The Faces permeates the whole LP, and not just because various Faces (or in fact all of them at some points) play on it. An almost autobiographical work, the tone is set by the opening title track. Written by Stewart and Ron Wood, 'Every Picture Tells A Story' is Stewart reminiscing over his early life as a Beatnik busker. The rest of the album followed *Gasoline Alley*'s formula – three Stewart songs (though two of them were written with others), a Dylan track, 'Tomorrow Is A Long Time', an Elvis track, 'That's All Right', the Temptations' '(I Know) I'm Losing You', plus two other lesser known songs, Theodore Anderson's 'Seems Like A Long Time' and Tim Hardin's 'Reason To Believe'. In addition, Stewart sneaks in a version of 'Amazing Grace', sung against Wood's bottleneck blues guitar.

Stewart's cover of '(I Know) I'm Losing You', played by The Faces, is the distillation of their live act into five and a half minutes of pure energy. Starting with Wood's edgy guitar riff and Lane's pulsating bass, Stewart's vocal rips through the song before McLagan's busy blues piano riffing and Jones' heavy, steady drumming drive the song along. The song ends following a pneumatic drum solo from Jones, before Stewart screams, 'I'm losing you.'

The song chosen to be the single off the album was 'Reason To Believe', a song about a man who has been cheated by his partner. Stewart brings to the song such emotion that it is almost impossible to believe that he hasn't lived it, the pleading, little-boy-lost quality that John Baldry spoke of caught on tape, Stewart's imploring voice set against Pete Sears' plaintive piano. The B-side of the single was another album track, ignored by the record company and almost never recorded.

'"Maggie May" wasn't even supposed to go on the album,' remembered Stewart. 'It was the last thing I wrote and nobody seemed to like it 'cos they said, "Oh, it hasn't got a chorus, we can't remember how it goes."'[2] It is a long-established truism in the music business that singles are required to have not just a chorus but a series of easy to remember 'hooks' which draw the listener in. While 'Maggie May' has no vocal chorus and, arguably, no noticeable guitar riff, what it does have is the basis of all folk music (and country and western, which is derived from folk): it tells a story. Classic folk music tells stories, whether of leaving home or lost love. If you don't have a story, you don't have a song, so the lyric is more important than the tune, something which is not true for pop music. 'Maggie May' tells the story of how Stewart lost his virginity.

'"Maggie May" is based on the truth,' recalls Stewart. 'It was my first shag where I lost my virginity and it lasted precisely twenty-eight seconds. It was the Bewley Jazz Festival and I was very young – I was about sixteen – and I lost my virginity to this rather large girl and I don't think her name was Maggie. But that's what the song's all about.'[3]

Stewart's talent – at its apex in 'Maggie May' – was to update the folk idiom, writing about something which most people go through – the end of an affair – but to add to it his 'little boy lost', the regret of moving on. The production of the song has the 'thin wild mercury' sound of Bob Dylan's *Blonde on Blonde*, with McLagan's Hammond organ slightly understated but filling out the sound, Ron Wood's guitar softer than usual, the drums steady without being busy, the acoustic guitars keeping time with the drums.

'I'd never really been a Dylan fanatic,' remembered Stewart, 'but I was so knocked out with *Blonde on Blonde* when Garth Hudson stepped into the picture with that beautiful organ sound, which Mac is the only one that can play like that. When I recorded "Maggie May" that was the sound I wanted on it – a lovely warm sound, acoustic-electric.'[4]

But 'Maggie May' isn't just acoustic-electric – it's folk music designed to be played at maximum volume, with all the rough edges left in. And finally, Stewart manages to make the song singable. Anyone hearing the song a couple of times on the radio could remember the words, could sing along with Rod, from the opening wake-up call to 'Maggie', to the cheeky reference to The Faces, the band that need some help, to the end of the song, where, despite all the evidence of the earlier verses where Stewart pleads his regret that the affair had ever started, he mourns his loss.

★

The album was a critical success, the *NME* calling it 'Stewart's brilliantly accomplished third solo set', despite the fact that Stewart again was over-reliant on cover versions – five out of the eight listed tracks were covers. Stewart's vocal performances were outstanding, and the arrangements of the covers more than compensated for the lack of self-penned songs. The brown art deco cover showed Stewart in 'soul singer' mode, microphone askew, eyes shut in tortured lament. Slightly understated, the album cover bore no relation to the reception the LP itself would receive over the coming months.

The album was released to coincide with The Faces' next visit to America in July. The tour was another major success, and slowly helped to push the LP and single up the charts. Robert Matheu, then an aspiring photographer living in Detroit, first discovered The Faces at this time.

'I first saw The Faces in '71 at the East Town Hall,' he recalls, 'when they took a lot of the run-down movie theatres and they started putting shows in there. I always felt that they made Detroit their home town base 'cos they would be there supporting Fleetwod Mac and they'd be back headlining a smaller venue. Quite consistently.

'One of the first times I met them, I snuck back with them after a Cobo Hall show – they were staying in a hotel right across the street. The way Detroit is, there's a river that runs along downtown and on the other side of the river is Canada, and Cobo Hall's right on the river and across the street is this hotel. They invited me over and I snuck over there with another couple of friends of mine. The Faces had all the furniture, the whole floor of the hotel, and they put it out in the hall-way. And they would have the party in the hallway. And more times than not they were asked to leave. But that hotel was pretty tolerant of them, and that became the rock 'n' roll hotel for a number of years.'

Their increased status had allowed them to make seemingly outlandish demands on their 'rider' (the list of conditions and requirements attached to the contract for the gig). In addition to the booze, meals and technical equipment, The Faces' rider was extended to include for the first time closed circuit television, filming the group on stage and projected on to two giant screens on either side of the stage. 'I think we were the first to use that, at a cost of $10,000 a night,' said Stewart, 'so that the people at the back of those big stadiums can see what's going on.'[5] As Stewart identified, the problem with playing increasingly large venues was that much of the audience couldn't see the stage, something that seemed inequitable considering the cost of a ticket; now it didn't matter where you were sitting, you could always see The Faces.

The rider also included (at Ian McLagan's insistence) a nine-foot Steinway grand piano which was to be tuned only after it had been placed in position on-stage. The rider contained the proviso that if the piano wasn't a nine-foot Steinway grand that any damage that may occur to it was to be at the expense of the concert promoter. McLagan then went out and bought an axe. When the group played Cobo Hall in Detroit, the promoter didn't come up with the Steinway, so during the final song, McLagan asked the roadies for the axe and demolished the piano.

The promoter said nothing, paid for the damage, and the next time they played the Cobo, the promoter supplied a 'Steinmeg' grand piano. McLagan, thinking that the promoter hadn't just ignored the request but had also presumed that McLagan was an idiot who couldn't tell the difference between 'Steinway' and 'Steinmeg', again asked for the axe. It was only as he was finishing his new demolition job that he realised that the Temptations' David Ruffin was about to join The Faces on stage to sing with them. McLagan was left with nothing to play on, and the band finished their set pianoless. Again, the promoter said nothing and paid for the damage, but some time later McLagan discovered that a 'Steinmeg' is a very old 'Steinway'. He had butchered a perfectly good vintage piano.

'David Ruffin played with The Faces a couple of times in Detroit,' remembers photographer Robert Matheu. 'Growing up in Detroit, that was the thing with us, with my gang of friends, Motown was a really important thing for us, as important as the Rolling Stones, or Led Zeppelin, or The Faces, or Alice Cooper. We really hung on to the Motown heritage.'

In the hotel after the show there was another huge party. 'We ran through a fire exit and up to the next floor, pushed the button and twenty kids came out of every elevator door,' remembered McLagan.[6] Because The Faces were now so big in the States, it had become impossible to keep their escapades under control. And, as is so often the way with a group of blokes abroad, the gang mentality kicked in. Tied together with each other, living together, going everywhere together, The Faces and their roadcrew saw everything as them against the world.

'We were all married,' remembered McLagan. 'My marriage didn't stop me shagging anyone I fancied. And girls were real keen and willing and ... so was I.'[7] Kenney Jones remembers it more straightforwardly. 'There were lots of great women around,' he recalled. 'Cor, lovely, stunning.'[8]

Paul Kantner of psychedelic rockers Jefferson Airplane says of his decision to recruit Grace Slick to the group, 'I said right away, "I want to sing with a woman."' A lot of feminists would consider this more oppression, but it only takes one woman singer to balance five or six males in a band.'[9] Kantner has a fundamental point: if there is a woman in a band, who is on an equal basis and is an integral part of the group, then the males in the band will adjust their behaviour accordingly. That isn't to say that the males will behave themselves entirely properly; but they will tone their behaviour down. It is something that writer Lucy O'Brien has encountered in her time as a music journalist.

'Being a journalist, a tour bus is much more smelly if it's a male roadcrew and a male band,' she says. 'It literally does get down to smelly socks and unclean toilets. I think that men don't want to be seen as completely crass, so they do behave a bit – not much, but a little bit more if there's a woman around. As a journalist, they see me more as an equal with them so I get treated with respect. More respect than the girlfriends, actually, and certainly the groupie hangers-on. I suppose I can really influence their profession in a way that their girlfriend can't.'

Fuelled by a massive intake of drink and drugs, The Faces had none of the 'balance' that Kantner spoke of. Part of rock 'n' roll legend is the dubious things that bands get up to when on tour, and those things themselves become legends. The Faces' contribution to this pantheon was the 'Surgery'.

'Any time one of the roadies found a pair of boilers who liked to be noticed and didn't object to getting naked in front of the band and crew,' remembered McLagan, 'we would all squeeze into one room where the girls would get undressed, ready for the operation. Someone even went to the lengths of carrying a surgical mask and stethoscope, but it was all very funny, with lots of stupid comments and general mayhem, falling over, laughter and probing with household objects. No-one ever got hurt, and it had very little to do with sex, although the girls invariably got all worked up, at which point we'd leave them to do or be done by whoever was willing, but never anyone in the band, because by that time we'd have hurried to the bar for a quick one before they closed.'[10]

Back in Britain in late August, the groundswell of support for The Faces eventually erupted as they continued to tour. The first signs of acceptance from the British music press came following the Weeley Festival, where they were supposed to be supporting T Rex. 'Weeley – A One Group Festival' squealed the cover of the *NME*, while the review was equally ecstatic. Apart from complaining about the organisation of the festival – apparently the organisers had learned nothing from the Rolling Stones' debacle at Altamont and had asked the Hell's Angels to provide the security – the paper couldn't have been happier with The Faces.

'No group generated the excitement of The Faces ... even Ron Wood's outrageous navy and yellow "yacht" outfit seemed conservative beside Rod Stewart's bright pink satin suit. No shirt – just a matching pink scarf ... Mr Stewart grabs hold of the mike stand –

inverts it and holds it above his head. Then it's back to the stomping, camping it up, marching and the comedy act ... The Faces may have thought they'd finished when they'd played for an hour but the audience weren't going to let them go. "Feel So Good" was an excellent choice of encore and it was an amazing sight to see an audience of around 100,000 all standing up and chanting back the chorus ... After they'd finished my sympathies were with the follow-up band, T Rex. After all, who could possibly follow or match the sheer brilliance of The Faces.'

The success at Weeley was followed by two riotous shows in London, at the Queen Elizabeth Hall, and another limelight-stealing appearance supporting The Who at Kennington Oval cricket ground in South London. '[The Faces weren't] so much a group as a musical gang,' remembered author Lloyd Bradley of the Oval gig. 'People were streaming out before the main attraction had finished their set, convinced they'd already seen the headliners.'[11]

The momentum generated by both The Faces and Rod Stewart on both sides of the Atlantic was beginning to pay off, with sales of Stewart's solo LP and 'Maggie May' soaring. By October, Rod Stewart, supported by The Faces, had achieved something never achieved before, and the front cover of the *NME* on 9 October 1971 told the story. 'Rod Chart Sensation' it read. *Every Picture Tells a Story* and 'Maggie May' were simultaneously top of the album and single charts respectively in both the UK and the USA. The single and album also went to the top of the charts in Canada, New Zealand and Australia. Rod Stewart was on top of the music business.

Unfortunately for the rest of The Faces, their names weren't attached. To the rest of the world, Rod was the star; The Faces were his backing band. The Number 1 status of 'Maggie May' in the UK gave Stewart an opportunity to appear on the BBC's *Top of the Pops*. Rather than take the musicians who had actually played on the record, Stewart took his mates, The Faces.

And suddenly there were The Faces on TV, all five of them along with DJ John Peel, whose reward for championing their music was to be dragooned on to the *Top of the Pops* stage, to sit on a stool behind Mac, self-consciously miming on a mandolin. Rod, Woody, Mac, Kenney and Ronnie with their grown-out Mod bouffant haircuts, Jones out front with Mac, steadily miming to the drums he didn't play, Woody and Ronnie hiding behind Kenney Jones, chatting and laughing and rushing around mischievously, Mac trying desperately to see what the others were up to behind him, and at the centre of the mayhem, Rod the Mod.

Rod, complete in his red velvet suit and black scarf, sitting on top of the world but for all the world looking like a bloke out for a laugh with his mates, flicking the mike stand over his head as though he's never really in control of it, smiling conspiratorially at Ronnie Lane, marching – strutting – backwards and forwards, waiting for the instrumental break when The Faces all turn to John Peel for his mandolin 'solo', and Ron Wood jumps off the stage to produce a football which they pass between themselves until Ronnie Lane whacks it and the ball exits stage left.

The lads had arrived, and that *Top of the Pops* appearance spoke to a generation of young, working-class men not interested in 'Progressive' rock and being serious, but interested instead in football and drinking and having a good time because of the banality of their own lives, trapped in council estates and limited horizons where the only outlet for ambition came on the football terraces at three o'clock on a Saturday afternoon. And for The Faces to take a football, with all the significance it held for 'yob' culture, on to *Top of the Pops* was an act of almost certainly unconscious subversion, taking a symbol of the working class onto a pop music show, into the homes of everyone who owned a television.

Over the next couple of years, barbers all over the country would be faced with young, working-class men demanding a 'Rod', the grown-out, spiky, ex-Mod bouffant now a symbol of class and allegiance. The scarves that Rod wore were a more stylised reflection of the scarves that football fans wore, the girls that Rod went out with the girls that everyone would like to go out with, the cars that Rod bought the cars everyone aspired to. And whether they were Rod's backing band or not, The Faces had also arrived.

'I remember "Maggie May" being Number 1 and it being a complete anthem and everyone loving it,' recalled Lucy O'Brien. 'He was Top of the Pops for a while, that was the thing, when you had that Number 1 record you really were "King of the World" and you became "the" celebrity. Now if someone gets to Number 1 – so what? Blink and you miss it.'

The problems The Faces had had with the British music press evaporated overnight. Rather than scrabbling to get space in the papers, they were now turning it down. 'I remember it being quite revolutionary when you'd go to a newsagent in the mid-Seventies and you'd see Rod Stewart ... in a national newspaper,' remembered journalist Chris Salewicz. 'Basically none of those papers had a clue about youth culture – it really was another world out there.'[12] The band had another short tour of America in October (including a sell-out gig at Madison Square Gardens, New York) plus they had a new LP to record.

Robert Matheu recalls that Stewart was at the height of his critical credibility following the release of *Every Picture*. 'Growing up in Detroit I was reading *Creem* magazine,' he remembers. 'Rod was up there – as far as the *Creem* writers went – around the time of *Every Picture Tells a Story*. I can even remember *Rolling Stone*. Rod had as much credibility at that moment as Dylan did, as far as a songwriter and taking American blues and folk music and interpreting them in his own ways.

'Listening to *Gasoline Alley* and *Every Picture Tells a Story*, just the arrangement they came up with for "Cut Across Shorty", which is a pretty simplistic, classic rockabilly song – the original arrangement that Carl Smith wrote in the Fifties is just a simple rockabilly tune – their arrangement was just amazing. On Rod's solo records he had a heavier hand on how things were done. On The Faces' records it was much more of a democracy.'

And Stewart had something else he had to do – the royalties from *Every Picture* were clearly already burning a hole in his pocket, and like any other big rock star, he was off to purchase new accommodation. The accommodation he chose was Cranbourne Court, a 32-room mansion near Windsor. 'There was a quantum leap to the money that came in with a million-, two-million-selling album,' remembered Stewart. 'But I managed to go through a lot of it very quickly. Like you do ...'[13]

Despite any lingering tension over Stewart's solo success, The Faces couldn't have been in better shape as they settled down to record their third album. It is, perhaps, a measure of their confidence – and their ambition – that they finally relented and allowed a producer into the studio. Glyn Johns brought the discipline that had been so lacking in their first two efforts, and Stewart and Wood emerged as a strong songwriting partnership. Recorded in between their now revelrous concerts, the album, named leeringly *A Nod is as Good as a Wink to a Blind Horse*, hones The Faces' live energy into sharp, rock-hard focus.

The LP opens with Wood's brooding guitar introduction to 'Miss Judy's Farm', a cool, hard blues, Bob Dylan's 'Maggie's Farm' updated for the Seventies by Stewart and Wood. McLagan and Lane's 'You're So Rude' follows, a teenage tale of being caught on the sofa with a girl by your parents. 'Love Lives Here' comes next, written by Wood, Stewart and Lane, a poignant observation of the redevelopment work which was finally taking place in London and other cities, with childhood landmarks – probably noticed only by those who grew up with them – knocked down to be replaced with new buildings. Lane's 'Last Orders Please' is almost a cockney, pub knees-up tune, from the title to McLagan's pub piano playing, a tale of meeting an old love.

The next track, 'Stay With Me', written by Stewart and Wood, was to be the single from the album and in many ways is the ultimate Faces' anthem. Two years on the road in Britain and America, with all the incumbent distractions and boredom that the road brings, along with the attitude of The Faces, their energy, their working-class roots, is encapsulated in four and a half minutes. After Ron Wood's simple opening chords, the drums of Jones herald Lane's bass, then Stewart's whoop (off in the background) is followed in by McLagan's Wurlitzer electric piano and they're rocking – but then they stop, McLagan's piano running down the scale until Wood's guitar starts again. But now it's different, it's slower, and before you know it The Faces are rocking again, but this time it's more steady, more laid back, more – well, more of a swagger. And what a swagger – it captures everything about The Faces' live shows – the booze, the 'we don't give a fuck' attitude and the girls, especially the girls. The attitude of the group to the groupies is laid bare, and Stewart leers through the song, offering cab fare and cologne as long as the girls clear off when the band have done with them.

'They're just shagging lyrics, I suppose,' says Stewart. 'There was quite a bit of shagging going on in those days.'[14] The song quickly became a live favourite, and audiences – male and female – regularly sang the chorus back to the band. 'We all lived the story of that song,' remembered McLagan. 'It was a very free time and there were drugs and it all fell into place very easily.'[15] Stewart himself remembered the times more punctiliously. 'The Faces would fuck anything with a pulse,' he said.

Ronnie Lane's self-reflective 'Debris' follows, a thoughtful examination of the way that a son has to re-evaluate his relationship with his father as he grows, his father first being a hero, but subsequently a friend. The next track is a rambling cover of Chuck Berry's 'Memphis (Tennessee)', followed by another Wood/Stewart tune, 'Too Bad', a song pitching The Faces as social outcasts whose aim is to obliterate social occasions. The song firmly places The Faces with the working class, with the wrong accents, the wrong clothes and a bad attitude. The album ends with another Wood/Stewart song, 'That's All You Need', a song about two brothers who choose different lives, but the brother who decides to go 'straight' doesn't make it. The track is a fairly straightforward if raucous blues featuring vicious guitar work from Wood.

*A Nod is as Good as a Wink* is probably The Faces' finest recorded work. Set amid their most productive and successful period, when the band were at their closest, it promises much and largely delivers it. Stewart and Wood's songwriting is at its peak, and Ronnie Lane's songs speak of everyday events and emotions. For once, Stewart's confidence seemed to have permeated the rest of the group, perhaps because of the integral role they had played for Stewart. The band – under Glyn Johns' direction – are sharper and more focused than before, and their confidence and power is obvious. However, Johns himself was not entirely happy with the experience.

'It was obvious to me when I first got involved that it was too much "Rod Stewart and his backing band",' he claimed later. 'That wasn't necessarily anyone's fault. Rod was a success and the band weren't. I doubt if I'd work with The Faces again. Too much hoo-hah went down in the end and I made myself unpopular. I'd like to work with them, though. Rod's vocal abilities are wider than he gives himself credit for. Again, he was the one person I never produced. You don't produce Rod Stewart. He has a particular way of recording and it works for him.'[16]

The press acclaimed the record, the *NME* comparing the band favourably to the Rolling Stones. 'This album is far superior to any put out by Messrs Jagger and Co. for a long time.' The public also acclaimed the record, and it entered the Top Twenty on New Year's Day, 1972, eventually rising to Number 2. In America the LP also entered the charts on New Year's Day, rising to Number 6. It seemed that some of Stewart's solo success was finally beginning to rub off on the band.

The film *Get Carter* starring Michael Caine was released in 1971. The story of a British gangster who goes home to Newcastle to avenge the murder of his brother, the film is gritty and grim, showing the seedier side of working-class life in the early Seventies. The movie stands in stark contrast to Caine's earlier work in the Sixties. Caine had made his name starring in bright, colourful films such as *Zulu* (1964) and more importantly *Alfie* (1966), the Harry Palmer series, and, seminally, *The Italian Job*, a knockabout movie about a robbery in Turin complete with a car chase involving Mini Coopers. The shift from bright movies with the latest fashions to a bleak vision of working-class life seemed apposite at the turn of the decade.

The Faces' private lives were also affected by their huge success in 1971. Stewart wasn't the only Face to have made a packet out of his solo success – Ron Wood's co-writing credits on Stewart's albums were making him a moderately wealthy man, and he too bought himself a larger house in Richmond. The three original Small Faces had married young, a particularly working-class trait in the years following the Second World War. Ian McLagan had married Sandy Sarjeant, a dancer from *Ready, Steady, Go*, Ronnie Lane married the singer Genevieve, whose real name was Sue, and Kenney Jones married Jan Osborn, band leader Tony Osborn's daughter. In 1971 Wood married his long-term girlfriend Krissie. Obviously The Faces' return from America with VD hadn't had a long-term effect on their relationships.

Wood and Stewart also treated themselves to new cars – Wood bought a Bentley and Stewart a Lamborghini. 'I bought a Lamborghini that I used to park outside,' remembered Stewart later. 'I used to wake up every night and look out of the window to make sure no-one had nicked it. I was really proud of it.'[17]

Stewart was also aware of the effect his success (and resultant fame) would have on his family. 'I was very pleased because all my family – two brothers, my sisters, my mum and dad – had always given me such great support and lent me a few bob when I was broke, a couple of quid here and a couple of quid there. So it was, like, thanks all of you, I've done it. That was wonderful.'[18] Rod also had a change of girlfriend at the end of '71, with Dee Harrington replacing Sarah Troops.

While their relationships may have been pressurised by their success, The Faces as a group seemed set for 1972.

# ELEVEN

# NEVER A
# DULL MOMENT

Even as The Faces and Rod Stewart had been wowing crowds in Britain and America in August of 1971, things elsewhere were taking a decided turn for the worse. Increasing sectarian attacks and the perceived success of the Provisional IRA had led the British Government to introduce 'Internment' – detention without trial – for those who were suspected of being involved with terrorism.

In the early morning gloom of 9 August, the sound of metal dust-bin lids being bashed on pavements could be heard around the cities of Northern Ireland. It was the sound of women warning the people in the surrounding streets that the Army were coming to take away their men. In the days that followed, an upsurge of violence led to the deaths of seventeen people, and sectarian violence led to thousands of people being forced to flee their homes, with scenes of blazing houses and soldiers in battledress standing behind riot shields, using armoured cars to move burning lorries out of the roads, and smashing crates full of bottles so they couldn't be used as petrol bombs. The violence continued through the autumn and into the winter of 1971, with strikes and campaigns of civil disobedience including rent strikes aimed at overturning Internment.

The situation in Northern Ireland was brought dramatically to the attention of ordinary people living in Britain when, on 31 October, the IRA exploded a bomb in the public area of the Post Office Tower in London. Until that point, the Post Office Tower had contained a public viewing area and a revolving restaurant. No-one was hurt in the explosion, as the bomb went off at 4.30 in the morning. After the bombing, the Post Office Tower closed to the public and was never re-opened. And bizarrely, a few weeks later, in an episode of *The Goodies* comedy television show titled 'Kitten Kong', the same Post Office Tower was shown being attacked by a giant white kitten. It just seemed to underline the schizophrenic nature of the times.

The turn of 1972 saw the campaign against Internment undertake marches. While The Faces were having a quiet time – a single appearance on *Top of the Pops* to promote 'Stay With Me' – the tension in Northern Ireland reached a new peak. On Sunday, 30 January an anti-Internment march through Derry led to the deaths of thirteen marchers with thirteen more being injured. Though the events of the day – which quickly became known as 'Bloody Sunday' – are still the subject of controversy, there is no dispute that the marchers were shot by the British Army. The fallout from these events was instant and dramatic.

The day effectively ended the Northern Ireland Civil Rights movement, and became fixed in the Nationalist consciousness as another in a long line of atrocities committed by the British against the Irish. It also acted as a major factor in boosting recruitment to the Provisional IRA. Tensions in the North were ratcheted further, the British Government announced an inquiry, and on 2 February, the day of the funerals of eleven of the dead, a crowd marched on the British Embassy in Dublin and burned it down. Twenty days later, the IRA exploded a bomb at the British Army Barracks at Aldershot killing seven people. The 'Troubles' in Northern Ireland were now firmly fixed in the public consciousness.

The domestic situation wasn't getting any better either – despite the Conservative government's attempts to reflate the economy during 1971, the economic situation was growing unstable, with unemployment rising towards the politically sensitive figure of one million people on the dole and inflation continuing to rise. And the relationship between the government and the trade unions was coming to a head. January 1972 saw the first confrontation between Heath's government and the National Union of Mineworkers (NUM). Britain's 280,000 miners came out on strike having rejected an increased pay offer of £2 per week.

The strike dragged on into February, and the miners picketed power stations in an attempt to prevent the movement of coal by road. The miners were supported by the railway workers, who refused to move coal trains, and there were violent incidents on the picket lines. The biggest of these took place at Saltley coke depot in Birmingham, where 6,000 trade unionists – not just miners – descended on the depot and successfully prevented supplies from being delivered. These non-mining trade unionists – known as 'flying pickets' – were well organised, and would concentrate on various sites and hold out until they were successful.

And rumbling on as a somewhat surreal backdrop was the debate the government was holding over whether Britain should enter the Common Market, the European trading bloc which had refused Britain membership on two previous occasions. The Labour Party – when in government – had wanted to join, and the Conservative government now also wanted to join. Negotiations regarding the terms of entry between Britain and the European Commission had been successful, and now the Conservatives had to get the necessary legislation through the British Parliament.

★

After the frenetic nature of 1971, 1972's first proper outings for The Faces were three sell-out dates at the newly renamed Finsbury Park Rainbow. The rock 'n' roll bubble which insulated groups from the harshness which epitomised Conservative Britain was punctured for the first time during the first of these shows: due to the miners' dispute, power stations were lowering their output, and low voltage at the venue meant that McLagan's organ ran out of tune. Despite this, the gigs were raucous, they were again well received, and it seemed that The Faces could do no wrong.

A short German tour followed in March, and a British tour began in April, but was interrupted by their short 'Rock 'n' Roll Circus' tour of America and another quick flit to Germany before resuming in May. The shows pretty much followed the same format: The Faces were ecstatically received, were in the process of getting drunk, and partied long into the night afterwards. Their show at the Camden Roundhouse followed the same format. Fresh back from watching his beloved Arsenal lose a bad-tempered FA Cup Final 1–0 to Leeds at Wembley, Rod Stewart led The Faces onto the stage to shouts of 'Rodney, Rodney' from the crowd, flicked up the mike stand and off they went.

'They always felt like they was just about to fall apart,' remembered Glen Matlock, 'but it just hung together somehow in a way that had a tension that was so good.'[1] The pain of watching Arsenal lose didn't affect Stewart's performance, and The Faces' boozy, coke-driven set ripped the place apart; the sweaty crowd, glad to forget the world outside, screaming their adulation along to 'Stay With Me' and 'Maggie May', just happy to be where they belonged. It was a scene often repeated on the tour.

In the meantime, Wood and Lane had accepted the job of composing the soundtrack to the movie, *Mahoney's Last Stand*, a story about a man from the city trying to make his living in the country. The soundtrack wasn't released until 1976. The tour of Britain continued until in mid-June they returned to America for a tour which lasted until mid-July. The events of the year before – when The Faces had returned from the States with VD – led to the group's management agreeing to fly their wives and girlfriends over to America for various portions of the tour.

Earlier in the year, Ronnie Lane's wife had discovered him in bed with her best friend and neighbour Kate McInnerney, and they had split up. Lane, who was now living in a house at the bottom of Wood's estate in Richmond, had started to be influenced by McInnerney's love of all things Romanesque. Recalling his early love of fairgrounds and his teenage days spent running the rides at Battersea Fairground, he let his old Mod bouffant straggle, and had begun wearing earrings.

The split between Lane and his wife also had an effect on the other wives and girlfriends, who while they knew that their partners were almost certainly up to no good, had had no proof of this (other than their doses of the clap) until Lane was caught in the act. Hence the wives' trips to America. But even this wasn't enough, and one evening, Krissie Wood decided to have it out with Ronnie. Usually this would have been fine, but Krissie Wood chose to have the discussion while The Faces were playing on stage.

'I saw her come on stage and thought, "Where the fuck's she going?"' remembered Kenney Jones. 'None of the others could see her because they had their backs turned.'[2] Krissie Wood was dressed in a feather boa, a big hat and a silk dress. And, to round the outfit off, she was very clearly very drunk and one of her breasts had popped out of the dress. She walked up to Ron Wood and tapped him on the back. Wood turned around in shock, and she started to wag her finger at him, shouting and pointing at an equally shocked Ronnie Lane. 'If you do to me what he did to Sue, I'm leaving you!' 'It was Rod who broke it up,' remembered Jones. 'He was so pissed off that he gobbed on her back, then hustled her off the stage. It was unbelievable.'[3]

By June 1972, the miners' dispute had already been settled – the government agreeing to pay them roughly three times their original offer – only for the dockworkers to strike. In June, three dockers who had been picketing a container depot refused to appear before the new National Industrial Relations Court. The new court ordered their arrest for contempt, and they were imprisoned. The situation rapidly escalated: within days 30,000 dockers were on strike, and the TUC was threatening a general strike if the dockers were not released. The Heath government, desperate for a way out of the corner it had painted itself into, used the Official Solicitor to challenge the Industrial Relations Court's ruling. Unsurprisingly, given the tension within the country, the challenge was successful, the ruling overturned, and the imprisoned dockers released. It wasn't the first – or the last – misjudgement of industrial relations the government would make, but it all added to the sense of a country split asunder.

For the first time since the war – and largely due to the worsening economic situation and against the background of the Northern Irish situation impinging onto the mainland – the British working class were flexing their metaphoric (and sometimes literal) muscle. But that summer also saw other dubious milestones. In July came the death of the hundredth British soldier in Northern Ireland, and the series of bombings, shootings and general mayhem – from all sides in the conflict – showed no signs of ceasing, despite the introduction of a 'ceasefire' on the part of the Provisional IRA in June. To underline the ineffectiveness of this, in Belfast on Friday, 21 July the IRA planted and exploded 22 bombs, which killed nine people and seriously injured around 130 others. The day became known as 'Bloody Friday'.

Following the success of the broadcasts of the 1970 World Cup, the BBC were more than happy to provide live coverage of the 1972 Munich Olympics, David Coleman's voice crackling out of the (increasingly colour) TV sets which had come to dominate every front room. In one of the first major live news events ever broadcast in Britain, Palestinian militants of the 'Black September' group attacked and killed nine Israeli athletes. As the drama unfolded, sports commentators like Coleman were forced to become news reporters for a stunned world audience. While – yet again – these events didn't affect Britain directly, it all added to the sense of a world increasingly violent and ever more out of control.

West Germany had their own group of terrorists to rival the IRA – the Baader-Meinhof gang were radical, left-wing terrorists, given to bank robberies, kidnappings (for ransoms) and dramatic shootouts with the police. Led by Andreas Baader and former journalist Ulrike Meinhof, and featuring such terrorist luminaries as Astrid Proll and 'Carlos the Jackal', the Baader-Meinhof gang were young, idealistic and looked like pop stars. Though ultimately unsuccessful (most of the gang would wind up in prison, dead or both), they were a constant feature of life in West Germany in the early Seventies and, somehow, a cause of slight relief in Britain: it didn't only happen here.

In between the touring and arguments with partners, Rod Stewart had gone back into the studio to record his follow-up to *Every Picture*. The pressure was on for Stewart, as record companies especially are loathe to change a winning formula, and *Every Picture* was certainly a winning formula. The same line-up was utilised again, and quickly fell into the old modus operandi – a couple of Stewart/Wood songs, a Stewart/Quittenton hit, a Dylan cover and a couple of R&B songs did the trick.

The new LP, *Never a Dull Moment*, opens with 'True Blue', a Stewart/Wood number prominently featuring McLagan's Wurlitzer electric piano, reframes Stewart's obsession with 'going home' and breaks down into the loose funk drumming that would turn up later in The Faces' story. Stewart's regular return to the theme of 'going home' reflects a common theme in both Scottish and Irish folk music. Both cultures – especially Irish culture – have been premised since the nineteenth century on the expectation that the majority of their citizens would have to emigrate in order to find work. This has meant that the music which came from those cultures was influenced by themes of leaving and hoping to return.

'Lost Paraguayos', a bluesy good-time Stewart/Wood song that rolls along on acoustic guitars complete with a Van Morrison-type horn riff on the outro could easily have been a Faces song – it wasn't just Wood's appearance on the track, it was the whole laid-back, rabble-rousing feel. Whatever else had been going on since he'd joined the group, Stewart had been learning something from their free and easy attitude.

While showing the song respect, Stewart's cover of Dylan's 'Mama, You Been On My Mind' is little more than perfunctory. 'Italian Girls', another Stewart/Wood composition, is again pretty ordinary. However, Stewart's cover of Jimi Hendrix's 'Angel' is impressive, though Stewart's attempt has nothing on the version The Faces were to play live. In The Faces' hands it became an anthem, a moment – more even than 'Stay With Me' – when the auditorium would become a single, swaying mass of adulation. Played at the climax of Faces shows, it was part terrace chant, part hymn, and it was to become the fans' own song.

After some fiddling about on the guitar which was actually given a name and a songwriting credit ('Interludings', credited to Art Wood, Ron's brother) comes the hit record for the album. 'You Wear It Well' is essentially 'Maggie May' spun around a couple of times and given a bit of a wash and scrub up. Almost a sequel to 'Maggie May', it did make concessions to the usual idea of a 'pop single' – there are identifiable riffs and the 'You wear it well' hook kept people's attention – but again Stewart comes through in the lyric and his performance of it.

The song was again produced with Dylan's *Blonde on Blonde* in mind, McLagan's Hammond a little more to the fore, but with the introduction of a violin riffing around the vocal in a style that comes from Celtic folk music. A story of someone trying to get in contact with a lover he has not seen for some time, and set loosely in the form of a letter, 'You Wear It Well' has all the poignancy and regret of 'Maggie May' but none of the venom. As with 'Maggie May', Stewart speaks in everyday words, calling on everyday, working-class experiences and drawing on familiar images such as parties and the all-day rock shows which were becoming common at football grounds around the country. And how better to win back a lost love than to compare her to the most glamorous woman on the planet, Jackie Kennedy Onassis? And, as the song comes to a disjointed end, Stewart almost comically wonders if the letter will ever arrive.

The album finishes with a slow blues, 'I'd Rather Go Blind', and a song by Sam Cooke – one of Stewart's musical heroes – 'Twistin' The Night Away'.

Overall, the LP is pretty much like *Every Picture*. The formula worked, the album and single selling incredibly well, but to a certain extent it was Stewart consolidating rather than advancing. Many of the songs from the LP would go on to be massive live favourites for The Faces, and it was a mark of how important Stewart's solo work was that The Faces were due to go to America to promote it in August.

The album was also well received in the music press. That The Faces were seen as an important group was now beyond doubt. In February, the *NME* had run an 'analysis' – written by Nick Logan – of what they called the 'mini-phenomenon' which was Slade, T Rex and The Faces. The 'mini-phenomenon' was 'a situation born out of three/four years of waiting in a post-Beatles limbo for a new real phenomenon to present itself for deification'. Logan had 'lumped' the three groups together because, he argued, they were catering for an audience – or audiences – which had been largely ignored by the music business over the preceding few years.

★

By the time *Never a Dull Moment* was released, Stewart and The Faces were considered to be one of the three hottest properties in British rock music, the other two being Marc Bolan and David Bowie. Bowie had just released *Ziggy Stardust and the Spiders from Mars*, his paean to other-worldliness, and was preparing to take the country by storm. Stewart and Bolan were both releasing LPs at the same time, and so they were reviewed together by Charles Shaar Murray in the *NME*.

Murray gave Bolan's *Slider* album a pasting, saying that '[Bolan's] music is chasing itself in circles and obsessively eating its own tail'. Stewart, however, was at the opposite extreme. The musicians who made the album were 'the best studio band since the one Dylan

Ronnie looks up

Woody gets down

... and Kenny looks around

Rod, gloved and ready

Rod, Ron and Woody – at the Party

He's only here for the beer

Ronnie and Rod Tell Everyone

Having a Real Good Time –
the Faces rip 'em up again

Mac and Woody chew the fat; new arrival Tetsu Yamauchi looks on

*Above:* Last Orders Please –
the Faces close to closing time

SPECIAL "BREAKIN' UP IS HARD TO DO" ISSUE

$1.00
NOV 1975
45P

**America's Only Rock 'n' Roll Magazine**

# creem

## ROD STEWART
### SLAPS FACES

**FACES** Turn The Other Cheek
Your Mother Wears Combat Boots!
**DALTREY** Responds to
**TOWNSHEND** Interview

**DEEP PURPLE:**
"Why I Quit"-BLACKMORE
"Why Me?"-TOMMY BOLIN

The Legacy of
**BUFFALO SPRINGFIELD:**
**STEPHEN STILLS**
Mellow Belly
**NEIL YOUNG**
In The Danger Zone
**RICHIE FURAY**
Jumps For Jesus

**MARSHALL TUCKER**
Good Ol' Bad Boys

- SPRINGSTEEN In The Jungle
- KEITH RICHARD In Bed
- CLAPTON • COOPER's Coupe
- BAY CITY ROLLERS

**EAGLES**
All-American Macho

GET YOUR
WAH WAH'S OUT!
CREEM's 3rd Annual GUITAR BREAK

*Right:* Rod and Britt
do the sailing thing

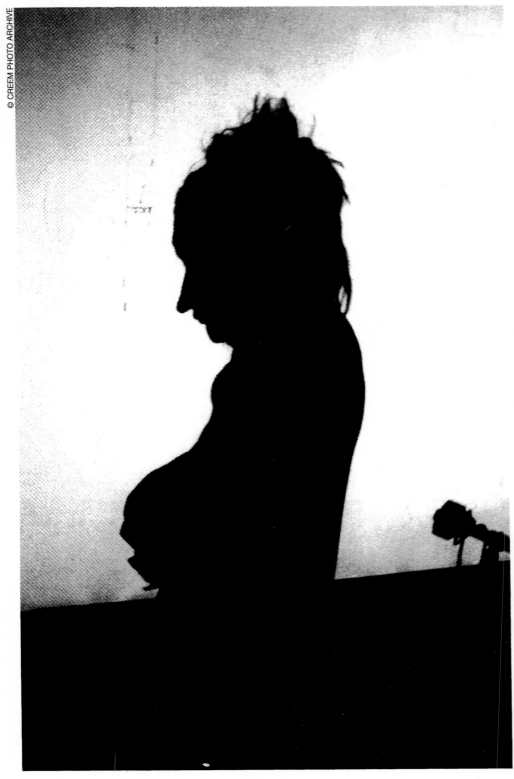

A Face apart

assembled for "Highway 61 Revisited" and "Blonde on Blonde"'. But Murray's review, while good for Stewart, contained a pointed dig at Stewart's mates. '"Never A Dull Moment?" Well, almost never. This is an album which is going to give me a lot of listening time over the next few months, and I'm glad it's in the house. I just wish that, one day, The Faces will make an album this good.'

With the album rising to Number 3 in the American charts, the final sentence of Murray's review stung the other Faces. But the irony of the opening line of the opening track of the album wasn't lost on them either: following the single pistol shot of Kenney Jones' snare drum, Stewart sings that he's never been a millionaire. Not yet, anyway.

At this point, Stewart and The Faces had the ability to speak to people in Britain in a way that no other pop artist seemed able.

'You would never say that The Faces were your favourite band, though,' remembered Kevin McDonald. 'You'd go and see them, and it was always an event, but it was difficult to see them as separate from Rod. To be honest, it was Rod's records that you bought. He did look like us ... Or maybe we looked like him. There were always loads of us with that haircut and we used to tie our scarves around our wrists like he did. You couldn't imagine him without them, though.'

Chris Sparks remembers the early Seventies as 'a sort of juncture of epochs. What I remember is all us lads – that's when I was going to Tottenham [Hotspur Football Club] – we were all halfway between being Suedeheads and something else. We all had Crombies [Abercrombie overcoats – one of the features of Skinhead dress] but we all had this strange, quite long hair which we'd grown out of crops. Flared sta-prest – big flares, but they were sta-prest, with big creases but they were very smart. They were an amalgam of Skinhead clothes and hippy clothes. Ben Shermans and flares and Crombies and long hair grown out of crops. We were ex-Suedeheads, but nothing. So it's quite a hybrid time. That was the time when you could be anything 'cos the hippy thing had ended and the Skinhead thing had ended and I guess the Mod thing had ended and nothing else had started and, in fact, nothing did start for years – 'til Punk. So there's five years when there really isn't anything.'

Journalist Lucy O'Brien views the 'absence' of subculture in a different way. 'In a sense, the subculture was "pop",' she argues. 'Pop was huge. It was mass culture, basically. But pop wasn't the pop we have now – it was David Bowie, Roxy Music, T Rex. Okay, there was Paper Lace and crap like that as well, but I think what was different is that pop was made by people who'd been touring musicians and who wrote their own stuff and who were older. They were bands that had been on the road, whether it was Wizzard or The Faces or Carole King; they were working musicians so the pop music you got was real, quality stuff, the stuff that obviously stays in your brain.

'I remember going to a friend's house and talking about David Bowie, and how much you loved Ziggy Stardust and the whole look of Ziggy Stardust, and she was eleven at the time. So what's considered subculture now was really mass culture then. David Bowie really was very mainstream. I remember girls at school having the Bowie cut, the Ziggy cut. Obviously there was also the teen stuff like The Osmonds and David Cassidy. I was into David Cassidy in a big way, posters on my bedroom wall. The more intelligent girls were into David Cassidy – the Osmonds were kind of smaltzy and crap and they were all Mormons.'

But O'Brien also remembers that there were few female pop stars in the early Seventies. 'In a way you could argue that the Seventies were a bit more regressive than the Sixties in terms of rock,' she argues. 'In the Sixties you did have a few prominent women, Marianne Faithfull, Janis Joplin, Grace Slick, women in the psychedelic scene doing really well. And then with Glam rock it was quite regressive.'

Carol Chaffer remembers fashion being eminently pliable. 'We used to wear these little crocheted skull-caps with our Oxford bags [trousers] and blazers,' she recalls. 'I don't know where it came from – it had no cultural connotations and it was something that I didn't see around us, and it was one of two things – first, that somebody round my area started wearing them and each subculture appropriates its own stuff, but I think it's probably more likely that somebody had just learned to crochet and so we all learned and that was just the easiest thing to make.'

Lucy O'Brien remembers the importance of clothes as a symbol of personality. 'Bright blue eyeshadow, spangly tops – I think it was a very bold time in terms of clothes,' she recalls. 'Really bright colours, and lots of stripes, everything was stripy this and stripy that. Subtlety just wasn't in the game. Wedges [shoes] were enormously popular. I had several pairs of wedges. It started off with platforms and then the part of the shoe between the heel and the sole got filled in. It went from being about "How big are your platforms?" to "How big are your wedges?" Some people came into school with enormous wedges. And that was an indication of how daring you were, how high your wedges were.'

Sue Westergaard also remembers women's clothes. 'We were supposed to wear bottle-green to school, a set uniform, white shirt, green tie, green skirt, but being the sort of school it was, as long as it was green it didn't really matter. I can remember having a red seer-sucker shirt with very pointy collars and a green jumper and a green wraparound mini-skirt. I can remember having black, patent leather shoes with beautiful yellow lines, beautiful leather lines, and platform shoes. Black, knee-high suede boots with a little platform. It was short skirts and platform boots, and in the summer Scholls and clogs – we used to wear clogs a lot. And no bra – in the sixth form I got told off, the head of the sixth form took me to one side and said he'd had complaints from members of staff because I wasn't wearing a bra, and would I wear a bra in future. I was completely nonplussed. I think about it now, but this guy – the head of sixth form – was a vicar, and he had to sit me alone in a room and tell me this. He must have been ever so embarrassed, but I didn't really mind. It had never crossed my mind that anyone would find this sixteen-year-old's tits interesting, bouncing around under this thin T-shirt and "granddad" vest. That's what we used to wear, granddad vests and mini-skirts, with boots.'

In the North of England there was a club scene which provided a substantive subculture for those who knew about it. 'Northern Soul' was a subculture based around the old Mod club scene, and premised on obscure soul records procured from secondhand record stores in America. Clubs such as the Wigan Casino would host all-night discos where those into Northern Soul would display their latest dance steps for an audience of young men, keen to be impressed. The movement was named 'Northern Soul' because the records were soul records and the clubs were in the North of England.

'I always felt that I belonged more with the pop side of things,' remembered Carol Chaffer. 'I was a Slade fan and a T Rex fan, that's what I felt suited my personality. The Faces were there, but they were slightly more grown-up. But my whole social life was Northern Soul, and that's simply because that was my peer group – at that age you try and run with the pack that's a couple of years older than you and you follow their direction – and it was simply that Northern Soul is all there was. So if you didn't go to the youth club and the Northern Soul clubs then you didn't have a social life other than going down the pub which would've made you more a biker/heavy metal type person, which I wasn't either. I was too young to go to the Wigan Casino although the older boys from the youth club did. I always felt the Northern Soul thing was very much a boys' thing because they all wanted to be DJs, they all bought the records, and for the girls I don't think it was that much fun. I liked some of the music and I still do, particularly the instrumental stuff, but it's not something that I would've bought or danced to.'

Chris Sparks sees The Faces as particularly apt for the times. 'The Faces were cool at that moment when everything else fell away. I guess they're a curiosity really, 'cos what they are is all the things they're not. They're not the Small Faces, that's the first thing they're not. And the second thing they're not is they're not the Rolling Stones. And the third thing they're not is they're not a "glitter" band which everyone else was doing. And they certainly weren't a sexy band in any sense of the word; they weren't "pop" stars although they were pop stars. They weren't actually quite rock 'n' roll stars because in those days, if you were rock 'n' roll stars you came from this select mix of people, so there was the Rolling Stones who were *the* band, and then there were people like Led Zeppelin. And that all came from John Mayall, basically. They were all very middle class. So The Faces weren't part of that. They're quite funny cos they're a band that aren't actually anything. They were kind of left-over Mods.'

Lucy O'Brien cites another reason for Stewart and The Faces' success. 'The Faces were so British,' she argues. 'Their sound was so British, 'cos they were drawing on that Celtic folk thing, that mixture of Celtic folk and R&B which has always been a strand in British music.'

Without the impetus that was apparent in British pop music during the Sixties – fuelled at first by a strange mixture of The Beatles' success and the adoption of American R&B by the Mods, and later by LSD and the invention of a British 'hippy' culture – the early Seventies seemed to drag. No dominant form of music appeared, and as Chris Sparks notes, no subculture appeared to replace hippy, Mod or Skinhead. Left to itself, British music fell back on the old traditions of music hall and pantomime. The emergence of David Bowie as the dominant musical figure of the early Seventies unleashed a whole new set of uncertainties, though not this time of class or social change.

David Bowie's *Ziggy Stardust* album and subsequent tour had created a storm in Britain. Bowie, dressed in make-up, dyed hair and lurid cat-suits, created 'a new sexually ambiguous image for those youngsters willing and brave enough to challenge the notoriously pedestrian stereotypes conventionally available to working-class men and women'.[4] The music itself was not radical, being instead a mish-mash of Sixties 'underground' music – pioneered by the Velvet Underground and Iggy Pop – and ordinary R&B pop riffs. Christened 'Glam rock', artists such as Gary Glitter, Alvin Stardust and The Sweet turned out simple, power-pop tunes for young teenagers. Bowie was unique in that he managed to attract a mass youth audience, and was at the top of a chain which included Roxy Music at the top end and Alvin Stardust, Gary Glitter and The Sweet at the bottom.

Others such as Slade and Marc Bolan adopted the elements to provide them with a ready-made, understandable image which undermined whatever musical credibility they may have had, while Roxy Music came directly from Bowie's *Ziggy* period but retained their credibility (for a while, at least). Even rockers such as Rod Stewart and Mick Jagger weren't averse to wearing the odd bit of blusher or eyeliner.

Bowie – as the erstwhile leader of Glitter or Glam rock – didn't seem to have any interest either in the socio-political issues of the day, or even in the effects of his sexual ambiguity, preferring instead to create himself outside of the world, removing himself from the ordinary banalities of existence in the early Seventies. Glam – and Bowie in particular – were premised on the idea of 'escape', 'from class, from

sex, from personality, from obvious commitment – into a fantasy past
… or a science-fiction future'.[5]

The question of sexuality and gender were all that Glam really
addressed, and though at one level (Bowie and Roxy Music) this was
done intelligently and subversively, at the other end (Gary Glitter, The
Sweet and eventually Marc Bolan), the artists were just schlock pop
groups trying to cash in on a fad, taking money from teenyboppers.

David Bowie aside, Glam rock, such as it was, couldn't hope to
appeal to a mass audience. In some ways it is easy to understand why
Glam rock was a success – even in limited terms – in Britain in the early
Seventies. Given the drabness of ordinary life, anything that looked
'larger than life' was bound to be exciting, plus the British were already
used to cross-dressing men through the tradition of pantomime.

'When I first started going out I tried to fit in with everyone else,'
recalled Carol Chaffer. 'That meant wearing blazers and Oxford bags
and stuff like that. But then I developed my own identity which was the
Marc Bolan influence, based on secondhand clothes, stuff that pop stars
on telly wore, so I had thigh-length black boots which I'd wear with cut-
off jeans, which nobody else would wear in my town.'

Though many serious artists – including, ultimately, Bowie
himself – turned their backs on Glam rock, the penchant for make-up
was infectious, and even artists not associated with Glam rock stole
something from it. The audience for Glam rock was divided into the
teenyboppers and older, more serious and self-conscious teenagers
into Bowie and Roxy Music alone among the Glam groups. It was in
this space that The Faces found their audience.

'I'd say pop music was a religion then,' recalls Lucy O'Brien.
'You'd go to school and everyone would know the words to the top
pop songs. Glam rock was huge, Gary Glitter was huge, T Rex were
huge, Rod Stewart and The Faces were huge.'

The Faces drew on the older Glam fans, but also on the countless others – grown-up Mods, ex-Skinheads and Suedeheads alienated by the sexual ambiguity and general frivolousness of Glam – who felt that there was nothing going on for them. The Faces' expression of their own brand of working-class values – boozing, womanising, football, driving fast cars – allied to their rough rendition of British R&B gave their audience some reflection of the lives they were living or, more importantly, aspired to.

Stewart's solo records – indistinguishable in the fans' eyes from those of The Faces – drew not just on the soul and R&B that the Mods had loved, but also on a particularly Celtic brand of folk music. Stewart's use of mandolin (which became a trademark of his early singles) and the violin (played as a fiddle, straight from the style of Irish and Scottish traditional music) came from a time of working-class certainty. This isn't to say that there was ever a time when being working class meant anything solid, but instead that there were some certainties – family, employment, community, football, some of which were imagined, some of which were real.

Stewart and The Faces may not have explicitly addressed any socio-political issues (though they did occasionally pop up in the odd lyric), but their lyrics did spring from ordinary, everyday life, from 'You're So Rude' to Cannon Street train station's cameo appearance in 'Bad 'N' Ruin'. But The Faces were especially about the gig, the party, and this is predominantly what they are remembered for. And these gigs were an affirmation, they provided a sense of belonging that, by the Seventies, came rarely – perhaps only on football terraces.

And, as opposed to the distance engendered by Bowie and the other Glam acts, The Faces – and Stewart – revelled in belonging, in bringing the fans along to the party. Everyone was invited, and it was an old-style knees-up, singalong, drunken revelry of a kind which had largely disappeared and is almost entirely absent today. It was simultaneously modern and traditional, it was working class and proud of it, and – unlike Bowie and the prog-rock groups of the day such as Genesis, Yes, and Emerson, Lake & Palmer – it was entirely unpsychedelic, and avoided being inward-looking or overly self-reflective as the music inspired by LSD tended to be.

Therefore there were, Sparks remembers, very few groups around that were actually likeable. One of the important factors for music fans (especially young men) is the credibility, the authenticity – both in musical form and lifestyle – of the group. This manifests itself not only in the bond between groups of young men, but also the icons they pledge their allegiance to – football clubs and pop groups. Though the choice of football club – certainly in the Seventies – was dictated by locale, the choice of pop group was more esoteric.

'Gary Glitter was children's stuff,' remembers Sparks. 'David Bowie was the serious stuff. Roxy Music were around too. Quite a lot of people would have a David Bowie, a Roxy Music and a Faces album – that would be a common combination for your thinking person in mid-teens. The people that bought The Faces wouldn't have bought Genesis. They [Genesis] were those sort of "Yes" people. They were a totally different thing. My brother did that, he was at university then. I don't think he even liked The Faces.'

Dave Phillips also remembers the early Seventies as a bleak time. 'The music I remember was Deep Purple, Yes, eternal one-hour organ solos. It was like the "art" side of music had vanished up its own anus. People were moving into becoming "discerning" rock listeners; it was a period when there were magazines like *Let It Rock* and there'd be articles on how to construct your own hi-fi system. It's when people started buying their own amplifiers and listening to that, all quite conservative, and at the consumer end there was pomp [progressive] rock and Glam rock. Girls liked T Rex, girls liked Glam rock, all those pretty, androgynous boys.'

'I liked Slade,' recalled Carol Chaffer, 'because they were quite poppy and quite simple, all their songs were quite simple and they were loud and they were fun. They were kids' songs. David Bowie was a bit more complex.'

Despite – or perhaps because of – their reputation as a womanising band, The Faces' fanbase was mostly male. 'The Faces were definitely a boys band,' remembers Sparks. 'I don't think girls were interested in them at all. None of the girls we hung out with were at all interested. All the girls were into Marc Bolan, who was definitely the happening thing for the girls. Bolan turned into a strange thing, he was the first kind of teenybop thing. Everybody liked David Bowie 'cos he was clever. But Rod Stewart was definitely what the lads used to aspire to.'

Lucy O'Brien agrees. 'The Faces were a reflection of working-class culture, that laddish escapism. I remember that being all around, it was par for the course. Girls were just "chicks" really. Drinking was a huge culture, 'cos drugs weren't that available, not in the way that they are now. Marijuana was more of a hippy thing.'

'There were very few women in the charts at that point,' says O'Brien. 'Suzi Quatro getting in the charts was important because she stood out, she was so distinctive, she was doing rock music and she was playing an instrument. And that was almost unheard of. She really was out there on her own. I don't think that it was exclusive, I just think that women didn't think that they could do it, it just wasn't their world. And their only relation to it was as "the girlfriend" or "the groupie".'

Carol Chaffer recalled the appeal of bands like T Rex to young women. 'Marc Bolan had good dresses that you would want to wear.

He had feather boas and vintage silk jackets and things: his outfits were very *Sex and the City*, the sort of thing that girls would've worn. For me, Marc Bolan more than anybody else was "Glam" rather than bands like The Sweet which were just bubblegum, throwaway. Marc Bolan's songs define for me what Glam was. His songs were very simple in structure, they were very anthemic, but they're still "pop", but he's still got a bit of artiness around the fringes. In the Sixties, my older sisters had liked The Herd and Peter Frampton and the Walker Brothers – they were more serious "artists", a bit more rocky and a bit more serious – and I put The Faces in that category. Older and more serious.'

Sue Westergaard didn't see it entirely the same way. 'I just thought The Faces were sexy,' she remembers. 'Because I went to this comprehensive school where all the blokes would play football, it was part of that. They were "blokey" blokes. They were lads, and that's what I liked about them. Like Slade – Noddy Holder and the others were "blokes" and Rod Stewart and The Faces were "blokes" and Marc Bolan wasn't, and Bowie wasn't but he was clever, and Roxy Music were intellectual. You liked people that you fancied, really, I think at that age. Marc Bolan was too little. I liked Noddy Holder, I liked Slade, 'cos he had this huge voice. Bolan was a bit too soppy for me. I liked Bowie and Roxy Music. Roxy Music were so stylish, they dressed so well. Quite a lot of the Glam bands were tacky; Roxy Music weren't tacky, they had class. Bowie had class too. Rod Stewart had a bit of style in those days, that pineapple haircut and the long scarves.'

The British audience for The Faces was therefore a mixed bunch. Sparks remembers seeing the range of Faces fans before a gig in London. 'I saw them at a place in Edmonton though I can't remember them at all. The only thing I remember about it is actually getting the tickets. I had a bunch of mates and we all decided to go – it might have been Christmas or Easter, a big gig. The queue were this incredible mix which we thought was very amusing. It had all these teeny-bopper girls there, and it also had loads of lads like us. There were loads of people like us in the queue. And there were a few black people as well in those days who used to go to those Faces gigs. Everybody felt a bit funny about the queue because there were certain people there you didn't want to be associated with, the very straight, teeny-boppery people. But I suppose that was what The Faces were about really. They were an amalgam, a collage of loads and loads of things.'

It was a collage which reflected the music scene in 1972. 'It was like a bricolage period, and that's why they're the band for it,' says Sparks. 'They're the bricolage band, bits of everything. A bit hippy – cos Ronnie Lane got quite hippy; a bit Mod-ish, but after Mods; a bit Skinheady; a bit yobby – Rod Stewart was a bit of a yob. And that was the period when they used to have those rock gigs at Charlton, and everyone would take those huge tins of Watney's down with them and drink fifteen pints of beer and take all those drugs and there were huge fights. I remember I went to one of those Charlton gigs and there were these massive fights between everyone, and even though they didn't play there, The Faces were all about that, it was all that territory. The Who got quite yobby around that time. They all went in for that kind of thing. So it was that kind of British yob culture. But The Faces' music was clever, the music's quite sensitive, actually. That was Ronnie Lane and Ronnie Wood's a great R&B guitarist. He should've been in The Yardbirds. I was learning the guitar at the time and I learned loads of those riffs he used to do, those great, chugging R&B riffs.'

Sue Westergaard remembers Rod Stewart and The Faces in a more everyday setting. 'I was at school,' she recalls, 'and I'd always done art. My brother was a musician and I was always the artist in the family, and in the art room at school when you were in the fourth and fifth year you could play records. But the only two records we had were *Every Picture* and *Never a Dull Moment*. I had the most fantastic art teacher, Francis Day, but we never bothered to ask why it was only those two records. I remember watching The Faces on *Top of the Pops* playing football and thinking they were so sexy. I said to my dad, "Hasn't he got a fantastic voice?" and my dad couldn't see it at all.'

But there was more than The Faces, Glam rock and 'progressive' rock going on. 'At that time we'd been to see *Jesus Christ Superstar*,' remembers Westergaard. 'My brother was always trying to write rock operas – it was the rock opera time, *Tommy* and all that. It was impressive – I despise Andrew Lloyd Webber but it was the first time you'd seen anything like that. The whole West End stage stuff was pretty amazing.'

★

After a couple of gigs in Britain (including the Reading Festival), The Faces duly made their way back to the States. The touring continued relentlessly through August and September. More hotel rooms were destroyed – manager Billy Gaff's being the favourite – and the band were eventually banned from the Holiday Inn chain of hotels. No matter, though – the group started booking hotels under the name of another British group, Fleetwood Mac. And Rod and the boys were exporting another aspect of British culture to their slightly bemused American audience.

'Rod would do the whole routine during the encore and kick out soccer balls into the audience,' recalls Robert Matheu. 'And because of that I started looking more at the *NME* and *Melody Maker* and was becoming more aware of their association with soccer. The kids that I used to hang out with in Detroit, we were aware that that was the big thing in England, but it was so extremely foreign to us. My brother's much older than me and he was never a music fan at all, he was more of the sports guy in the family – he liked football and he liked baseball and hockey. And 'cos of the way that Rod dressed, with the yellow chiffon and everything, it always had that gay stigma attached to it. Even the kids that I went to school with that were in bands like his would call him a faggot, and the same thing with Ron Wood. But this was the music that I was attracted to, along with Bowie, and Alice Cooper, and my friends and I actually emulated that look to some extent. I don't think I was into eye-shadow or anything, but there was definitely polka-dot shirts and a lot of scarves.'

The partying continued apace. When they played the Hollywood Bowl, one of the most prestigious gigs in America, The Faces once again took the party on stage. McLagan rented a suit: 'Like the one Groucho Marx used to wear,' he later remembered. 'The audience brought picnic baskets and bottles of wine and the smell of pot wafted up on to the stage. The tux came with all the trimmings, white tie, waistcoat, braces, cufflinks and collar studs. I wore white basketball boots instead of evening dress, but the *pièce de résistance* was the white carnation in my lapel into which I poured copious amounts of the finest Colombian coke. I could pull the carnation to my nostril, do a hefty line in plain view of the audience, and no-one suspected. No-one except Ronnie and Woody, who knew I'd done it and kept sliding over to the piano for a sniff while I played.'[6]

News of the tour's success filtered back to Britain, where Stewart's on-stage assessment of the Hollywood Bowl gig – 'It's better than a Nuremberg rally' – gave The Faces another headline on another page.

# TWELVE

# BORSTAL BOYS

Back in England at the end of September, The Faces were under pressure to record their fourth LP. There had been no product from the group – single or album – since the start of 1972, and the record company were starting to get edgy. Huge live concerts and million-selling Rod Stewart solo LPs were all very well, but The Faces as a band were signed to a separate label, Warner Brothers. The Faces' own profile was kept high in the media largely due to Stewart's success. The band appeared with him on TV to promote 'You Wear It Well', and it was the same old Faces of the *Top of the Pops* 'Maggie May' appearance, Kenney Jones again nervously miming to drums he didn't play, but this time Stewart allowed Martin Quittenton to mime to his own acoustic guitar. But The Faces had to record something to capitalise on their success with Stewart.

In late 1972, before The Faces made their way into the studio, another group released a record featuring Stewart on lead vocals. In the late Sixties, between engagements with Jeff Beck and becoming a Face, Stewart had done a friend a favour and recorded a guide vocal on a demo of a song. 'A mate of mine was running this secondhand car sales showroom,' remembered Stewart. 'He said, "I've got this demo, would you mind coming down and doing a vocal so I can get a singer to copy it?" I said, "Oh yeah, of course." So I went down, did it in two takes.'[1]

The song was 'In A Broken Dream' which was released under the banner of 'Python Lee Jackson'. 'There was no contract, no nothing,' remembered Billy Gaff. 'I think Rod was duped into doing it and suddenly, of course, he became very famous and bang! Out it comes. And, to this day, I still don't know who owns it or whose it is.'[2] The dispute may have been very real, but it kept Stewart in the charts and in the press.

'All I got paid was a set of carpets for my car,' remembered Stewart. 'He said, "You can take them." I thought, "That's fine, it only took me ten minutes," and then of course it was released.'[3] The other effect of the single was to subtly reaffirm in the public's mind the role of Rod Stewart as a solo performer. He could make records with any old band.

The Faces moved into Olympic Sounds Studios at the end of September 1972, along with producer Glyn Johns, to write and record an album. Even before they arrived at the studio, a rift had developed in the band, but not the rift that had been festering since their first American tour. During the year, Ronnie Lane had become increasingly distant from the rest of the group, and had taken to driving to gigs separately in a hired Land Rover in Britain, or a rented Winnebago in the USA. His appearance had also taken a change for the worse. Increasingly, as The Faces' and Stewart's music had been apposite for the large stadiums they were playing in America, Lane's songs seemed inappropriate, their more reflective, sensitive nature more suited to smaller venues such as those the band used to play in Britain, or for listening to at home.

Stewart's solo success, along with the fact that the main song-writing axis in The Faces had quickly become Wood and Stewart, must have hurt Lane the most. McLagan would complain the loudest, but Lane had the most to lose. In the Small Faces, despite Steve Marriott's role as the undoubted band-leader, Lane had shared the majority of the songwriting credits and therefore had a privileged position. Now, despite The Faces having once been his band when Marriott quit, he was relegated to a bit-player, even though that was quite an integral 'bit'.

And there were other slights, not just felt by Lane, but also by McLagan and Jones. Sandy Sarjeant recounted one such affront to author Terry Rawlings. 'All the girls had gone to New York and we were in a hotel … We'd all been out the night before, after the gig. Everyone was all hyper, we'd gone clubbing … the drinking and drugs were absolutely ridiculous. I remember trying to find a chemist for Mac because he was in a real mess. All the girls were due to leave as the boys went on to LA. When I got back to the hotel Ronnie [Lane], Mac and Kenney were all sitting around feeling like shit – they were really deflated because they'd just been told by Reception that Woody and Rod had already flown to LA without them.'[4]

The process of recording an album can often be dull for those band members not constantly and directly involved. Since the way The Faces worked was to lay down the basic track – drums, bass, guitar, keyboards, guide vocal – and then fix anything that needed fixing while waiting for Stewart to complete his vocal, Kenney Jones' work would be completed quite early in the sessions. Things weren't helped in that, from early in the piece, it became obvious that Stewart had lost interest in recording with The Faces.

'Rod wasn't even there for the first two weeks of sessions,' remembered McLagan. 'We had most of the tracks finished before he even came down to the studio. And when he came down he'd say, "I don't like that," and he'd be a real downer … It was very disheartening … And when it came down to Rod singing [the songs], either he didn't like the words because he hadn't written any – they were either Ronnie's words or Woody's words – or he didn't like the tune, or he didn't like the key, or he didn't like the way we played it, so it virtually meant that most of the tracks were blown out.'[5]

There were problems, too, with the song that would go on to be the album's title track, 'Ooh La La'. 'We recorded [it] about four times,' remembered McLagan. 'Rod was supposed to sing it, but didn't like the key and the way we'd done it, so we did it again and he didn't like the words. Then Ronnie Lane tried to sing it but it wasn't in his key and it didn't suit his voice at the time. Eventually Woody sang it.'[6]

In between the acrimonious recording sessions, the band managed to fit in a show at the Empire Pool, Wembley, and Stewart released his second single off his *Never a Dull Moment* LP, his cover of Hendrix's 'Angel'. It was a measure of the state of The Faces that when Stewart asked them back on to *Top of the Pops* to promote the record, though Jones yet again mimed along to someone else's drumming, and McLagan and Wood mucked about at the back of the class, Ronnie Lane could pretend no longer. He sent along a lifesize cardboard cut-out of himself instead.

The recording sessions dragged on into the winter, suspended in December for a major tour of Britain. Though on stage they were the same old Faces, drinking, laughing and falling over, the tetchiness and bitchiness returned when they were back in the studio. The recording sessions dragged past Christmas, past January and into February. The first fruits of their labours appeared in early 1973, when the single 'Cindy Incidentally' was released, obviously as both a sop to a record company demanding product from their act, but also as a taster for the forthcoming LP. Another routine hit, it wasn't quite appreciated by all members of the group.

'It came out of a pub session when every sentence you spoke had to mention the word "incidentally",' remembered Wood later. 'Like, "I'll have a pint of Guinness, incidentally."'[7]

Speaking in an interview – ironically to promote the single – McLagan began what was to become a feature of The Faces' press interviews in the future: slagging off the group's product or, later, the group itself. 'It doesn't really lead anywhere and I think it'd be nice if it did,' said McLagan. 'Actually, we've been thinking of re-recording it for the album – adding a climax perhaps.'[8]

★

The new single from The Faces was released into a Britain which had changed, though the change went unnoticed by most people. On 1 January 1973, Britain joined the Common Market, effectively ending years of exclusion from what was then the world's largest trading bloc (outside of the Soviet Union-dominated Eastern Bloc). In the space of two years, the country's money had changed (with decimalisation) and now the British were supposed to think of themselves as European. Initially, joining the Common Market made little apparent difference to the British. Daily life continued much as it had before: the strikes, the random violence shown on TV, either from Northern Ireland, football terraces or the occasional picket line, the struggle to get to work, the boozy weekends.

'It was a very unsophisticated time,' recalls Carol Chaffer. 'Then there were only two types of sugar in the shops, and only one type of car that was a family saloon. It was unsophisticated and simpler and easier. More things were set in terms of social expectations, the way society operated, the roles people played.'

Meanwhile, out in the North Atlantic at the end of 1972, British fishermen had been involved in what came to be known as the 'Second Cod War' (there had been an earlier 'Cod War' in the Fifties). News reports showed Icelandic coastal patrol vessels bearing down on British trawlers who were fishing within the unilaterally declared '50-mile limit' around Iceland's coast. And, interminably, there were the pictures of cars pulling up outside 10 Downing Street, for trade union leaders to emerge, peering suspiciously at the collected TV cameras and reporters before entering the building to negotiate with Prime Minister Heath over beer and sandwiches, their regular appearances watched only by a small group of vaguely interested people lining the street opposite held back only by a couple of token crowd control barriers and a few bored policemen.

Daily life for teenagers was also unchanged. Chris Sparks used to spend his weekends hanging out at a club in North London. 'The Tottenham Royal was a serious club in Tottenham,' he remembered. 'It was a James Brown zone. It had quite a lot of black people in it when there were just no black people around. That's where I met my first legitimate Rude Boys. It was so cool. It was a Mod place, it was all Mod music and black music and it was very, very dodgy. I loved it. They had seriously dangerous people there and they had seriously dangerous fights there with knives and stuff. And you'd get loads of 'French Blues' there and that kind of thing, so that's where I seriously encountered drugs for the first time. I guess that by the time I got there that whole thing was coming to an end.'

As with The Faces themselves, drugs played a large part in the social lives of young people. The drug of choice in the early Seventies was Mandrax, a barbiturate manufactured as a sleeping tablet, and known in America as 'Qualudes' or 'Ludes'.

'You used to get them like you'd get "Blues", take two and you'd drink with it,' remembers Sparks. 'It was a downer. One thing that it did was you could feel no pain, so you could get really hurt and not know. When you were on Mandrax you felt like you were being really cool, but actually on the outside you just looked like you were very, very drunk. And it made you fantastically randy – you can have sex for ages with Mandrax, which is very good if you're drunk, which is one of the reasons it was popular with girls. Well, they were called Randy Mandies.'

Sparks remembers that there was a direct link between Mandrax and the violence on the football terraces. 'We used to take them before we went to Spurs,' he remembers, ''cos people would hit you and you wouldn't care. So in fact a lot of the terrace violence that I witnessed at Spurs around this time, down at the Park Lane End, was because everybody was just absolutely out of it on Mandrax so you could batter the shit out of each other and say, "Oh that was fun." It was only the next day that you would feel it.

'I did actually see a guy walk into a moving bus – the bus was pulling off and he walked into it and it hit him. The bus stopped and he just got up and got on the bus and he had no idea at all that he was really bashed up – he had his jaw broken. And he didn't even know that he'd even walked into the bus. The other thing about it was that it was totally unpsychedelic, it was for people who didn't want to be psychedelic. It was a drug for brutal stuff. And it was almost a weekend necessary; you would have to have Mandrax, condoms and speed for your weekend activity. I suppose people have ecstasy now – but it was more basic than ecstasy, it did brutalise you. People got very violent; it made you very open to violence added to the fact that you couldn't feel any pain. So it was the perfect drug for the time. And speed, of course, remained popular. And in the early Seventies you could still get French Blues. They were barbiturate and speed together, so you were kind of up and down at the same time. You were really very cool on those. They gave you a sustained high that didn't really go mad like it does on ordinary amphetamines.'

The reason for young people's reliance on prescription drugs such as Mandrax and amphetamines was that drugs such as cocaine and heroin were too expensive for regular use, and as such were seen as the preserve of the rich and famous. As Sparks says, the brutalising effects of drugs such as Mandrax were appropriate to a time when everything seemed much more basic.

However, the more basic times didn't stretch to everyone. Sue Westergaard didn't come into contact with the drug culture until much later. 'I went to a big comprehensive school, and all the blokes came from Deptford,' she recalled. 'They were just solid, working-class blokes and they didn't take drugs, those guys. It never even crossed my mind, I never came across it, I was never offered anything, until I left school.'

Further North, however, Carol Chaffer found that drugs were easier to come across. 'When I grew up there were two lots of drugs about,' Chaffer recalls. 'With the Northern Soul thing, some of the older boys were going to all-nighters at Wigan Casino and were taking speed and French Blues. But then the other part of Todmorden was Hebden Bridge and the huge hippy culture which was very Sixties, very dopey, alternative, hang out, drop out. There was a lot of dope in Hebden Bridge.'

★

Before the end of the LP recording sessions, and even before the release of 'Cindy Incidentally', Ron Wood was taking his own steps away from

The Faces, hanging out with his own celebrity mates. Eric Clapton was planning two concerts at London's Finsbury Park Rainbow to mark his comeback from heroin addiction, and he wanted Wood to play in his all-star band which also featured Pete Townshend and Steve Winwood. Wood took up the offer, and found he was on equal billing with Clapton, Townshend et al. Such company would have turned anyone's head, even the self-effacing Wood. And thus the gulf between Stewart, Wood and the other Faces stretched just a little more.

Before the new album was released, The Faces found themselves on a European tour, playing in Italy and Holland before returning to Britain for more dates. In between they managed to fit in a promotional show at the Paris Theatre for BBC Radio 1.

'We used to have the greatest time with that Liverpool supporter, John Peel,' remembered Wood. 'He was great to go round the pub with and get totally pissed, then back into the BBC studios and go out live on air. Never having any idea about the set list or who was doing what, giving each other piggy-back rides to the stage, with Ronnie Lane always on my or Rod's back.'[9] It is, perhaps, an indication of Wood's state at the session that though The Faces played 'as live', the 'concert' wasn't actually broadcast until a couple of weeks later. Even the staid old BBC weren't stupid enough to allow The Faces to be broadcast live, risking mayhem over the airwaves.

Finally the album was completed and released. *Ooh La La* came complete with a sleeve featuring a picture of turn-of-the-century Italian theatre and cinema star Ettore Petrolini. Petrolini had performed with the 'Futurists', an Italian art movement who were in favour of 'progress' and 'speed'. If the edges of the *Ooh La La* cover were pressed, it moved Petrolini's eyes and opened his mouth. Such were the foibles of the Seventies. The record inside contained ten tracks that were if anything slightly disappointing. Ever since The

Beatles' *Sgt Pepper* sessions in 1966/67, any group ensconced in the studio for a long period of time were considered to be embarking on their 'masterpiece'. The Small Faces themselves had done the same thing when recording *Ogden's Nut Gone Flake*. So, given the real circumstances of this recording – Stewart's nonchalance, everyone else's ambiguity towards the project – it's a wonder anything came out of it at all. But the disappointment should have been tempered with a modicum of objectivity, for *Ooh La La* is not a bad album.

The opening track, Stewart and Wood's 'Silicone Grown', is a tough, tongue-in-cheek observation on women who have breast enlargement surgery. The song is full of cheeky references to keeping abreast of the times and comparing women to the Haig Museum. Described by Wood as 'our style of amphetamine rock',[10] Stewart's lyric also hints at events across the Atlantic, where the Watergate scandal was very gradually beginning to engulf then President Richard Nixon with a sly reference to the White House. The single, 'Cindy Incidentally', follows. Written by Wood, Stewart and McLagan, the song is based around a piano-riff doubled on Wood's guitar. Stewart's lyric tells of a couple's need to move on, and perhaps points to where Stewart saw his future, describing a last party before he says goodbye to his old life.

Lane and Stewart combined to write track three, 'Flags And Banners'. A lament premised upon a dream, and utilising images of the American Civil War, referring to the grey uniforms of the South, it meanders to an end without ever going anywhere. 'My Fault' – another Wood/Stewart/McLagan tune – is on the face of it a hard-rocking statement of defiance and self-identity. Stewart demands to be taken as he is, and that no-one should try to change him. But the bridge to the song is more regretful, and as the song goes on it seems to be more about self-justification than anything else, Stewart's lyric insisting that even if he's always drunk it's down to him. But as well as self-justification, Stewart also manages to drag in a picture from the news of the day, threatening to plant a bomb if he doesn't get his own way. The events in Northern Ireland – the apparently limitless bombings and shootings – were starting to seep into the world of popular music.

Another intrusion was demonstrated in the next track. Preceded by the wail of a siren, McLagan, Wood and Stewart's 'Borstal Boys' is ostensibly a simple song about the inmates of one of the country's penal institutions for young offenders. Borstals were so named because the first young offenders institution was at Borstal Prison in Kent. To write and record a song on this subject was simply to reflect the general feeling in Britain that young people were increasingly out of control – plus there had also been some debate as to whether the Borstal system worked (it was eventually abolished in 1982) – but there is more to it than just that. *Borstal Boy* was also the title of a novel written by Irish author Brendan Behan. The novel is based upon Behan's own experience of being sent to a Borstal at sixteen for his part in a foiled IRA bomb plot – Behan was arrested in Liverpool carrying explosives and was sentenced to eighteen months. On his release he returned to the IRA and was again arrested for shooting at a policeman, for which he was sentenced to fourteen years, though he served only four.

So though The Faces' song 'Borstal Boys' appears to be a simple tale of life inside a Borstal – along with accounts of how the inmates got there – it seems impossible to believe that Stewart (let alone the other members of the group) was unaware of the song title's origins. Ian McLagan's family were Irish, and it seems unthinkable that they would have left him unaware, if not of Behan in particular, then of Irish culture in general.

A perfunctory instrumental, 'Fly In The Ointment', follows, according to McLagan, 'a total throwaway and ... only put on the album to piss Rod off'.[11] The next track, Stewart and Lane's 'If I'm On The Late Side', is a moody, reflective soul tune, in the style of Otis Redding's 'Try A Little Tenderness' but with a more subdued Stewart vocal as opposed to Redding's passion and McLagan's Hammond rumbling soothingly in the background. Ronnie Lane's 'Glad And Sorry' probably says more about Lane's state of mind during the recording than it says about The Faces or the times. Slow and intro-verted, the song displays a deep resignation that was never really a part of The Faces' stage personas. Lane sings it almost directly at Stewart, his bitterness at his own reduced role within the group now obvious. By this point, Lane's disaffection with his role in The Faces and with Stewart's attitude in particular seems to have been complete.

Lane also wrote the next track, 'Just Another Honky', though Stewart sings it. Another slow, disjointed song, the lyric tells of a rela-tionship in turmoil. And in the chorus, Lane puts words into Stewart's mouth that Lane probably wanted to hear, that Lane is free to leave if that's what he wants.

The final track on the LP is the title track. Penned by Wood and Lane, 'Ooh La La' is a folky singalong, a return to the 'nudge, nudge, wink, wink' days of the Small Faces and The Faces before it was all huge stadiums, vast quantities of drugs and private jets. The song tells of a grandfather's advice to a young man on the subject of women, and his subsequent discovery that Granddad was right. Women aren't to be trusted, Lane argues, because young men are too trusting. Unlike most rock or pop songs on the subject of love, Lane correctly identifies the fact that it's often young men rather than young women who have their hearts broken. Poignant, passionate and world-weary, 'Ooh La La' sums up Lane's life as a Face, and the final chorus could be a eulogy to his time with the band. And then there's just Ron Wood's sweet acoustic guitar riffing and the album drifts away into the fade-out.

Writing in the *NME*, Charles Shaar Murray's verdict on the album was 'short but sweet', and even by the standards of the vinyl age the LP was short – most albums would contain between 35 and 40 minutes of music but *Ooh La La* clocks in at just over 30 minutes. But the *NME*'s review – while picking apart the musicianship and complaining that 'The Faces have never made a bad record, but compared to Roderick's personal music adventures they've always sounded a trifle superficial, somewhat shallow, curiously unfinished' – was largely benevolent. 'It'll go down in rock history as a goodie,' Murray writes.[12]

But even at the party to launch the album to the press, there was something hollow at the heart of The Faces' good-natured roistering. Stewart gave an interview to *Melody Maker* deriding the LP as 'a bloody mess', but that didn't wash with the public and the album raced up the charts both in the UK and America, where it reached Number 21.

Even so, the rift between Stewart and Lane had reached the point of no return. It was only a matter of time before something broke down.

# THIRTEEN

# A SPIV OR
# A TEDDY BOY?

Like any close group of people who had been through shared experiences, The Faces had their own language and their own phrases which meant nothing to anyone else. 'I'm leaving the group' was one such phrase for The Faces, a semi-sarcastic reflection of their status as pop stars, a phrase that was shouted by band members 'whenever there wasn't enough ice in the drink, or the eggs were too runny,' remembered McLagan.[1] 'Every time there was a problem, you used to say, "I'm leaving the group,"' recalled Wood.[2]

After the release of *Ooh La La*, The Faces were back in America, on tour to support the album. As part of the stage show, a backdrop was built featuring luminaries such as actress Barbara Windsor, footballer Georgie Best, Stewart's hero Al Jolson, Richard Nixon and Marilyn Monroe. They also had palm trees and their portable drinks trolley. Unfortunately, the stages in many of the venues weren't big enough to accommodate the 21-section backdrop, though this didn't seem to bother The Faces – their shambolic, drunken stage show would've worked in the pubs they'd started out in.

But things were very different for The Faces in 1973. The band flew from gig to gig in a privately rented Hansa Jet. The groupies and ordinary fans would be at their hotels before they even arrived. Gigs sold out within hours of tickets being made available. And out in front of the stage set, Ronnie Lane was now so semi-detached from the rest of the group that every outburst from any band member was considered to be of vast proportions. As the group's plane flew in over St Louis for yet another show, the pilot pointed out another disaster area: the Mississippi had burst its banks.

The Faces were playing in Providence, Rhode Island, when the first explosion occurred. As they left the stage, Stewart, dressed in his usual satin trousers, feather boa and mascara (Stewart's gesture towards Glam rock), looked aghast at Ronnie Lane. Lane was dressed in a checked three-piece suit and looked less like a rock star than an East End market stall owner in his Sunday best.

'What are you,' jeered Stewart, 'a fucking spiv or a Teddy Boy?' This was a calculated comment – as an old Mod, Lane would have considered Teddy Boys to be the old enemy.

'I'd rather be a fucking Teddy Boy than a prostitute who's going through the change of life,'[3] Lane replied, punctuating his reply by taking a swing at the singer. A full-scale fight developed in the dressing room until one of the group's roadcrew pulled Lane off Stewart. The next day, the group – minus Lane – made their way by plane to the next gig. After some persuasion, Lane was convinced to go along, but hired a car and drove himself.

Just as the group were about to take the stage eight days later for the penultimate show of the tour, Ronnie Lane said to McLagan, 'I'm leaving the group.' This time he meant it.

'It was always a joke until Ronnie said it that day,' remembered McLagan.[4] At the time, McLagan responded with another stock Faces phrase, 'Bollocks, you cunt.'[5] But Lane was serious, told McLagan so and implied that McLagan should leave the group with him. All McLagan could do was reply, 'Fuck off, you cunt.'

Later, while on stage, Lane approached McLagan and swore at him mid-song. McLagan finally lost his rag and went for Lane, kicking him and chasing him off the stage. After the gig, Stewart, Wood, Jones and McLagan held a band meeting to decide what they would do next, but it was too soon. 'We drank and talked and threw peanuts and laughed for a moment, then we talked and drank and became quite morose,' remembered McLagan.[6]

Lane agreed to finish both the American tour and the three dates they had left in Britain before he left. The shows took on a semi-surreal flavour, the tension between Lane and the rest of the group somehow resolved, Lane himself almost relieved, the boozy raucousness undiminished. The last show they played together was in June in Edmonton, England, where they were greeted by banners reading, 'Goodbye Ronnie We Love You'. They rounded off the show with a drunken rendition of 'We'll Meet Again' before Stewart told the crowd, 'We're off down the pub.'

'Too late,' said Lane. 'They're shut.'

Stewart puts the success of the Lane-era Faces down to the extraordinary mix of personalities. 'Woody and I were – I suppose – the two glamorous ones up front, the singer and the guitar player,' he says. 'Ronnie Lane was the engine of the group because he epitomised what the Small Faces and The Faces were about. Kenney was the heart of it because he's a little cockney guy and a really aggressive little drummer. And Mac, who was a little bit of all of us. We all shared the same haircut. And one hairdryer. We were really close mates. I don't think you get many bands nowadays that are real, close soul brothers like we were. For me it fell apart when Ronnie left. He was the soul of the band. He was the true cockney sparrow.'[7]

The task now facing The Faces was to find a replacement for Lane. They originally approached Andy Fraser, who had played with Free, and Phil Chen, but both of them declined. They then approached Tetsu Yamauchi, a Japanese session bassist who had replaced Fraser in Free. Yamauchi was available and was up for it, and so was asked to join. However, the British Government and the Musicians Union conspired to deny Yamauchi a work permit, on the premise that he was depriving a British musician of work. Some neat legal footwork from Gaff and associated lawyers persuaded the Employment Ministry to change its decision a month later. Tetsu was in.

The group decamped to Ibiza to rehearse with their new bass player and to try and write some new material. There was a European tour organised to begin in July, and Yamauchi had to be brought up to speed with The Faces' own particular brand of stage show. But when the tour began, The Faces realised that they may have taken on more than they'd bargained for. Yamauchi – on more than one occasion – had to be tied to an amplifier to keep him upright.

'His problem was he believed all he'd read about our boozing,' recalled McLagan later. 'Though we all liked a drink, we'd pace ourselves, being professional drinkers like Dean Martin. Tetsu never understood that, and Rod swears he saw his breakfast tray being delivered one morning with a bottle of Teachers on it ... His playing was fine when he was relatively sober, but that was relatively rare.'[8]

At the time, Yamauchi was distanced from the other Faces, unable to break into a close-knit group who had been together – if in two groups – for nearly ten years. Interviews given at the time show The Faces self-consciously defending Lane's departure and Yamauchi's arrival. 'I think the band is much better since Ronnie left,' claimed McLagan. 'Tetsu's a different sort of bass player and he's given us a kick up the arse. Tetsu's a bass player first and foremost, whereas Ronnie wasn't.'[9]

There was a new Rod Stewart LP to coincide with the tour, this time a compilation. *Sing it Again, Rod* was little more than a consolidation of his position, but it was product, and it sold reasonably well both in the UK and the US, where it reached Number 31. Perhaps more importantly, though, it reflected his stature as a recording artist. He had recorded four albums as a solo artist and four more as a Face; he had Number 1 singles and albums on both sides of the Atlantic; he was seen as one of the top artists in rock. His friends and peers now included the Rolling Stones, Elton John and Paul McCartney, figures who were forming the new aristocracy of celebrity.

And now that Ronnie Lane had quit The Faces, the charade that they were anything other than Stewart's backing group was – outside of the endless denials in the press – extinguished. While Ronnie Lane was with The Faces, there was some truth – and some pretence – that they were a serious recording outfit. Unlike Stewart and Wood, Lane had no vehicle for his own writing output outside of The Faces, and the pressure to record mostly came from him. Lane's replacement – Yamauchi – had no writing pretensions, and anyway was just happy to be in a working band where he could drink all he wanted.

The band continued to play live, performing at the Reading

Festival before making their way to America for yet another tour. In an interview given to James Johnson of the *NME*, Billy Gaff unwittingly added fuel to the increasing rumours that Stewart would split from The Faces.

'To me Rod Stewart will always be a great performer,' said Gaff. 'I'm one hundred per cent sure he'll be singing in twenty years' time simply because he can manage any sort of material. Just lately I've been trying to persuade him to try things like "I've Grown Accustomed To Your Face" because I think he could even handle material like that. In fact, I think he'd do it tremendously. He could even slip it on an album and get away with it.'[10]

The end of August saw another Stewart solo single, a cover of Goffin and King's 'Oh No Not My Baby' backed with a Faces track, 'Jodie', written by Stewart, Wood and McLagan. At the time Stewart described the release as, 'A bona fide single … just right for me market – the tartan hordes, that's what I call 'em.'[11] The single was credited to 'Rod & The Faces – and a bottle of Campari'. The diminished position of The Faces was becoming increasingly explicit.

★

Although the Conservative Party had come to power in 1970 committed to withdrawing government money from the economy (and having slated the previous Labour government for spending too much money), by spring 1972 the slump in the economy, complemented neatly by a rapid rise in inflation, meant that they would have to pump more money into the economy to stop British industry going down the tubes. In a massive reverse of their original policy, they started to help ailing industries, most notably Rolls-Royce – who were in trouble over the delivery of RB II engines for the American Lockheed TriStar – and Upper Clyde Shipbuilders in Glasgow.

By January 1973 the government had introduced a Price

Commission and a Pay Board, whose functions were to regulate prices, dividends and rents in accordance with the government policy set out in the Price and Pay Code. From the end of March 1973 until the autumn, there were to be no pay increases for any group of employees of more than £1 per week and the Pay Board had to be notified of any settlement involving less than 1,000 employees. No pay award was to be made by a company with more than 1,000 employees without the Pay Board's approval. It became an offence in law to strike, threaten to strike, or do anything else to try and force an employer to contravene any order of the Pay Board.

Unsurprisingly, the trade unions were less than enthusiastic. On Valentine's Day, 1973, Britain's gas workers began a campaign of strikes and overtime bans to support their claim for wage increases. Within a day nearly four million homes had reductions in gas pressure and over 600 industrial plants had to close because of a lack of gas. Before the end of the month – and for the first time in its history – 200,000 civil servants went on strike in support of their pay claim. The gulf between the rulers and the ruled had not seemed so great since the General Strike in 1926.

By the early Seventies, the Middle East was dominated by continuing conflict between Israel and its closest neighbours. The creation of the State of Israel in 1946 had left both the Palestinians who were already there and states such as Egypt and Jordan highly aggrieved. In 1967, the 'Six Day War' between Israel and Syria, Jordan and Egypt had left Israel as the dominant military power in the area. While events in the Middle East seemed a very long way away to a Britain still trying to come to terms with the war in Northern Ireland (a war which was increasingly being brought to the streets of Britain), by 1973 these events would have a very direct effect on Britain.

The Yom Kippur War of October 1973 led the Organisation of

Petroleum Exporting Countries (OPEC) – a coalition of oil-rich, Arab, Palestinian-supporting states in the Middle East – to raise the price of oil by 400 per cent, claiming they were retaliating for Western support for Israel. The effect on the oil-reliant Western economies was drastic, causing inflation to rise rapidly. Western economies run on oil, whether in the manufacture of goods or their distribution, let alone the petrol that ordinary people put in their cars. Any increase in the price of oil acted to raise all prices of all goods and affected everyone. The British government and the British people were suddenly battered by an economic whirlwind over which they could never dream of having any control. The most that either government or people could hope to do was to alleviate the worst economic excesses.

And, in the end, Ronnie Lane wasn't the only deserter in 1973. American Vice-President Spiro Agnew was forced to resign when it became glaringly obvious that he was guilty of tax evasion, for which he was ultimately fined $10,000 and put on three years' probation. His boss, President Richard Nixon, was also subject to rumours regarding the probity of his election campaign in 1972. Nixon appointed Gerald Ford as Agnew's successor, and prepared his bunker for the rocky year ahead.

★

Leaving strike-bound Britain behind, in September The Faces set off for their ninth tour of the USA. They were possibly the biggest draw in the States at that time, and the demand for them led to an apparently limitless itinerary. From Richmond through Houston, Dallas, Denver, Tucson, Oakland and Las Vegas, playing in sports stadiums and arenas to packed houses, The Faces ripped up audiences and hotels as they went.

'[The Faces were] generally breaking rooms up, [with] televisions thrown into swimming pools,' remembered Billy Gaff (BBC doc).

'Whenever there was trouble, Stewart was at the forefront of it, but when everybody got arrested he was nowhere to be seen. The money that I spent paying hotel damages was quite dramatic.'

In Tucson, there was even more trouble. After the show there was the usual pool-side party, complete with loads of kids and extensive boozing. Then someone realised that there was a model train that ran around the outside of the hotel. So – logically – the party moved on to the model train, which wasn't built to take the weight of the various assembled Faces let alone the assorted liggers who decided to board it … and it didn't take long before – with a crunch – the train fell over, spilling laughing partyers everywhere.

'I decided it was time for bed and ran before there was any more trouble,' remembered McLagan.[12] The next he knew of the matter was the next morning, when he was woken by the local sheriff, armed and taking the whole thing very seriously. As ever, McLagan in particular and The Faces in general denied all knowledge, though the event took its own place within The Faces' mythology as the 'derailment'.

The tour lasted until mid-October, when the band returned to Britain to prepare for a major British tour. In order to have some product to promote – to keep the record company happy – the band went into Morgan Sound Studios to record a single. The result, Stewart and Wood's 'Pool Hall Richard', was Faces-by-numbers, a straightforward rocker without any of the subtlety of their earlier work, though it could be argued that there hadn't particularly been much subtlety about that either. Driven by Wood's chunky rhythm and blues guitar and Yamauchi's plodding bass, Stewart just screams over the top of the resulting noise.

★

But at the end of 1973, subtlety wasn't at the forefront of the British consciousness. The dispute between the National Union of Mineworkers

– under their leader Joe Gormley – and the government, which had simmered throughout 1973, finally came to a head at the end of the year. November saw the miners undertake an overtime ban, severely depleting the stocks of coal. Successive British governments had been deliberately increasing Britain's dependence on oil rather than coal for power generation, and following the OPEC price increase earlier in 1973, oil and petrol were already in short supply. The British economy had entered a position that became known as 'stagflation' – the economy was stagnant (i.e. not growing – it is assumed by economists that an economy has to grow by two to three per cent each year just to stay still) allied to rapidly rising inflation. As inflation increased – by 1975 it would be over twenty-four per cent per year – so wage demands increased to try and keep pace, prices rose dramatically – and people started to worry.

The deteriorating fuel situation was exacerbated by an 'out-of-hours' ban by electricity power workers, limiting the ability of the Central Electricity Generating Board to cope with the shortages which were building up at various power stations. As a result, on 13 November, the government declared a State of Emergency. The government issued orders restricting the use of electricity to heat space, except in people's homes and certain other places. The use of electricity for advertising, displays or floodlighting was prohibited. Another trade union, the Amalgamated Society of Locomotive Engineers and Firemen (ASLEF) decided to ban Sunday, overtime and rest-day working, considerably worsening the situation as this disrupted the delivery of coal to power stations, as well as inconveniencing thousands of passengers, especially in the South-East of England. The government refused to strike a deal with the miners, and instead decided to take them on. It was announced that from 1 January 1974, electricity was to be provided to industry on three, specified days per week (the 'three-day week').

A blanket speed limit of 50 miles per hour was to be imposed on all roads (the first time there was a speed limit imposed on Britain's burgeoning motorway network since Labour's Barbara Castle had done so in the late Sixties) and a maximum heating limit introduced on all commercial premises and offices. And, as if to add insult to the injury of proposed blanket evening power cuts which would affect the country on a regionally variable basis, TV companies would be forced to stop broadcasting after 10.30 pm each evening. Not only were people forced to stay at home and be subjected to random power cuts, even if the television worked, they weren't allowed to watch it.

Even before the 'three-day week' the government imposed a 'five-day week' before Christmas. Anxious retailers, worried about the effect on Christmas shopping, resorted to lighting their shops over the weekends with candles and gas lamps, and anxious shoppers scoured news reports for any inkling that they would be able to get food for Christmas, let alone gifts. In the cold, grey December rain, people trudged from queue to queue, trying to pick up whatever they could before the country shut down.

Despite the worsening situation – and just before the power cuts were to begin – The Faces embarked on another, month-long British tour, which culminated in yet another riotous show in Edmonton on Christmas Eve. The Faces, it seemed, could party while the world outside fell apart. Suddenly 'Pool Hall Richard' seemed an apt theme tune to Heath's Britain. With the success of the tour, The Faces' future as a live phenomenon seemed assured.

More questionable was their future as a band.

# FOURTEEN

# A STUDY IN DISINTEGRATION

At the turn of the New Year, Britain could not have seemed a bleaker place. There were – on the restricted TV service – regular broadcasts by grim-faced ministers and the grimmer-faced Prime Minister. Every evening, families would scour the evening papers to see which areas – defined by postcode – would be blacked out. Children and adults went to bed in rooms lit only by candles, which themselves were now at a premium.

'It was really boring,' remembered Carol Chaffer. 'It was exciting at first, because we'd get candles and it was dark, and it was something different, but what I realised was how much light we live in all the time because suddenly the streetlights went out and that was a darkness that we weren't used to at all. But then it just became really boring 'cos candlelight's not enough to do anything.'

There were also food shortages caused by the three-day week – bread couldn't be baked, milk couldn't be pasteurised and the shortage of petrol meant that other goods couldn't be distributed to shops. Queues developed at bakeries and there were empty shelves in relatively new supermarkets where bemused shoppers aimlessly walked down aisles looking for products which just weren't there, with toilet roll especially in short supply.

As firms could only open for three days in a week, workers could only work for three days a week, and therefore only received three days' pay. Unfortunately, rent still had to be paid for seven days, and many households were in dire financial need.

'I was working down in Cricklewood,' remembers Richard Amos. 'They had a building arm and we were working from a complex on site. With the three-day week you were given so much time when the electricity was on and then it was turned off. And we used to work when we got electricity. Unlike a lot of offices, who shut when the electricity went out, we used to come in when it went on and go home when it went off. So we could be working from five in the morning 'til one in the afternoon; and then maybe one in the afternoon until ten at night.'

'I don't remember the strikes and the blackouts as a bad thing,' says Sue Westergaard. 'We were brought up in a Marxist household, our dad was a Marxist sociologist, so we were in this household where you were on the side of people who were striking because they were all underpaid, but of course it was all serious. I remember my dad had to ride to work on a bike – which is quite a long way, from Eltham [in South London] to the Strand, for a man who's never ridden a bike or done a stroke of exercise in his life. I don't remember it as being particularly a bad thing.' Meanwhile Heath was still refusing to cut a deal with the miners, and was instead preparing for a General Election. The misery continued.

For The Faces, 1974 opened with the release of a live album, *Coast to Coast – Overture and Beginners*. The LP – compiled from two gigs at Anaheim and Los Angeles on the previous year's American tour – was supposed to showcase the forum in which The Faces were at their best – live performance. Nonetheless, Stewart re-recorded or fixed many of his vocal performances later in the relative safety of the studio. The album was disappointing, and was roundly slated in the press. Released as part of Stewart's Mercury deal rather than as part of The Faces' Warner Brothers deal, the album was credited to 'Rod Stewart and The Faces', and was seen as a cynical move on Stewart's part to get himself a step closer to ending his deal with Mercury – the deal would have been for five or six albums, and this LP was one less he would have to record. Writing in the *NME*, Charles Shaar Murray's review sums up the general antipathy to the record.

'Ladies and gentlemen,' he begins, 'a study in disintegration. When The Faces began their current incarnation, their boozy looseness helped to add some riotous vibes to a tight, powerful, hell-for-leather set. Just an extra little something to liven up the act, kind of like a rock and roll Dean Martin. Now, several gold records and a few years of gigging later, they've indulged themselves to such an extent that their music is virtually unlistenable … Once upon a time The Faces were one of the most genuinely exciting bands in the country. On the evidence of all the gigs I've seen (with one exception) they are now a painful travesty of their former selves. Maybe this album was released simply to get Rod out of his Mercury contract; I neither know nor care … To continue on this basis is a disservice to both the band

and to those members of their audience who can tell a bad set from a good one, and who are financing this disintegration.'[1]

Of the eleven tracks on the album only three were Faces songs. Later, McLagan would defend the record, claiming it to be the best they'd ever done. 'In my mind, anybody who disagrees is totally wrong,' he told the *NME*. 'I'd just tell them to screw it and go and listen to something else … Things were really steamin' on that tour and if it didn't sound like it to some people it did to me. The feel was incredible. The album sold a lot better than *Ooh La La* and that took about a year and a half to make. There must be a message in that somewhere …'[2]

Leaving the bad press, the power cuts and the national antagonism behind them, The Faces took off for a month-long tour of the Far East. The tour began in Auckland (where McLagan took an axe to a substandard piano at the end of the show) and New Zealand, before traipsing through Australia, Hong Kong (where they played in the football stadium) and Japan. When The Faces arrived in Japan, their fame had preceded them and they were treated to a Beatle-esque reception, complete with kids at the airport bearing banners which variously read, 'Faces', 'Rod and The Faces', and even 'Tetsu and The Faces'.

For once, Yamauchi was a definite asset, breaking the language barrier and introducing the band and each song to their audiences, who politely applauded each number. Yamauchi also came to McLagan's aid in their Tokyo hotel: McLagan – among others – was playing football in the corridor outside their hotel room when an American tourist came out to complain about the noise.

'One of us said something like, "Get lost, you shithead" and he got angry for some reason,' remembers McLagan. 'He ran into his room and we continued booting the ball about, but then he came back wielding a wooden shoe-tree. He came thrashing at me with this thing and caught me on the cheek, drawing blood. Rod and Woody disappeared into their rooms, but Tetsu wasn't going to take that and he went all Japanese and beat the living crap out of him.'[3] McLagan discovered later that Yamauchi was a black belt in Kendo.

★

While The Faces had been away, a series of frantic discussions, proposals and threats bounced between the warring British government and National Union of Mineworkers. As January passed and the Labour opposition sat and quietly enjoyed the government's self-inflicted predicament, the Trade Union Congress also became involved in an attempt to broker a peace deal but to no avail. When, on 21 January, Heath's government threatened the NUM with a return to a four- or five-day week, the union responded by balloting their membership on all-out strike action.

By 1 February, the TUC's negotiations with the government had reached stalemate: there would be no new offer to the NUM. On the following day the result of the NUM's ballot was announced, showing 81 per cent in favour of a strike. The Executive of the NUM announced that the strike would begin on Saturday, 9 February. Heath's government, faced with a showdown, called an election for 28 February on the question, 'Who governs Britain?'

The question seemed to go further than just the government's run-ins with the unions – even before Heath announced the date of the election, the IRA planted a bomb on a coach carrying British soldiers and their families. The bomb exploded as the coach travelled up the M62 and eleven people were killed at the scene and another died a few days later.

In an attempt to bring some sense of normality to the country, the restrictions on TV broadcasting were lifted for the duration of the election campaign – God forbid that the British people should be denied a full menu of politics – but the campaign took place against a background of power cuts, the other restrictions which remained in place, further violence in Northern Ireland and another IRA bombing, this time in Buckinghamshire, which injured ten people. The British public duly gave their verdict: they weren't quite sure who ran the country, but it obviously wasn't the Conservative Party. Labour won 301 seats to the Conservatives' 297, but no party had enough seats to hold an overall majority making it a 'hung' Parliament.

For several days, Heath's Conservatives tried to do a deal with a resurgent Liberal Party (they had doubled their representation and now had fourteen seats) to try and create a coalition government, but Jeremy Thorpe's Liberals couldn't agree on a deal that would hold the Liberal Party together. The Scottish Nationalist Party had also done well from the election, increasing their representation from a single seat at the 1970 election to seven. Heath's inability to broker a deal with the Liberals meant that Harold Wilson's Labour Party returned as a minority government and within a few days had done a deal with the NUM that saw the end of the power cuts and the three-day week. The country's other economic problems, however, weren't so easy to deal with.

Another feature of the continuing crises was a further rise in support for the Far Right. May saw clashes as members of the National Front marched through the centre of London. In Red Lion Square in Holborn, they were met by members of the nascent Socialist Workers Party, and police struggled to keep the two sides apart. The National Front marchers, complete with drums and oversized Union flags, seemed to be attempting to ape the marching bands of the Unionists in Northern Ireland. Between the militant trade unions and the National Front, the political landscape of Britain seemed to be increasingly polarised. Despite the growing power of the trade unions, for the radical Left of the late Sixties, things didn't seem to be heading their way.

Richard Amos remembers the change from the Sixties to the Seventies as a shift from carefree times to a careworn world. 'The Sixties was just utterly different,' he recalls. 'It was colourful. People were happy. I don't know if it was chemically induced or what. It was certainly a colourful, happy period. Everybody used to do basically what they wanted. It was peaceful as well. Whereas the Seventies felt a bit harsh, very sharp-edged. The early Seventies was going backwards again.'

★

Returning to a relatively quiet Britain, The Faces were at a loose end. That is to say that The Faces as a group were at a loose end – both Stewart and Wood had projects they were more predisposed to work on. Stewart began work on his new album, though for the first time with no members of The Faces other than the very occasional Ron Wood. Wood himself had decided that he wanted to make an album, and had settled down in his own recording studio in his house in Richmond to record it. As well as all his fellow conspirators from The Faces, Wood also drafted in his rock aristo friends, among them Mick Jagger, Keith Richards and Mick Taylor from the Stones; Martin Quittenton and Mick Waller from Stewart's solo work; and ex-Beatle George Harrison and Sly Stone's drummer, Andy Newmark.

'That album cost around £40,000 and that was just the booze,' remembered Wood. 'I was going to set up a bar and charge for drinks for all the people that just dropped in. Everyone had roadies and friends with them. Then the neighbours got a bit annoyed at the constant rehearsals. So I don't think you can say it was well organised. Fun, but definitely lacking on the organisation front.'⁴

All of this left Kenney Jones and Ian McLagan a little lost, and Yamauchi missing somewhere in Japan. 'It's strange when you've struggled in groups for ten years to be finally almost retired,'

McLagan told the *NME*. 'I don't want to be retired and I can't afford to be, but at present it's like the group is so successful there's nowhere you can bloody work. We wanted to play in Britain, but we did it before Christmas ... We've just done the Far East and we can't play America again 'til there's another album out. I'm getting bored to tears right now.'[5]

The summer of 1974 brought another World Cup, this time in less glamorous (compared to Mexico 1970) West Germany. As if to reflect the mood of the country, England had failed to qualify, knocked out on a dismal night at Wembley in 1973 when they couldn't beat Poland whose goalkeeper, Tomachevsky, described as a 'clown' by manager and football pundit Brian Clough, defied everything England could throw at him. Scotland, however, did qualify, and made their way to the tournament with high hopes. With a squad which included such luminaries of British football as Bruce Rioch, Joe Jordan and Billy Bremner, they failed to win a single game in their qualifying group (though they didn't lose either) and returned home in ignominy.

The stars of the tournament this time were not the highly fancied holders Brazil, but were instead Holland, who had invented 'total football', a system where, aside from the goalkeeper, each player was expected to be able to play in every position. Based on the highly successful Ajax club side from Amsterdam, and centred on the supremely gifted Johann Cruyff, the system got Holland as far as the World Cup final, where they were beaten by a sturdy, hard-working West German side led by Franz Beckenbaur, but also featuring the prodigious goal-scorer Gerd Muller. With their long hair and vast sideburns, the German team looked like they could have been members of the Baader-Meinhof gang.

While the world was engrossed by the World Cup, the only work The Faces had was a gig at the Buxton Festival in early July. The organisers offered the group so much money to play that the band arranged for the Memphis Horns to augment their sound. The Memphis Horns were the house brass section of the legendary 'Fame' studios in Tennessee where artists such as Wilson Pickett and Aretha Franklin had recorded some of their best work. Early July saw The Faces at Shepperton Studios rehearsing for the Buxton gig. While they ran through their numbers in their usual knockabout manner, the more professional Memphis Horns, unsure quite what they were supposed to add, sat quietly in a corner studiously working out their parts. Despite the apparent lack of organisation, The Faces' appearance at Buxton was the high spot of an otherwise dreary event.

'We'd only had four days to rehearse with them [the Memphis Horns],' said Stewart. 'So they had to fall back on their great old Otis Redding intros. The crowd might not've known who the Memphis Horns were, but they bloody well recognised those licks!'[6]

Mid-July saw Ron Wood and his own band – including McLagan and Keith Richards – play three nights at the Kilburn Gaumont. The gigs were played in front of a largely mystified audience, who had come expecting something somewhere between The Faces and the Rolling Stones and instead were treated to a set which they didn't know, as Wood's solo LP was not released until later in the year. But the 'solo' gig, allied to the stories in the press of Wood's 'solo' LP, fuelled the rumours about the end of The Faces.

'There's none of this "split" thing in the air at all,' said Wood at the time. 'There's just a lot of chemistry with everybody in the band right now, and this album and show is a good outlet for me, just as it's a good outlet for Rod to sing at Elton's show, or Tetsu to play with Stomu Yamash'ta, or for the Small Faces to reunite for a couple of gigs. Everybody is letting off steam in different directions and looking forward to getting together again. It can't do The Faces any harm, especially if you get in a rut with the music-paper-buying public who get to know a group year after year. The best from The Faces is yet to come.'[7]

And, as if to spite Stewart and Wood, Kenney Jones went into the studio to record his own single, 'Ready Or Not'. When released in October, it sank without trace.

The Faces then headed off to Belgium for a one-off festival show, and then back in America, playing a few festivals. But the America they returned to was in crisis. At the end of July, President Richard Nixon had articles of impeachment raised against him by the House Judiciary Committee for his part in the Watergate scandal. Nixon was implicated in a burglary of the Democratic Party offices in the Watergate Hotel complex in Washington. The accusation against Nixon was that he had used his position as President not just to organise the burglary, but more importantly, to cover it up. On 8 August Nixon resigned, the first American President to do so. His recently appointed (and unelected) Vice-President, Gerald Ford, was sworn in as President the next day. Britain – and the rest of the world – looked on aghast as it seemed that America (and 'Tricky Dicky,' as Nixon had become known) had imploded.

★

For The Faces, everything else was on hold, as Stewart's LP – though completed – hadn't been released. There was a dispute between Stewart, his record company for his solo deal, Mercury, and the company that The Faces were on (and Stewart was about to sign to), Warner Brothers. When Stewart's initial solo deal with Mercury expired in 1972, Mercury claimed that Stewart had signed an extension. Stewart had initially thought that the deal had ended with the

*Coast to Coast* album; Mercury insisted that there was still one more LP to be delivered.

In the meantime, Stewart had signed a new solo deal with Warner Brothers, who thought that his new album, *Smiler*, would be released on their label. Everything had been proceeding normally with the release of the LP until the Vice-President of Warner Brothers, Joe Smith, arrived at Mercury's offices with a court injunction preventing the album's release. The legal wrangles left Stewart bemused.

'It's like writing a letter home and then not having a stamp to send it,' he said. 'All this fighting back and forth. The album will come out in September, and then the thing goes to the courts. Winner takes all.'[8]

And amid the lethargy, yet another rumour appeared in the press, not least due to Ronnie Wood's interview earlier in the year: Jones and McLagan were going to reform the original Small Faces with Steve Marriott – whose group Humble Pie was falling apart – and Ronnie Lane, whose group Slim Chance were going nowhere. But Stewart remained defiant about The Faces.

'[We're] in a stronger position, I think,' he told the *NME*. 'Everybody's working out their own things, and I think we'll come back to the band as stronger individuals. We'll pull that strength together because The Faces is a personal thing, if you know what I mean.'[9]

However, Stewart was less confident about The Faces' future as a recording outfit. 'Well, we've tried it in the studio four times, and it's never really worked out the way it should've,' he said. 'My albums have always been better than Faces albums, always. We won't make another Faces album, I think we'll just cut singles from now on. You know, go for the great performance and cancel out the rest. But maybe I shouldn't be saying this … maybe the lads want to make another album.'[10] It spoke volumes about the state of The Faces that Stewart hadn't bothered to ask them.

Come September, The Faces were undertaking their biggest and longest European tour. But their long absence from touring and their lack of record releases was beginning to show: the venues weren't quite as large as they were used to, and some of the venues weren't sold out. It didn't take them long to realise that they would have to work harder than they had for a couple of years.

'It's strange, really,' said Stewart, 'that in five years we haven't really been over there [in Europe]. I had an interview with a French journalist the other day and I thought, "This'd be good, y'know … new questions and all that," but the first thing he said was, "Give me your history."'[11]

★

Back in the States, the precarious position of the Presidency took another twist when President Gerald Ford gave his predecessor a 'full, free, absolute pardon'. 'Tricky Dicky' had got away with it after all.

Wood's solo LP was released to little acclaim and less sales. Stewart released a solo single, 'Farewell', as a sampler for his forthcoming album and so The Faces would have something to support on tour. And the tour dragged on. And on. Twenty-three dates covering most of Europe – West Germany, Sweden, France, Denmark, Holland, Italy, Spain, Belgium, Norway, and a cancelled show in Switzerland – spilled over into November. And despite their penchant for partying, The Faces were beginning to sober up. At the Buxton festival earlier in the year, The Faces had celebrated their success by showering their roadcrew with orange juice.

'God, I'd hate to think that anybody ever bought a ticket to see a Faces show because they wanted to see a bunch of drunks staggering about,' claimed Stewart in direct contradiction of his statements at the start of The Faces' adventure.[12]

Even as the tour continued Kenney Jones was concerned about

the state of the group. 'I think we've come together a lot,' he told the *NME*. 'We needed the break and we've needed a few days on tour to sort things out among ourselves. I think we're ready to play England now. We should be really good.'

Midway through the tour, they stopped off in a studio in Munich and in two days wrote, rehearsed and recorded the track which was to become their next single. Despite Stewart's claim that The Faces were no longer a recording group, they seemed to have regained some of the spirit of *A Nod is as Good as a Wink*.

It had been known since the result of the election of February 1974 that there would be another election before long, and Harold Wilson duly called it for 10 October. The introduction of the formal 'Social Contract' between the trade unions and the Labour government had put a lid on some of the worst disputes, though there remained the problems of rising inflation (between 1973 and 1974 it had reached sixteen per cent) and a deterioration in general living standards.

The situation in Northern Ireland had also worsened. An attempt by the government to impose the 'Sunningdale Agreement' – which effectively enforced power-sharing between all sides – was opposed by the majority of Protestants, and May had seen a General Strike called by the Ulster Workers Council, enforced (it was alleged) by a campaign of 'persuasion' by Loyalist paramilitaries. Eventually, after fourteen days of marches, shootings and the Dublin and Monaghan bombings – four bombs were planted by Loyalist paramilitaries killing 33 people – the Northern Ireland Secretary Merlyn Rees was forced to resume direct rule over Northern Ireland.

Despite Rees's announcing the phased end of internment in July, the IRA again bombed mainland Britain, this time in Birmingham, Manchester and a little later, the Tower of London, a bomb that killed one person and injured forty-one others. The shootings in the Province continued through the summer, and even as the General Election campaign rumbled on, the IRA planted two more bombs in two pubs in Guildford. The pubs were chosen because they were frequented by British soldiers. The bombs killed five people and injured fifty-four others.

The mournful tones of Stewart's new single, 'Farewell', provided a soundtrack to a Britain that felt like a country under siege. 'I love you and I miss you,' he sang. He could have been talking to an earlier time. The other reflection of the times was the sitcom *Whatever Happened to the Likely Lads?*, a sequel to the Sixties' *Likely Lads*. The theme tune, performed by Manfred Mann, ostensibly looking to the future but heavily tinged with regret seemed to sum it all up. Premised around how two young men had changed since the Sixties – one had become a proto-yuppie, the other a drifter – the melancholy which underpinned the show was endemic.

The General Election campaign was fought by Labour on the slogan, 'Labour Keeps Its Promises', with Wilson ever happy to recall the 'three-day week' as 'the dark ages'. Heath's Conservatives and Jeremy Thorpe's Liberals, however, focused on the serious problems the country faced, and talked openly of a Government of National Unity, thereby recalling the crisis that faced Britain in 1940 when Europe had fallen to the Nazis and the last time there had been a Government of National Unity.

★

On 4 October – the day before the Guildford pub bombings – Stewart's long-completed *Smiler* album was released. The album's thirteen tracks included two instrumentals, 'Lochinvar' and 'I've Grown Accustomed To Her Face', the obligatory Dylan cover, 'Girl From The North Country', along with Elton John's 'Let Me Be Your

Car' and Paul McCartney's 'Mine For Me'. Stewart combined with Quittenton again for the single, 'Farewell', but the rest of the album was Stewart on auto-pilot. The album didn't contain a 'Maggie May', and if anything was more of a vehicle for Stewart's vocal range, a vinyl audition. The painting of Stewart which adorned the cover, surrounded by tartan, made him appear more alone than he had before.

'The solo records of Rod's that I love are *Gasoline Alley* and *Every Picture Tells a Story*,' remembers Robert Matheu. 'Then I shifted at that point into *A Nod's as Good as a Wink* and *Ooh La La*. In those years those were the four records that I loved. I didn't particularly like *Smiler*. I think *Smiler* suffered because of the production, the bad mastering; it was always a muddy record and it never seemed to have as much of a heart to it as the other two.'

The album climbed to Number 13 in America, proving that Stewart was established there as a major artist. But he couldn't keep to the old formula for ever, certainly if he wanted to continue his success, something he had publicly acknowledged before the year was out.

'It's time to get back to the *Gasoline Alley* type of thing now, I think,' he told the *NME*. 'I just know that I'll have given up listening to *Smiler* long before I ever forget about *Gasoline Alley*. That was my favourite album. It's getting a bit too samey now.' The fans, the music business and The Faces waited to see what he would do next.

The General Election on 10 October hadn't provided Wilson with the majority he had wanted or expected – the opinion polls had shown Labour with a lead of up to ten per cent. He did have a majority, but only of three, not enough to get a government through a full term (it's usually expected that a government could lose ten or more MPs during its life through death or resignation and losses in the subsequent by-elections).

The election was notable for the rise of the Nationalist parties – the Scottish Nationalists increased their representation from seven to eleven MPs (all gained from the Conservatives) and Plaid Cymru from two to three. Enoch Powell, whose inflammatory speech in 1968 had heightened the issue of race and immigration, had left the Conservative Party over the issue of Britain's membership of the Common Market, and was returned as an Ulster Unionist MP. The other notable feature of the election was the increased presence of the explicitly racist National Front, who fielded ninety candidates. Though none of them was elected, it did show their increasing confidence, especially in areas of the country with a high number of immigrants.

The Labour government carried on with their policies towards the economy, attempting to right what was an increasingly listing ship. The 'Social Contract' contained wage restraint and price controls, and in an effort to balance the economic books, the government imposed substantial income tax increases. Since taxes were already considered high, this move was to drive many wealthy people to consider leaving the country for a less harsh tax regime. The Rolling Stones were among those who had already taken the odd tax year off, as it were. The increasingly antagonistic relationship between rock's elite and government – first documented in George Harrison's 'Taxman' on The Beatles' *Revolver* album and pursued through drugs busts in the late Sixties and Seventies – would get no better.

But there seemed to be some hope for the British economy – in the Sixties, it had been discovered that there were oil reserves in the North Sea. The government realised that there was money to be made from exploiting (selling) the rights for exploration and drilling for the oil to the major oil companies. Such was the anticipation of a huge windfall that Prime Minister Harold Wilson was moved to joke that Britain could now join OPEC. No-one laughed for long.

★

On their return from the European dates, The Faces were flung straight into a massive British tour, but just before they were due to begin, there was another IRA attack on a pub in London – in early November, a bomb was flung through the window of the King's Arms in Woolwich, London, killing an off-duty soldier and a civilian. Journalist Lucy O'Brien recalls that it didn't feel safe even to go out in the evening.

'It was scary as hell,' she says. 'Northern Ireland was the big issue, one of the biggest issues; it just impinged on everyone's consciousness in a scary way because there was so much violence at that time. There were bombs going off on the "mainland" as well as in Northern Ireland. We were living in Southampton at the time and there were a few IRA cells there.'

People still flocked to see The Faces, though. While Europe had been quite pleased to see them, back in Britain The Faces were as huge as ever. A week into the tour, Warner Brothers released the new Faces single, 'You Can Make Me Dance, Sing Or Anything', a loose, funky, up-beat workout reminiscent of the feel of the end of 'True Blue', backed with 'As Long As You Tell Him'.

Reviewing the song in *Sounds*, DJ John Peel was more than enthusiastic. 'This single is the one that marks The Faces' first major development since "First Step". Neither side here is a rocker in the traditional sense, and neither is an "Angel" or an "I'd Rather Go Blind". This is second-generation Faces music, inspired by Bobby Womack rather than Chuck Berry ... As good as "Dance" is, "As Long As You Tell Him" is even better. The playing of the band is a revelation, no flash, no riot, just perfectly appropriate and quite electrifying music. To read young Rod's

251

interviews and to hear the boy talk you'd believe he regards sensitivity in singing with some suspicion. Yet on records like this no other white popular singer could match our Rod for a moment for expression or sensitivity … this is THE Faces record, one of the most beautiful records I've ever heard, and if they decided not to record again then I hope you'll join me in selecting a heavy cudgel from the hedgerow and marching on their homes with violence in our hearts.'

The evening before the single was released, the IRA exploded two bombs in two pubs in Birmingham, the Mulberry Bush and the Tavern in the Town. A total of twenty-one people were killed. There was widespread outrage among the British people at the series of attacks on pubs, the main criticism being that the government were not doing enough to counter the threat from the IRA. In response, the British government rushed through the Prevention of Terrorism Act, giving them the power to detain suspects without charge for up to seven days and exclude anyone thought to be a threat.

These were difficult days for ordinary Irish people living in the UK, whose accents made them appear suspicious to the British. In addition, the increasingly vocal National Front demanded the repatriation of Irish people generally and that anyone found to be a member of the IRA should be hanged. While these views were not widely reported, nor remotely popular, they did nothing to lessen the general nervousness which descended on the large Irish community in the country.

'You Can Make Me Dance …' did creditably well and the tour went like a rocket, finishing with four nights at the Glasgow Apollo followed by three riotous nights in Kilburn Gaumont. In Glasgow, the Lord Provost gave Stewart the freedom of the city. At the town hall, Stewart beat his chest and threw his arms open to the crowd below. The backstage visitors grew increasingly glamorous, increasingly 'showbiz': when The Faces played Lewisham, Paul and Linda McCartney joined them on stage. At Kilburn, Gary Glitter in a huge fur coat appeared on stage to sing the end of 'Maggie May'. Elton John turned up to three shows in a row. Alvin Stardust came to hang out backstage.

But when the band invited Keith Richards on stage with them and he overdid his guitar solo, Stewart scowled and slid his finger across his throat. And, perhaps, more importantly, though the songwriting credit for 'You Can Make Me Dance ...' went to all the members of the group – as if in an attempt to portray a united front on the part of Stewart and the band – the single itself was credited to 'Rod Stewart and The Faces'. There was no hiding the fact any more – even at best, The Faces were just an appendage to Stewart.

'Rod was a huge star,' says Billy Gaff. 'He'd had Number 1 after Number 1. It just wasn't a group any more. It was Rod Stewart.'[13]

Summing up the year for The Faces, Stewart admitted that it had been difficult. 'There was a lot of arguing, certainly,' Stewart told Nick Kent. 'It got really bad at times ... You've got to remember the situation we were in when Ronnie Lane left the band because ... well, at the very beginning, and this is something that a lot of people don't know, but Ronnie was very much the leader of The Faces. He had the final say on virtually everything. And the whole band was into emulating the "Booker T" thing ... that's what they were aiming for and it was all a bit awkward because it wasn't really together.'[14]

By this point it wasn't only Stewart who was suspected of harbouring ambitions which didn't include The Faces. As well as his solo album, it was becoming well known in the music business and widely reported in the music press that Ron Wood was being courted by the Rolling Stones. Wood and Keith Richards were already close friends – Richards had been staying in the house at the end of Wood's drive – and Richards had played both on Wood's solo LP and with Wood's solo live band. In addition, Wood had played on some Rolling Stones recording sessions. When Mick Taylor quit the Stones at the end of 1974, The Faces were quick to deny all rumours about Wood's possible defection.

'I don't think it'll happen,' said Stewart. 'I really don't ... even though we haven't had a heart to heart or anything, I mean, Ronnie's my best mate. There's never been anyone closer to me than Woody.'[15]

Wood himself felt pressured enough to release a statement to the press on the last day of the year. 'People obviously would think that I'm joining the Stones due to my supposed social connections with them,' he said. 'This, however, is just not true – for though I respect them immensely, my position in The Faces is of far greater personal importance.'[16]

But at the end of 1974 it was sometimes hard to tell one way or another. The Faces had studio time booked for January and a massive American tour booked to begin in February. It seemed that all the rumours of a split were premature. December also saw a strike by bakery workers which led to short supplies of bread. Queues duly formed outside shops, and bread was rationed – by the shops – to two loaves per family. It even led to the hijacking of a bread van in East London. And in Northern Ireland, the IRA called a ceasefire over Christmas.

Between The Faces' indecision, trade union belligerence and the vague glimmer of hope in Northern Ireland, it seemed like business as usual.

# FIFTEEN

# MUSIC FOR HOUSEWIVES

The Faces spent some time in January at London's AIR Studios over-looking Oxford Circus. They recorded around five songs with which they were (seemingly) very pleased. 'It was the first sign of an album being fucking good,' recalled Kenney Jones. 'For once it had a great deal of excitement in the actual track, and the numbers were sounding nice too. All it needed was good vocals and a good mix and whatever you put on them. If we'd continued like that and finished the album instead of going to the States we'd have made a winner album.'[1]

But the American tour was booked, and so February saw The Faces back in New York, playing before rapturous audiences, flying across the country, back in their home away from home in Cobo Hall,

Detroit, drinking and partying and doing what they did best – playing live. In Los Angeles they booked themselves into the Record Plant recording studios to work further on the session that they had started in London, but to no avail.

'When we got there, it's like anything in LA,' remembered Jones. 'We got there and everyone said, "Let's go into the studio at midnight." As far as I'm concerned I don't fit into that. That's my problem: I like going there at two in the afternoon. But I did, I went there at twelve o'clock, only everyone's idea of twelve o'clock is one o'clock. And then you get all these liggers hanging about, all these famous guitarists, other famous people popping in and out, and you end up talking to them for ages and nobody would be playing, and it ceased to become what we wanted it to be. Everything falls apart in LA if you want to make a record. I thought we were going to come back and work on the tracks, but instead of that Woody started his album and Rod stayed in the States. So how could we do it? Nobody else wanted to do it. It was all very selfish.'[2]

Back in Britain, industrial mayhem remained the order of the day. The oil crisis had a further knock-on effect, with the demand for oil tankers collapsing and the demands for new tankers evaporating. The dockyards all over Britain which had built some of the most famous ships in the world (including the 'supertankers') were in dire trouble. February saw more deaths in London, though this time not due to terrorism. At Moorgate tube station, thirty-five people died when a tube train overran the buffers and crashed into the end of a tunnel. Television pictures of dazed commuters, covered in a film of blood mixed with dust, sent a shockwave through London's passengers – it was the first major disaster on the London Underground.

And in March, strikes by dustcart drivers in Glasgow led to the

Army being brought in to remove the rubbish that had started to pile up. Rather than defending themselves against rock-throwing teenagers, the soldiers now found themselves carrying bags of rubbish away from Glasgow's tenements and chasing rats through the piles of rubbish, armed only with steel bars.

★

Insulated from the everyday trials of life back home, the general mayhem and debauchery associated with The Faces on tour continued remorselessly. When Stewart found out that President Gerald Ford and his family had gone to see George Harrison on his tour, Stewart issued an invitation to Ford's daughters to come to The Faces' Washington show. Only one of the daughters – Susan – came to the show, along with a few friends. Billy Gaff and the band's press officer Tony Toon made sure that the press got pictures of her chatting with the group backstage, but immediately afterwards Stewart, who felt snubbed by the White House, jetted off to New York for a party being thrown by Led Zeppelin.

When the band returned to their hotel they discovered that as a 'thank you' gesture to Stewart, Ford had sent a dinner invitation to him. Stewart was stranded in New York, which was becoming fogbound. All civilian flights were grounded, as was Stewart. And to make matters worse, Toon had planted a story in the British press that Stewart was dating Susan Ford. Stewart sent a bouquet of red roses to the White House as an apology.

Back in New York for a show in a sold-out Madison Square Gardens, the band played another blistering set. 'Ronnie called me into his room backstage after the gig,' recalls Jones. 'There was blood everywhere. His nose had fucking come away at the top with all the coke he'd been doing. And he made this looking-down-nose face and said, "Fuck me, Kenney, I can see the sink from here!" Anyway, we cleaned him up and stuck his nose back on with gaffer-tape, then put on this huge pair of dark glasses to hide the join. But he wasn't worried, only said, "I'll just get one of those things that Stephen Stills has got, he's had a couple."'[3] Wood subsequently had a plastic septum inserted in his nose.

But it wasn't only Wood's nose that was in danger, and some members of the group took to using pessaries rather than snorting their cocaine – they would empty the pessary out and then refill it with cocaine before using it, mistakenly thinking that this would cause them less physical damage. They discovered the truth before any serious damage was done and the band's intestines remained intact.

When the tour finished in March, The Faces were due to return to Britain. Their 'end-of-tour' party, thrown at a glamorous Hollywood restaurant named The Greenhouse, was graced with the presence of the great and good from Hollywood and rock's 'A'-list celebrities: Paul and Linda McCartney, Cher, Greg Allman, Joni Mitchell, and Ryan O'Neal among the faces to meet The Faces. Billy Gaff had no problem in announcing that the tour had gone so well that it would extend through the year, with a break from June to July to allow Stewart to make a new album, followed by a short UK tour and the strong possibility of a new Faces LP.

However, the band made their way back to Britain without Stewart, who announced that he was going to make his next record in America. Stewart's life was certainly changing – in the spring of 1975 he had met Britt Ekland, actress, model and celebrity wife (she had previously been married to Peter Sellers). Ekland was pure Hollywood, and was certainly a step into the big leagues for the boy from the Archway Road. And in keeping with the big leagues, Stewart was looking to recruit the best session players for his next recording project: Booker T & The MGs, the Memphis Horns and guitarist Jesse Ed Davis. For the first time there would be no Faces on a Rod Stewart record.

Wood's initial reaction was to reassemble his studio band and, along with Bobby Womack, to make a start on his second solo LP. But it wasn't long before a better offer came along. The Rolling Stones had been in pursuit of Ron Wood for some time. Back in 1969, when the singerless Faces were in their early, stuttering rehearsals in the Rolling Stones' studio in Bermondsey, they had tried to get Wood on the phone to ask him to join following Brian Jones' departure and subsequent death. Unfortunately, they got the other 'Ron' (Lane) who, well aware of who was calling and of the situation, told them, 'He's quite happy where he is.' At the end of 1974, the offer came up again.

'I was at a party for Eric Clapton at Robert Stigwood's house,' remembered Wood. 'Mick Taylor told Mick Jagger that he was definitely leaving, told him right in the middle of this do, and Mick was shocked, he wasn't happy, and came up to me and said, "Mick Taylor's just told me he's leaving and there's a whole tour lined up." But I still said, "Well, I don't want to break up The Faces, but give me a call if you get stuck, keep in touch." The Stones had everyone wanting to join – Steve Marriott, even Wayne Perkins. Clapton auditioned too, but he didn't work out. The Stones were holding auditions for the band in Germany and I got a call from Mick to come out. I went and they'd rented a load of rooms in the Munich Hilton. Jeff Beck was in a room next to me.'[4]

★

The spring and summer of 1975 were dominated by the debate over whether Britain should stay in the Common Market. The re-elected Labour government had stated that there would be a national referendum on the matter, and in a remarkable political move, Wilson allowed his ministers to argue publically on the subject. The debate rolled on through May and June, and in early July the vote took place on the question, 'Do you think the UK should stay in the European Community?', the outcome to be decided by a simple majority of the votes cast. Over seventeen million voters answered 'yes' against over eight million 'no' votes. Britain had linked its future to Europe.

While political attention was hypnotised by the European debate, another political decision had taken place in February which would have larger implications for the future of Britain. As a 'failed' leader, Ted Heath was ejected by the Conservative Party. In what was, at the time, a major shock, the Conservatives replaced him with a woman, Margaret Thatcher. Thatcher's sole claim to fame had been that as Education Minister in Heath's government she had overseen the abolition of free school milk. Now, little known outside of the Conservative Party, she was ready to bring her own brand of right-wing economic fundamentalism allied to proto-Victorian social values to bear on her own party.

Later in the year the Labour government passed a piece of social legislation that was to have a dramatic effect on the lives of many women. Led by Barbara Castle, Parliament passed the Sex Discrimination Act which, allied to the 1970 Equal Pay Act, meant that for the first time it was no longer permissible to discriminate against women in the workplace simply because they were women. Though the effects took time to set in, it would lead to the social acceptance of women's rights to be taken seriously in work.

Meanwhile, the South Vietnamese government finally fell after the Americans' withdrawal. Cambodia also fell to Pol Pot's Khamir Rouge. When the new regime cut off communications to the rest of the world, a bloodbath was feared. Those fears – it was discovered later – were to be realised. And unemployment in Britain reached the figure of one million. Inflation was now so out of control that the Chancellor,

Dennis Healey, imposed a severe budget with swinging tax increases. A proposed hike in Value Added Tax to twenty-five per cent on 'luxury' goods led to a stampede in the shops to buy televisions, fridges and other electrical goods.

But not everything was grim. For young people in Britain, the early to mid-Seventies provided a high point for music on terrestrial television.

'We used to go to Granada TV studios to watch them making a music show,' remembered Carol Chaffer. 'Granada was really, really good at that time in putting on loads of music shows. Local youth clubs in Manchester and the area around used to be invited along to get tickets to see the shows being recorded, so we used to go to those. It was called 45. I saw Slade and Roxy Music.'

Pop music was still seen at the time to be a big enough cultural and social event that television companies would make shows devoted solely to pop groups. The television companies felt that they had to make an effort to reach a young audience, and pop music was seen to provide a link. It was also important for commercial companies such as Granada, who relied on advertisements for their income, to reach the young audience as it was perceived that they still had a disposable income despite the relative austerity of the times.

★

Because Stewart was to be in America for the foreseeable future – it was an open secret that he was going to stay out of Britain for twelve months to avoid British income tax – all the talk of a British tour had ended up as just talk. It didn't seem to be a problem for Wood to use the few months' vacation he would have as a Face to fill in as a Stone. While Stewart's reasons for going were at first claimed to be artistic – he wanted to work with the legendary session players – it very quickly became apparent that there was more to it.

'It wasn't rocket science, there was nothing to it,' remembers Billy Gaff. 'Taxation in America at the time was, I think, a maximum forty-five per cent; here it was eighty-three per cent. And that was the only reason.'[5]

It was also an emotional decision for Stewart. 'It was a real close toss-up,' he recalled. 'I remember I had a wonderful night with Elton [John] where he called me a traitor. We were playing "Land Of Hope And Glory", the "Last Night Of The Proms", and he was going, "How could you leave this, how could you leave this?" And he was absolutely right, you know? It was a real struggle, it really was, with the football and everything.'[6]

But there were other factors. Stewart had turned thirty and had been in and around the music business in one form or another for over ten years. He had had four years of major success, built around the formula of a 'folky' single (e.g. 'Maggie May'), a couple of rock songs (e.g. 'True Blue'), and the raucous stage shows of The Faces. In the Seventies, rock was the preserve of young men, the general consideration being that with a few exceptions – the top of rock's hierarchy such as Clapton and the ex-Beatles – anyone over thirty was in trouble. If Stewart was to continue his success – at any level – he would have to shift his audience away from the young football fans in Britain and towards an audience close to his own age (or older).

'You never know how long you're gonna last in this business,' remembered Stewart. 'I thought, "God, I've gotta put some money in the bank, it might be all over next year."'[7]

Another consideration was Stewart's new woman. Britt Ekland was definitely 'A'-list in terms of celebrity, and his relationship with her saw Stewart permanently promoted to the tabloid front pages. In interviews with the music press over the previous year, he had been trying to down-play the more riotous elements of life on the road with

The Faces (though life on the road with The Faces had remained pretty much the same). But having got a sniff of the Hollywood high-life with Ekland, Stewart wasn't keen to give it up.

On 9 May 1975, Stewart announced from Los Angeles that he had become a tax exile. He was going to apply for American citizenship and had instructed Billy Gaff to sell off all he owned in Britain. By June he had recanted his conversion, claiming instead that he was merely working abroad for a few months. None of this was helped by a disastrous press conference called in Dublin in July 1975 to launch his new album, *Atlantic Crossing*.

The debacle began with Stewart and Ekland landing at Heathrow Airport for a stopover, and then refusing to leave the International Lounge. Some newspapers reported that this was because he was avoiding a writ for £750,000 in unpaid taxes, reports that were denied by Stewart who subsequently claimed to have issued writs against the papers. Stewart and Ekland were then forced to fly to Amsterdam to connect with a flight to Dublin. They arrived for the press conference late, were further delayed by the need to prepare a statement regarding Stewart's tax position for the papers, and the whole thing was conducted in an atmosphere of frustrated irritation on the part of the assembled press and TV corps and bemused, almost aggressive self-justification on the part of Stewart and Ekland. The interviews continued into the next day when the atmosphere had calmed a little.

'I believe this album is the best one I've ever done,' Stewart told the *NME*. 'I definitely needed new blood around me. Suddenly I've seen the light of day. This is what I should have been doing two years ago.' Stewart claimed that working without his old group had been refreshing. 'It's the first time I've recorded without Woody or Mickey Waller,' he said. 'It's a complete change – not that much of a change that you'd hear it, but the musicianship is a lot more polished, which is what I wanted, and at last I've found a rhythm section I can really get into.'[8]

What Stewart was implying was that freed of The Faces, he had finally made a proper, grown-up record. Two of The Faces – McLagan and Jones – had been formally invited to the press launch, but unsurprisingly chose to stay in England. If relations between The Faces were strained, they would be strained further by Stewart's comments at the press conference and the interviews that followed.

Stewart also announced his plan to play a show in early 1976 at the Royal Albert Hall in London with Booker T & The MGs and a full orchestra (the show was subsequently cancelled when Al Jackson, the MGs drummer, was shot dead at his home in Memphis). But what of The Faces? 'We'll be down in Miami in three weeks to start rehearsing and obviously there's going to be a lot of ego floating around,' he told the *NME*. It was always a possibility.

*Atlantic Crossing* was certainly Stewart's most 'grown-up' LP to date. Stewart decided to divide the album's two sides into a 'Fast Half' and a 'Slow Half'. The 'Fast Half' – and the album – begins with 'Three Time Loser', a straightforward R&B track written by Stewart on the subject of venereal disease. Tightly produced, it lacks the spontaneity associated with Stewart's earlier recordings. 'Alright For An Hour', written by Stewart and guitarist Jesse Ed Davis, is an attempt to incorporate the rhythm of reggae which was, at the time, breaking on to the world market through the success of Bob Marley & The Wailers. Unfortunately, in common with many of the established artists who tried to assimilate reggae, it merely sounded like a pale imitation of the original.

'All In The Name of Rock 'N' Roll' follows, again written by Stewart, another chugging R&B number in the vein of the Rolling Stones' 'Bitch' from their *Sticky Fingers* LP which survives simply because the production and the Memphis Horns hide the fact that the song doesn't go anywhere. Dobie Gray's 'Drift Away', written by Mentor Williams, belies its placing on the 'Fast Half' of the album, and is a competent cover which doesn't match Gray's version. The final track of the half, 'Stone Cold Sober', was penned by Stewart and guitarist Steve Cropper and opens with Cropper's steady riffing. However, it's merely another competent R&B song augmented by the Memphis Horns.

The 'Slow Half' opens with Stewart's version of Danny Whitten's 'I Don't Want To Talk About It'. The track which most recalls Stewart's earlier work, the recording manages – more than any other on the album – to recapture the 'little boy lost' poignancy identified by Long John Baldry ten years before. Even the addition of strings – arranged by Arif Mardin – doesn't reduce Stewart's effectiveness. The next track, 'It's Not The Spotlight', written by Goldberg and Goffin, is a ballad-by-numbers, while Stewart's cover of the Isley Brothers' 'This Old Heart Of Mine' tries to take the old soul stomper into Al Green territory and as such is the most inventive track on the album. Stewart's own 'Still Love You' follows, a song which if anything is reminiscent of Stewart's collaborations with Ronnie Lane. Gavin Sutherland's epic 'Sailing', yet another Stewart track on the theme of 'going home', closes the album.

Although the rhythm section might have been one of the tightest – and most professional – around, what they added in polish they subtracted in energy, for what Stewart failed to appreciate was that for Booker T & The MGs, Stewart's LP was just another session, just another job. That isn't to denigrate their undoubted ability or professionalism; it's just that playing session after session would eventually wear anyone down, and Booker T & The MGs had been playing sessions for ever. Stewart's singing was again technically as good as it had ever been, but the whole album lacked the raw edge that Wood and the gang brought to the studio. Hidden within the grooves of the album were only hints of Stewart's past; what was missing was the sense of what had made Stewart and The Faces' earlier recordings so likeable. There was no sense of fun. The album sounded like someone going to work rather than a band having a good time.

The other omission, especially in the writing, was the Celtic folk influence which had permeated all of Stewart's earlier work. Without that folk feel in the songwriting, and without the edge supplied by Wood et al., the album sounds inauthentic. That this could be true seems contradictory, since Stewart was working with some of the musicians who had made the authentic soul recordings that Stewart and The Faces loved so much. Perhaps it's just that Stewart was being untrue or inauthentic to himself.

The cover featured slick artwork featuring Stewart bestriding the Atlantic, complete with the Houses of Parliament (replete with Scottish flag) and New York's skyscrapers. The sleevenotes listed the eminent names who had worked on the album, but unlike his earlier covers, there was no message from Stewart and no mention of The Faces.

The single from the album, 'Sailing', was a massive Number 1, seemingly endlessly the final song on *Top of the Pops*, the promotional film that Stewart had made for it – him, heavily made up, in a sailor suit, sitting on a yacht, trying to look wistful – a never-ending source of irritation for his legion of football-supporting fans. But somehow the song made its way to the terraces, the words changed to something more suitable for armies of young men to bellow with each other in between throwing toilet rolls at the footballers who played on pitches in such bad condition that they resembled the Somme – 'We are [insert name of team], we are [insert name], super [name], coming in.' Or, in the case of one group of particularly miserable fans from

South-East London football club Millwall, 'No-one likes us / No-one likes / No-one likes us / We don't care'. (Millwall's supporters had – and to some extent retain – a notorious image in the media for being particularly violent, and it was – and remains – a truism in British football that indeed no-one does like them.)

The song remains a terrace favourite to this day, even though the terraces and the hooligans have disappeared, replaced by seats and largely better-heeled fans. With 'Sailing', Stewart had pulled off his final coup: he'd made what journalist and Faces fan Lester Bangs would describe as 'music for housewives'; and he'd got his brothers on the terraces to sing it. But not everyone was happy with Stewart's version.

'I remember hearing "Sailing" by the Sutherland Brothers and Quiver on the *Old Grey Whistle Test*,' recalls Sue Westergaard, 'and I loved it then 'cos it was just a gentle little song with one of those funny bits of film that they used to have on the show. But not Rod Stewart's version.'

Up in Todmorden, Carol Chaffer was also appalled by Stewart's new direction. 'I remember "Sailing" and I thought, "My God, how can anyone like this music?" Dreadful. I started going out with my first long-term boyfriend then, and he used to like that and I was so embarrassed.'

But whatever the impressions of his fans in Britain, the album had the effect that Stewart desired – it was a massive hit everywhere, and gained him a new audience. When Stewart was asked whether the apparent career shift meant that he had abandoned his old audience, he denied it. 'No. I love all that,' he told the *NME*. 'I love the football and I'll always love the football. I'd die by it.'[9]

★

Ron Wood had completed his second solo album in time to join the Rolling Stones' American tour, and a month into the tour the record was released, to little acclaim and just as few sales. The Faces were due to start rehearsals in Miami but they were put on hold when Jagger announced an extension to the Rolling Stones' successful tour, thereby press-ganging Wood to stay with them. Not that Wood especially needed press-ganging – one of the reasons why Wood was in a band at all was his early love of the Rolling Stones. It was his boyhood dream come true.

In the meantime, Kenney Jones had given an interview where he complained that Stewart's decision to stay in America had left him unemployed and out of pocket. 'I feel pretty browned off,' said Jones. 'Ever since Rod moved to the States everything's got disorganised. The Faces haven't worked in four months and I've lost £80,000 because we're not playing Wembley any longer.'[10]

It wasn't just Wembley – The Faces had been tentatively scheduled to play concerts at a series of football grounds around Britain. The Faces' office replied to Jones' complaints by telling the press, 'There hasn't been any official reply and there isn't going to be one. The matter is being dealt with internally.' The possible album that Billy Gaff had trailed in May was also now on hold, pending the return of their singer and guitarist.

Stewart's defence of his own absence was to point out that the British tour couldn't have taken place anyway due to Wood's secondment to the Stones, and to disclose that he was less than pleased with the Stones' decision to extend their tour.

'We've had to cancel three concerts in Miami at a loss of £20,000,' Stewart complained to the press, 'because there won't be enough time to rehearse new numbers with Ronnie. I'm particularly fed up because I feel the Stones should have let me know about their tour extension earlier.'

Despite the rehearsals now due to start in Miami in early August, it was beginning to look like the leading Faces were jockeying for position in the race to the exit. But no-one wanted to carry the can.

'We're probably further away from each other than we've ever been,' said Stewart. 'There's a lot of bullshit goes down. We have a go at each other behind each other's backs, we never say the best things about each other, but when we're together we're the best of mates always. If that was to change then I'd be very surprised.'[11] Stewart went on to tell the London *Evening Standard*, 'If the Faces are going to break up, it'll be in the next few months. I love 'em as blokes, but we've got a lot to talk about.'[12] Even years later, Stewart was still not keen to accept responsibility for the deteriorating situation in The Faces.

'Jagger swore to me, "I'm never gonna nick Woody from The Faces,"' remembered Stewart later. 'I said, "Yeah, you lying bastard, of course you will."

'And, of course, he did.'[13]

# SIXTEEN

# I'LL JUST STAY HERE

By the time the five Faces reunited in Miami for the rehearsals, there was much to be discussed. Aside from the bitching and backbiting which had continued in the press through the summer, there was also the matter of Stewart's desired new format for the live shows. Kenney Jones, though, was optimistic.

'I'd been playing with a lot of different people too,' remembered Jones, 'like Paul and Linda McCartney ... and what with Rod playing with Steve Cropper and 'Duck' Dunn, and Ronnie playing with the Stones, I thought the added experience would have made The Faces sound better. I knew Rod wanted the band to sound like his studio records, and we could have done it. But we never delivered it because we were still getting pissed as ever. And Ronnie had gone away as a Face and come back as a Rolling Stone.'[1]

Stewart, however, was less optimistic. 'If it doesn't work out in rehearsal then we just won't tour,' he told *Creem* magazine. 'If it doesn't sound how I want it to sound, that's it. I want it to sound like something new, like the record I've made. We've got to be a lot more disciplined. We've got to tighten up. We always looked at touring like it was party time, which it should be, but it's time we proved ourselves. It's time we took the blinkers off.'[2]

Ian McLagan, whose work through the summer had largely been within Ron Wood's gift, was not at all happy at the way things were going. The way the tour was being organised made it clear that from Stewart's point of view, The Faces were now explicitly nothing more than his backing band. McLagan's approach seemed to be to try and keep The Faces alive through sheer force of his own determination.

'We're going into the studio in November,' he told the *Evening Standard*, 'and if Rod isn't going to sing on the numbers we'll do them ourselves ... If Rod does decide to leave we'll carry on by ourselves. The pressure is on him to leave at the moment because he's constantly being told he's a Hollywood star and a dedicated leader of fashion. Perhaps he should go solo and try it. Since he's always changing his mind about things, he's going to find it very difficult to be boss unless he's with friends. I hope it won't come to that. I think he still cares about The Faces but he's up in the air at the moment, being feted by all the people around him. I feel hurt, but realistically I suppose it was bound to happen. Personally I'd just like a bloody phone call or something. At present I get directives through about five different people. He'll say he wants strings on the next tour or he wants us all over for a meeting in Miami. If he wants to act just like that, he will have to hire some musicians on a wage.'[3]

Stewart's demands for the new tour were relatively simple, though in their own way demeaning to the other Faces. He wanted a string section to augment their overall sound, something which both McLagan and Wood thought unnecessary, 'because it wouldn't be rock 'n' roll any more, it wouldn't be The Faces, it would be crap'[4] and especially since McLagan could get a synthesiser which could replicate string parts closely enough for live work. He also wanted to bring in another guitarist, claiming that Wood's time with the Stones would have made him too much of a rhythm guitarist and not enough of a lead guitarist, something which had never bothered anyone in The Faces before and had certainly never held them back.

Despite McLagan's bloody-minded obstinacy, Stewart got his way. It was probably the case that McLagan, Jones and the unconsulted Yamauchi could see the writing on the wall as to the future of the group. Given that the writing was also on the billboards outside every gig, where the billing wasn't just 'Rod Stewart and The Faces' but read 'ROD STEWART and The Faces', they would have to have been blind to miss it.

The tour was to be a massive money-spinner, lasting two and a half months, over forty dates covering the whole of North America from New York to Los Angeles, from Hawaii to Toronto, Canada. And so on 15 August, The Faces took the stage at West Palm Beach Auditorium in Florida. For the first time they were officially Rod Stewart's backing group; for the first time they were augmented by a small string section conducted by Jimmy Horowitz, the man who had first put them in touch with Billy Gaff; and they were joined onstage by guitarist Jesse Ed Davis.

Once upon a time the five of them had been enough, but that was back when Ronnie Lane was still there, Stewart's 'true cockney sparrow', and the whole show was for the party and the laugh and the general, genuine, all-round fun of it all. It was a business now, or, more importantly, Rod Stewart was a business now.

'Getting back to The Faces that time [after touring with the Rolling Stones],' said Wood later, 'I realised how unprofessional we'd always been, and how much more organised the Stones were. In The Faces we'd all treated it too much as a laugh. The Stones had set lists and everything worked out beforehand, they knew exactly what they were going to do. They all worked together, they were the most professional band in the world. Spontaneity is all right, but for years in The Faces we never even used to work from a set list – you wouldn't know what number you were going to play next and we'd all be shouting at each other, "What number are we doing now?"'[5]

Despite all of this, The Faces could still rip the crowds up, and they did, all the way through the tour. This was their biggest-grossing tour in terms of money, attendances and casual mayhem. But there was absolutely no doubt any more that it had become the Rod Stewart show. Apart from his separate billing, he also took Britt Ekland with him everywhere, their faces adorning newspapers and magazines wherever they went.

'I suppose we are a fairly interesting couple,' Ekland told *Rolling Stone* magazine. 'I guess we are, or people wouldn't want to write about us or photograph us. That's OK. I don't mind. I think my life is really exciting ... It is important that people should know about you. Obviously they think that your life is a little more exciting than theirs, otherwise they wouldn't want to read about you. And if it isn't – you should make it a little more exciting.'[6]

Eckland rode with Stewart in his limousine. Ekland stayed with him in his hotel room. Now when there was trouble, Stewart was nowhere to be found because he was nowhere near it. Well, apart from one occasion in Hawaii, when the hotel had double-booked Stewart and Ekland's room with Jeff Wald, the manager and husband of singer Helen Reddy. A row developed where Wald swore at Ekland, and she and Stewart decided they couldn't be bothered to argue and instead headed back to Los Angeles. But not before Stewart and the other Faces drew on years of experience to sabotage the room. While Wald was arguing with the hotel management and Stewart and Ekland packed their bags, they flooded the bathroom, broke the phone, fatally weakened the legs of the bed and generally wrecked the room.

When Wald got into his new room and discovered it was a disaster area, he demanded The Faces be ejected from the hotel. When that didn't work, he physically attacked McLagan. The police were called, and with The Faces pulling their best 'working-class innocents' act ('who, me, guv?') they got away with it.

Another cloud hanging over the heads of The Faces was the position of Ron Wood. Speaking to *Creem* magazine (November 1975) he insisted that membership of the Stones was 'hardly an idea of any foundation. It's just an arrangement if I've got the time ... for instance, I've got to do a December tour of Europe with them for nine or ten days. We just work it out each time. And I don't think it will harm any relationship with The Faces. This working relationship between the two bands can only go on so long, but while there's no tension, and while it's helping both bands, it's no reason to make a major thing out of it.'

By the end of September, The Faces' tour was going so well that Stewart was moved to tell *Melody Maker*, 'At first it seemed like we would break up. But we're playing better, it sounds tighter. I'll be honest ... I think we'll stay together.'[7] By October he was almost exuberant.

'It dawned on me last night how good everybody in the group is,' said Stewart. 'So I'll tell you what. I'll change my mind from what I said a few nights ago. I'll be as bold as to say that even if Woody does leave – and he should make up his mind sooner or later, though I think that he genuinely does want to tour with both bands – even if he did join them, I think I would stay with the band. Find somebody else. Even if Woody does go. I'd miss him. Christ. But I've realised how good the others are ...

'I mean, I'd be willing to have a go at a Faces album. If I get another solo album done in December and if we go to Australia and Japan ... I think we should record there. Australia. There's one incredible studio in Sydney. If we did it nice and quiet, and thought about it. I just don't want anyone to be waiting for it, so they can knock it, which is what's always happened ... I think now we've had enough time to think about it, to look back at what we've done, we could create something really good ... I'd give anything to produce it. Or even get Tom Dowd or somebody in to produce it for us. I'd do it if I was asked. I really would, and I think I could get an album done in a month ... I'm willing to try.'[8]

This interview probably says more about the effects of extensive touring – especially when it's going well – on the human condition than of Stewart's future plans. Kenney Jones' response, when told of Stewart's plans to record in Australia, was wry.

'He just likes to confuse the press,' Jones told *Melody Maker*. 'I think it's OK now. [The Faces] will end when it's meant to end, but we're playing pretty good right now. I don't think about a break-up.'[9]

'Their last tour was pretty much a farewell tour,' remembers Robert Matheu. 'It wasn't billed as that but we kinda knew that that was going to be it. In the beginning of that fall tour, in September of '75, it must have been the second or third time that I'd met Ron Wood and they were getting ready for Toronto. I ended up spending a very long night that lasted for three days in the Sheraton Hotel with Ron Wood and Bobby Womack and I just had an amazingly good time. I was working at a Detroit radio station and I was just starting my involvement with *Creem* magazine and Ronnie Wood always loved *Creem*. I must have been seventeen. And they would just sit around and play guitars all night, and various other things we did back then …

'I think one of the nights we went to the Playboy Club and closed that down. I think Woody gave money to keep us there late. At about four in the morning we took all the girls back to the hotel room for another day or so. Ronnie was showing me wardrobe cases full of clothes that Mick Jagger had given him from that summer's Stones tour that Mick never wore. So he had all these great clothes And he'd be playing live tapes or tapes of these jam sessions, him and Jeff Beck. It was a good time. Because of that I got turned on to Bobby Womack 'cos I was never into that particular brand of American R&B music and I learned a lot from Wood about that.'

Notwithstanding Stewart's ideas regarding Australia and Jones' dispassionate assessment, The Faces did go into a studio in Nashville for a couple of days to cut some new material. Nothing ever came of it.

★

While The Faces had been fighting among themselves, the situation in Northern Ireland had changed. The IRA ceasefire which had come into force over Christmas 1974 had lasted into January, only to end with a series of bomb blasts in Belfast, London and Manchester at the end of January. However, a further 'truce' was declared in February, though this did not stop the spiral of explosions and shootings in Northern Ireland. During the summer and into the autumn, the trials took place of those accused of the pub bombings in Birmingham and Guildford the previous summer. Those convicted – the 'Birmingham Six' and the 'Guildford Four' – were released during the Nineties when their convictions were found to be unsafe.

And the autumn saw the bombs back in Britain – the IRA attacked the Hilton Hotel in London, an army barracks in Caterham, Oxford Street and Green Park underground station in London, murdered Ross McWhirter (an outspoken critic of IRA violence) at his home in Enfield, and threw a bomb into a restaurant in Walton Street, London. The sense of danger – especially in the capital – was all-pervasive.

Danger wasn't the preserve of Londoners, though; through the streets and buildings of Beirut, Lebanese right-wing Christians battled left-wing Muslims and Palestinian groups. Before long, the city would be devastated by the battles, and though the Lebanese were ultimately victorious and the Palestinians ejected from the city, Beirut would become a synonym for devastated cities everywhere.

The Faces didn't play in Britain in 1975, nor did they release any records. In their absence, the music sensations of 1975 were instead two other groups, the first a Swedish pop group called Abba, who had won the Eurovision Song Contest in 1974. Manufacturing highly produced, self-written, synthesised pop, they were by the end of the year a worldwide sensation following their massive hit 'SOS'.

The other group were five young lads from Scotland called the Bay City Rollers who produced bland teen anthems. Dressed in jump suits edged with tartan, complete with blow-waved hair and tartan scarves tied around their wrists, they looked like nothing less than Rod Stewart's bastard offspring, a cleaned-up version of Stewart's time with The Faces. Their song titles gave the game away – 'Shang-A-Lang', 'Bye Bye Baby' and 'Give A Little Love' were saccharin-sweet sops to teenage 'love', and they were hugely successful. 'Rollermania' was as much a national phenomena as 'Beatlemania' had been eleven years before.

'There was an awfully long time when there wasn't anything,' remembers Sue Westergaard. 'It was just soppy, with groups like Brotherhood of Man and the Bay City Rollers. It was awfully dull, dull stuff, nothing at all.'

In the meantime, David Bowie had dropped his 'other worldly' personas and had donned a 'soul-boy' suit and haircut to promote his slick, poppy *Young Americans* LP. It seemed that if even Bowie could be tamed and with Stewart ensconsed in Los Angeles, any menace that pop music had held seemed to have been neutered. The Faces – apparently the only defence against the encroaching monster of bland pop – were wobbling, and Kenney Jones' confidence seemed out of place.

It was probably never Jones' place to think about a break-up anyway. When the tour finished on 1 November 1975, there was no talk of a split. Rod Stewart simply made his way back to Beverly Hills along with Billy Gaff, who was now living in LA and proffering himself as Stewart's personal manager, Ron Wood made his way to Jamaica for a short holiday with Keith Richards before returning to Britain to rehearse for the Stones' tour, and Ian McLagan, Kenney Jones and a still disconnected Tetsu Yamauchi made their way back to England. The music press still wanted to talk to The Faces about their future and McLagan and Jones were happy to talk about what they knew was happening – which was nothing, but with the vague outline of possible plans. In actuality, they were just waiting for Stewart to take himself out of their misery.

And to round off the year neatly, the *Daily Mirror* of 19 December 1975 bore the headline, 'Why Rock Star Rod Is Quitting The Faces.' Stewart, the *Mirror* reported, had said, 'I have only just made up my mind. But I'm definitely quitting this time.'

Stewart's press officer, Tony Toon, commented, 'Rod feels he can no longer work in a situation where the group's lead guitarist Ron Wood seems to be permanently "on loan" to the Rolling Stones.'

Billy Gaff waded in with, 'Rod thinks the world of Ron Wood. I have repeatedly tried to telephone Ron, who is touring with the Rolling Stones. I have left messages for him to call me, but I've heard nothing.'

McLagan added, 'I won't believe he is leaving The Faces until I hear it from his own lips.'

And Jones' contribution was a pragmatic, 'If this means the end of The Faces, I'm not bothered. I expect I will survive.'

No-one bothered to ask Yamauchi what he thought, and Wood was presumed lost somewhere in Europe with the Rolling Stones, which he was, trying to decide whether to make his stay with the Rolling Stones permanent.

'I got an English newspaper,' Wood told the BBC, 'and it said, "Rod Stewart Quits Faces" and I thought, "Well, that makes my decision simple, then – I'll just stay here."'[10]

McLagan remembered later that it was typical of Stewart's general attitude at that time. 'It was, "Pull the ladder up, I'm all right, grab the headline and fuck 'em all save one,"' he wrote later.

'Merry Christmas, Rod.'[11]

# EPILOGUE

# 'LAST ORDERS, PLEASE'

'There was this terrible trough in the mid-Seventies,' remembers singer and songwriter Billy Bragg. 'England didn't qualify for the 1974 World Cup, Miss Hall our English teacher left school, and The Faces split.'[1]

By the end of 1975, Britain was on the cusp of fundamental change. The welfare state, which had underpinned the social fabric of the country for almost thirty years, was creaking at the seams as rising unemployment, inflation and disputes between government and trade unions put it under strain. Bolstered by their success in bringing down the Conservative government in 1974, the trade unions' relationship with the government was again on the verge of breaking down. Harold Wilson, the dominant figure in British politics for a decade, would resign within a year to be replaced by James Callaghan, who as Chancellor had devalued the pound in 1967.

Margaret Thatcher, still unproven as leader of the Conservative Party, was trying to move out of the shadow of Ted Heath, still highly visible due to the referendum on the Common Market. Heath had made no secret of the fact that he was bitter about being ousted from the leadership of the Conservative Party, but Thatcher was already beginning to make noises about 'thrift, patriotism, self-help, hard work and responsibility to family',[2] which, allied to the complete breakdown of relations between government and unions later in the decade would sweep her to power.

'In the Sixties you could not imagine there being a Thatcher or that type of government,' says Dave Phillips. 'That type of politics seemed dead and buried. I think it was a reflection of our own hubris; we had very little experience and we were projecting out of a very narrow experience and we simply couldn't comprehend the scale of the forces that were at work. Things in the first half of the Seventies were just dreary and in the second half they got bad because things just got worse and worse. It just became like the 1940s really.'

Dick Hebdige sees the shift from the Sixties to the Seventies as predicated on the prevalence of certain drugs. 'My theory about the 1960s is that the whole thing ran on speed,' he recalls. 'Everybody from archetypal "alienated housewives" ("Mother's Little Helper") to military personnel, to anorexics to people with mild weight problems, to the art/fashion/music crowds, to students and professors writing papers, to prize fighters, bank blaggers, wages snatchers and stick-up men, to Soho Mods and Brighton Mods and Welwyn Garden City Mods and Mods in Leeds and Glasgow and Huddersfield and Newcastle were leaping about for most of that decade on uppers. Even Andy Warhol's "Factory" in New York ran on speed (he said he made *Sleep* in which a clique member is filmed snoozing for eight hours because he regarded sleep as a dying art). Dexedrine, ephedrine, amphetamine and its infinite derivatives fuelled the Sixties and shaped, at a physiological level, the entire febrile 1960s structure of feeling: the rabid neophilia, the nervousness, the multiple neuroses, the permanent sense of impending entropy, the persistent undertow of sadism and violence, the impatience with stasis and the past, the obsession with action and with making things happen. After the rush, the come down. I don't think amphetamine dependency is sustainable over long periods of time for individuals without a crack up or heart failure. The same, no doubt, applies to an entire amphetamine-dependent cultural formation.'

Not everything went badly during the period immediately following the end of The Faces. The 1975 Equal Opportunities Act went some way towards improving the position of women in Britain, and, perhaps more importantly, it helped to change the cultural climate that women were forced to live within.

'I remember that changing and shifting a lot during and after the Punk era,' recalls Lucy O'Brien. 'My generation were in the vanguard of not getting married immediately and not having children immediately and going to university and having a career. I think that by 1980 it was five years after the Equal Opportunities Act and that's when it really started to kick in, that feeling of, "Well, we can do what we want, we can be lawyers, we can be doctors."'

America, shell-shocked by the twin blows of Vietnam and the implosion of Richard Nixon's presidency, looked to simpler things from a simpler time with the emergence of 'the future of rock 'n' roll': at the end of 1975, Bruce Springsteen was hailed as rock's saviour and the 1976 presidential election saw former peanut farmer and Democratic Party candidate Jimmy Carter gain power.

★

Back in London, four old friends reunited to appear in a promotional film to help sell an eight-year-old song to new fans. Bereft of a lead singer for the second time in five years, the Small Faces turned to Steve Marriott and a re-released 'Itchycoo Park' in a short-lived attempt to revitalise their careers. Even Ronnie Lane was back on board for a while.

In another part of London, however, a group of young Faces fans – using some equipment and songs stolen from The Faces – were cranking out the first chords of a musical revolution that would explode over London and the world in the following year. Rehearsing at the end of the King's Road, John Lydon, Paul Cook, Steve Jones and Glen Matlock – the Sex Pistols – were beginning their long march to infamy by churning out their own versions of 'What'cha Gonna Do About It', 'All Or Nothing' and the songs Rod and The Faces used to cover.

And it wasn't just Wood who stayed where he was. Stewart also stayed where he was, in Los Angeles, living the 'celebrity couple' life with Britt Ekland. He asked Kenney Jones to tour with him in 1976, but Jones withdrew at the last moment in a gesture of solidarity to Ian McLagan. Meanwhile, Tetsu Yamauchi simply withdrew into obscurity.

★

The dreary sameness of life in Britain simply carried on. But it would carry on without The Faces. 'All the people who started the Punk bands were the people who were listening to The Faces, though there's no connection,' says Chris Sparks. 'If you think about the age group, people like The Clash, all their resentments, all the things they talk about in 1977 is the stuff that goes on during 1971, '72 and so on.' And for that generation, The Faces – along with David Bowie – were their only respite from the unending drabness.

'As a kid trying to get in a band you'd look at them and think, "They get up to all that? Sounds great!"' remembered Sex Pistol Glen Matlock.

'That's what you British boys liked about The Faces,' says Robert Matheu. 'It's the "lads" thing.'

But their position in music history has now been relegated to that of a backing group for Stewart. 'They were all unlucky to be in the band except Rod Stewart, who was just completely lucky,' says Chris Sparks, 'because he ended up fronting a band of really grade-A musicians, which they were – each and every one of them is still a grade-A musician and talented songwriter. He wouldn't have got anywhere without them. Without him they could have been great. They got lost in that Rod Stewart image – not a Mod, not a hippy, not a rock 'n' roller. He's never had a base in any kind of subculture which all the other bands had. He's a nothing man.'

Jonno Pavitt sees Stewart in an equally dull light. 'If the Small Faces had carried on, who knows what would have happened?' he argues. 'The difference between The Faces and the Small Faces was Rod Stewart. And Rod Stewart took himself far too seriously. And he seemed to me to be somebody who was in it for what he could get out of it. I don't think he was in it for the music, even though he probably loved it. And anyone who wears a straw boater hat a few years later ...

'Look at Marriott – when Humble Pie were bigger in America than they were here, he didn't do all the things that Rod Stewart did. Another difference between Steve Marriott and Rod Stewart is that if you listen to the lyrics, you've got lots of Marriott songs that say, "Would you still love me if I wasn't a big, rich, famous guy? Would you marry me anyway?" How many of them just say "I need loving?" They're really not self-assured. Anything by Rod Stewart, he just expects birds to love him. Rod Stewart's got that big, brash, "I'm better than you are" attitude. Steve Marriott is more, "I am rich and famous and that, but I'm still not quite sure."'

Lucy O'Brien doesn't agree. 'I think Rod Stewart made The Faces pop stars,' she argues. 'He was always the pop star. It's that thing about charisma and how he operates and he is "the star". And the rest are the satellites. He's got front, so there he was fronting the band, and he took them and made them legendary. He's got a great voice 'cos it's so distinctive. It's got a lot of soul in it, but it's so utterly recognisable. He sort of lost the plot, really, after *Atlantic Crossing*.'

Stewart's own assessment of The Faces is also more positive. 'I think we'd gone the distance,' he says. 'The five years we had together were like a marriage. It's better to be together five years than twenty boring years. We had five brilliant years together. I have no regrets whatsoever.'[3]

★

Regardless of Stewart's decision to go to America or Wood's decision to go to the Stones, The Faces had, in their own way, lit up British pop music for five years.

'That's the nature of them. That's what's so glorious about them,' says Lucy O'Brien. 'They didn't hang around like Dire Straits or something trying to make album after album after album. They had those glorious years and the whole thing imploded because that was the nature of them. They were so fierce and full-on. It had its time and that was it. It's a bit like the two series of *Fawlty Towers*, it's that British thing, you sort of do it and that's it, you don't have to keep milking it. I'm sure the various members would have wanted it a different way, but I suppose Rod Stewart broke up the party.'

But if nothing else, the music that Stewart made in the early Seventies, both with The Faces and apart from them, helped to define an era for a generation which would subsequently attempt to wipe it all away in the amphetamine ferocity that was Punk rock.

'[The Faces] were a bit of a blueprint, really,' says O'Brien. 'Before Punk it drifted into pub rock with Dr Feelgood and bands like that. They were a similar tradition, drawing on R&B and quite speedy, that speedy culture with that Celtic thing going on in there as well. Early Punk was very Mod anyway in its influences.'

For many of those who lived the arc of The Faces' career, though, it is all very different. 'I haven't got anything by The Faces now,' says Chris Sparks. 'I've done that thing of buying old CDs, I've got *Led Zeppelin I* – not that I listen to it, but I've got it – but I would never go and get a Faces CD 'cos they're just bleak, they're just a bleak experience.'

When The Faces split, **Ian McLagan** found himself to be an in-demand keyboard player. He went on to play with Bob Dylan, the Rolling Stones and Keith Richards' New Barbarians among others, before recording his own solo album and touring in his own right with the Bump Band. During the Nineties, McLagan also found himself in demand by younger musicians, and worked with Billy Bragg and Paul Weller among others. He went on to write a success-ful autobiography in the late Nineties. He currently lives in Austin, Texas, when he's not on tour.

**Kenney Jones**' assessment that he would be OK after The Faces was correct. Following the demise of the reformed Small Faces and the death of Keith Moon, Kenney Jones joined The Who and stayed with them until they split in the early Eighties. After a brief band project – The Law – Jones took a break from the music business, though he was at the fore-front of the Small Faces' successful legal battles to receive their royalties. He now runs a polo club in Surrey. He still occasionally records.

After his time as a Face, **Ron Wood** continued to stay quite happily where he was. Still a Rolling Stone, he also recorded and toured in his own right, his most notable albums being *Gimme Some Neck*, released in 1979, and *Not For Beginners*, released in 2001. Wood has also appeared as a guest for numerous other artists including Bob Dylan and George Harrison. His artwork is in demand, and he still lives in Richmond with his family. There are no signs of Ron Wood leaving the group.

**Tetsu Yamauchi**'s post-Faces career is as well documented as his pre-Faces career. He lives in Japan and continues to work.

Following his announcement that he was leaving the Faces, **Rod Stewart** put together a new band and continued to release commercially successful singles and albums throughout the Seventies and Eighties. His later work, however, was not well received by the critics. Stewart's departure to America and 'superstardom' just before the explosion on to the world of Punk (which he and The Faces had unintentionally aided) left those in Britain with the suspicion that Stewart had sold out, though a vast army of fans around the world never lost their love for him.

'Everyone hates Rod Stewart because he wore that straw boater and sang "Hot Legs",' says Jonno Pavitt. 'And he sang "Sailing". And he wore Lycra. A lot of people probably heard of him through The Faces, and they thought he was one of the lads. Which he – now – so obviously wasn't. He was the football fans' favourite – you went straight from watching football to go and see The Faces. And then you realised that he was just totally in it for the money.'

Robert Matheu has another theory for some of Stewart's sartorial mistakes. 'After working with and going to see Rod live for twenty-seven years, I had no idea that he's actually colour-blind,' he says. 'I was photographing him for *Mojo* magazine and he came down in this suit with a dreadful shirt, and I said, "I like the suit but not the shirt." He went back up to change and his manager said, "Well, after all, he is colour-blind." Well, that would explain most of the Eighties.'

During the late Nineties, Stewart attempted to recapture his early, more gritty appeal through a series of albums which began with *Unplugged and Seated*, a live set recorded for MTV where he was reunited with Ronnie Wood. He also revisited his days with The Faces when he finally sang Ronnie Lane's 'Ooh La La', and on the album *When We Were the New Boys* he covered material written by Nineties bands including Skunk Anansie and Oasis.

'Rod's appeal over the years is that he's the fella at the pub down the road, the guy next door,' says John Baldry. 'But the Rod Stewart that I know is much more unique than that.'[4]

'He comes across very confident,' says Ron Wood, 'but underneath he still gets nervous, very worried, he still wants to give his best. Which is a great thing for someone who just doesn't take it for granted. He still puts his heart and soul into it when he can. Rod can still cut it ... he just needs a kick up the arse.'[5] Despite a brush with throat cancer for which he had surgery in the late Nineties, Rod Stewart continues to write, record and tour and he divides his time between his homes in Los Angeles and Essex.

★

After walking out on the Small Faces, **Steve Marriott** formed Humble Pie with Peter Frampton, and the group enjoyed success both in the UK and in America. When that folded he formed the All Stars which included Alexis Korner, before recording a patchy solo LP. Marriott joined McLagan, Lane and Jones for the brief Small Faces reunion, ostensibly to make a promotional film to support a re-released 'Itchycoo Park'. Ronnie Lane was not interested in a long-term reunion, but the other Small Faces – sans Ronnie Lane – stayed together for two LPs, *Playmates* released in 1977 and *Seventy-Eight in the Shade* released in 1978. Both albums vanished into the void created by Punk, which had burst into the consciousness not just of the music business but of the country as a whole. Although the Small Faces were heroes to many involved with Punk, their time was seen to have passed. 'The Small Faces went through a stage when they weren't important,' says Jonno Pavitt. 'I think that's because everybody else was being all pompous. In the early Eighties and Nineties when everybody was "I am, I am, I am," they weren't important.'

When the reunion ended, Marriott reformed Humble Pie for a couple of albums in the early Eighties. Through the remainder of the Eighties Marriott went on the road with his own groups, Packet of Three, the Next Band and the DTs, churning out his own brand of British R&B and Small Faces songs to old fans and those too young to remember him first time around.

'Any man who finishes off a song by saying "I'm just a fat, bald, sweating midget" doesn't take himself too seriously,' says Pavitt, who went to watch Marriott's gigs regularly during the Eighties and Nineties. 'And when he sang it you'd think, "But we all wish we were." Any man who can make you wish you were a sweaty, bald midget as well can't be all bad. He just made you wish you'd seen him with a better backing band, really. The energy that this guy could still give.'

Following a new, short collaboration with Frampton in America, where Marriott was yet again attempting to reconstruct Humble Pie, Steve Marriott died tragically in a fire at his home in Arkesden, Essex, on 20 April 1991. He was forty-four years old.

'I cried when I found out he'd died,' says Pavitt. 'Just because I wouldn't be able to go and see him play again. Well, that and half a dozen Fosters. If he'd lived longer, he'd be huge now. When all that Brit Pop came in in the mid-Nineties, he would've ridden in on the back of that. He would've been this likable old uncle. I reckon that Paul Weller has got all the love and affection from the generation that Marriott would've got back if he'd been alive. I think that when you're young and you like a band, you think that anything before that time doesn't exist, and anything that goes on after that time, you think they're copying the band that you liked.

'So a lot of people now will base it on The Jam, and now they've moved on to that Ocean Colour Scene thing as well. And what they want is somebody who sounds like The Jam, so they go on to Ocean Colour Scene. And what people got with The Jam is that they sounded and looked like the Small Faces. And I don't know who you'd have had before that. 'Cos the Small Faces were doing black R&B, and you weren't going to get that in Stepney, were you? So Weller's probably the guy who's benefited most out of all this.

'The Small Faces were important because the other big bands like The Beatles got into that "political" stuff, like "Working Class Hero" and stuff, and the Rolling Stones – Keith Richards aside – became mansion house-owning stadium rockers. But the Small Faces, possibly 'cos of the time they split up, just seemed to be into it for the money, the music, the drugs, the fun. I think when the fun stopped is when they did. The reason I still think the Small Faces are magnificent is Steve Marriott's voice. And that's all there is to it. Full stop.'

★

When his time with The Faces ended, **Ronnie Lane** put his own band together, called Slim Chance. After some initial success, he took the band on the road on the ambitious Passing Show tour, complete with a circus tent, clowns and fire-eaters. Although it was well received critically, the show was a huge drain financially and Lane eventually had to close it down. He recorded three albums with Slim Chance, *Anymore for Anymore*, *Ronnie Lane's Slim Chance* and *One for the Road* before splitting the group. He recorded an album with Pete Townshend, named *Rough Mix*, which was critically well received.

Diagnosed with multiple sclerosis in 1977, Lane began to withdraw from the music business, though he did release a further solo LP, *See Me*. He was involved in the organisation of a series of high-profile concerts to raise money for Action for Research into Multiple Sclerosis and did continue to record and occasionally play live. Increasingly affected by the symptoms of the debilitating disease, Lane moved to America to get away from the English weather, eventually winding up in Trinidad, Colorado. He appeared at a couple of Faces' live reunions, most notably at the Brit Awards in 1993 when Rolling Stone Bill Wyman took over the seriously ill Lane's role on bass.

In common with many other musicians from the Sixties and early Seventies, Lane and the other Small Faces were forced to go to court in order to obtain royalty and other payments they were due. Before their successful court case, when the huge financial cost of his treatment spiralled beyond Lane's means, his old partners-in-crime, Rod Stewart and Ron Wood, helped him out.

'When Ronnie's health really deteriorated it was Ronnie Wood and Rod Stewart,' recalled McLagan. 'They both paid for all his medical bills and chipped in financially. Carte blanche. Whenever Ronnie wanted. Which just goes to show that you're in a band like Faces or the Small Faces and you're in it for ever.'[6]

'Yeah, well, you obviously take care of someone if they're ill,' says Wood. 'And if they're hurting for money and then you've got some, then yeah.'[7]

Ronnie Lane's health continued to deteriorate throughout the Nineties, and on 4 July 1997 he finally succumbed to the disease aged 51.

'He's better now,' says McLagan. 'He's dancing. He's doing the Ronnie Lane strut in the sky.'[8]

★

Despite regular rumours that The Faces would reform for a tour or one-off shows, little ever materialised. And, given Stewart's analogy with a marriage, it's probably for the best – remarriages rarely work, and Stewart himself had moved so far from the group's origins that reconciliation was never on the cards. As ever with pop groups, re-examining their story is difficult – trite comments about 'what we're left with is their music' are irrelevant and cretinous, since popular music is a product of its time no matter how good the music may appear in retrospect. But then we also have to deal with the arrogance of pop music, peddled by those who argue bizarrely and unrelent-ingly as if it could really last for ever, especially during periods when the music is uninventive, uninnovative and unimportant.

The most pernicious argument they peddle is that pop music will resurrect itself. This is clearly nonsense. As a branch of music in general (from Bach to Irish folk tunes), pop music arrived late and offered little. Though, it should be said, this is not to diminish in any way the work of Lennon and McCartney, nor Marriott and Lane, nor Stewart and Wood (on a good day), nor any of those writers and performers who have brought us songs that we remember and cher-ish. Pop music is always of its time and – more importantly – is always, always the preserve of those people who bought it and the lifestyle that went with it.

The Faces were of their time, and in the end their most important legacy in terms of pop music is that they (unwittingly) held a foot in the rapidly closing door of popular culture that Punk rock would later kick open. It may seem ironic now, but Rod Stewart was a folk hero to many involved in the last, great, British youth subculture (Punk).

But that still leaves the problem of how to sum up the Faces. Perhaps it's better not to – not least because the surviving Faces are much as they were: Woody's still a Stone, Mac's still playing Hammond, Kenney's still doing okay and Rod – well, he's still Rod. And finally there's Ronnie Lane, Rod's 'cockney sparrow', the Face who couldn't deal with their success and bailed out first. Mac put it best: he's still doing 'the Ronnie Lane strut in the sky.'

# CODA

# LONG PLAYER

Back in the Glasgow tower block - the flat no longer rented but bought in the 'Right-To-Buy' frenzy of the mid-Eighties - there are now hundreds of channels on satellite TV, but they're all still shite, just like it was in the Seventies. In a corner of the living-room, next to the Dolby 5.1 Surround Sound CD-DVD music system, rests a rack full of old vinyl LPs, dusty, unplayed and ignored for years. Hidden among them are albums by David Bowie, the Clash, the Jam, and, some-where, The Faces and Rod Stewart, but nowadays there's no record player to play them on any more, the CD- player having long-since assumed precedence. And, like every-one else, we're all sitting around watching crap-TV when, abruptly, on *Top of the Pops 2*, there's *Maggie May*, and then it's Rod and the Faces again, strutting and posing and cavorting, and suddenly the volume's whacked up and somehow everything feels right for once and we're up on our feet again for the sake of *Auld Lang Syne*, singing along, whooping the words, wishing the haircut, the attitude and the birds, and then every-body's laughing at the kid tottering in his pyjamas …

# DISCOGRAPHY

This discography is not exhaustive and is based around releases relevant to this book.


## STEVE MARRIOTT

### Single
Give Her My Regards / Imaginary Love
    (released 1963, Decca F11619)


## THE BIRDS

### Singles
You Don't Love Me (You Don't Care) / You're On My Mind
    (released 1964, Decca F12031)
Next In Line / Leaving Here
    (released 1965, Decca F12140)
No Good Without You Baby / How Can It Be
    (released 1965, Decca F12257)

## THE MULESKINNERS

### Singles

Back Door Man / Need Your Lovin'
   (released 1965, Fontana TF527)


## SMALL FACES

### Singles

What'cha Gonna Do About It / What's A Matter Baby
   (released 1965, Decca F12276)
Sha La La La Lee / Grow Your Own
   (released 1966, Decca F12317)
Hey Girl / Almost Grown
   (released 1966, Decca F12393)
All Or Nothing / Understanding
   (released 1966, Decca F12470)
My Mind's Eye / I Can't Dance With You
   (released 1966, Decca F12500)
I Can't Make It / Just Passing
   (released 1967, Decca F12565)
Patterns / E Too D
   (released 1967, Decca F12619)
Here Comes The Nice / Talk To You
   (released 1967, Immediate IM050)
Itchycoo Park / I'm Only Dreaming
   (released 1967, Immediate IM057)
Tin Soldier / I Feel Much Better
   (released 1967, Immediate IM062)

Lazy Sunday / Rolling Over
  (released 1968, Immediate IM064)
The Universal / Donkey Rides, A Penny A Glass
  (released 1968, Immediate IM069)
Afterglow (Of Your Love) / Wham Bam Thank You Mam
  (released 1969, Immediate IM077)

## Albums

*Small Faces*

(released 1966, Decca LK4790)

Shake / Come On Children / You Better Believe It / It's Too Late / One Night Stand / What'cha Gonna Do About It / Sorry She's Mine / Own Up / You Need Loving / Don't Stop What You Are Doing / E Too D / Sha La La La Lee

*From the Beginning*

(released 1967, Decca LK4879)

Runaway / My Mind's Eye / Yesterday, Today and Tomorrow / That Man / My Way Of Giving / Hey Girl / Tell Me Have You Ever Seen Me / Take This Hurt Off Me / All Or Nothing / Baby Don't Do It / Plum Nellie / Sha-la-la-la-lee / You've Really Got A Hold On Me / What'cha Gonna Do About It

*Small Faces*

(released 1967, Immediate IMLP008)

(Tell Me) Have You Ever Seen Me / Something I Want To Tell You / Feeling Lonely / Happy Boys Happy / Things Are Going To Get Better / My Way Of Giving / Green Circles / Become Like You / Get Yourself Together / All Our Yesterdays / Talk To You / Show Me The Way / Up The Wooden Hills To Bedfordshire / Eddie's Dreaming

*Ogden's Nut Gone Flake*
(released 1968, Immediate IMLP012)
Ogden's Nut Gone Flake / Afterglow / Long Ago And Worlds Apart / Rene / Song Of A Baker / Lazy Sunday / Happiness Stan / Rollin' Over / The Hungry Intruder / The Journey / Mad John / Happy Days Toy Town

*The Autumn Stone*
(released 1969, Immediate IMAL012)
Here Come The Nice / Autumn Stone / Collibosher / All Or Nothing (live) / Red Balloon / Lazy Sunday / Rollin' Over (live) / If I Were A Carpenter (live) / Every Little Bit Hurts (live) / My Mind's Eye / Tin Soldier / Just Passing / Call It Something Nice / I Can't Make It / Afterglow / Sha La La La Lee / The Universal / Itchycoo Park / Hey Girl / Wide Eyed Girl On The Wall / What'cha Gonna Do About It / Wham Bam Thank You Mam

## JEFF BECK/ JEFF BECK GROUP

**Singles**
Tallyman / Rock My Plimsoul
    (released 1967, Columbia DB8227)
Love Is Blue / I've Been Drinking
    (released 1968, Columbia DB8359)

**Albums**
*Truth*
(released 1968, Columbia SCX6293)
Shapes Of Things / Let Me Love You / Morning Dew / You Shook Me

/ Ol' Man River / Greensleeves / Rock My Plimsoul / Beck's Bolero
/ Blues De Luxe / I Ain't Superstitious

*Beck-Ola*
(released 1969, Columbia SCX6351)
All Shook Up / Spanish Boots / Girl From Mill Valley / Jailhouse
Rock / Plynth (Water Down The Drain) / The Hangman's Knee / Rice
Pudding

## ROD STEWART

### Singles
Good Morning Little Schoolgirl /
 I'm Gonna Move To The Outskirts Of Town
    (released 1964, Decca F11996)
The Day Will Come / Why Does It Go On
    (released 1965, Columbia DB7766)
Shake / I Just Got Some
    (released 1966, Columbia DB7892)
Little Misunderstood / So Much To Say
    (released 1968, Immediate IM60)
Handbags And Gladrags / Man Of Constant Sorrow
    (released 1970, Mercury 73031)
In A Broken Dream / Doing Fine (with Python Lee Jackson)
    (released 1970, Youngblood YB1017)
Reason To Believe / Maggie May
    (released 1971, Mercury 73224)
You Wear It Well / Lost Paraguayos
    (released 1972, Mercury 6052 171)

Angel / What Made Milwaukee Famous (Has Made A Loser Out Of Me)
(released 1972, Mercury 6052 198)

Oh No Not My Baby / Jodie
(released 1973, Mercury 6052 371)

Farewell / Bring It On Home To Me – You Send Me
(released 1974, Mercury 6167 033)

It's All Over Now / Handbags And Gladrags
(released 1975, Mercury 6167 327)

Sailing / Stone Cold Sober
(released 1975, Warner Bros K16600)

This Old Heart Of Mine / All In The Name Of Rock 'N' Roll
(released 1975, 7 Riva 1)

**Albums**

*An Old Raincoat Won't Ever Let You Down*
(released 1970, Vertigo VO4)
Street Fighting Man / Man Of Constant Sorrow / Blind Prayer / Handbags And Gladrags / An Old Raincoat Won't Ever Let You Down / I Wouldn't Ever Change A Thing / Cindy's Lament / Dirty Old Town

*Gasoline Alley*
(released 1970, Vertigo 6360 500)
Gasoline Alley / It's All Over Now / Only A Hobo / My Way Of Giving / Country Comfort / Cut Across Shorty / Lady Day / Jo's Lament / You're My Girl (I Don't Want To Discuss It)

*Every Picture Tells a Story*
(released 1971, Mercury 6338)
Every Picture Tells A Story / Seems Like A Long Time / That's All

Right / Tomorrow Is A Long Time / Maggie May / Mandolin Wind / (I Know) I'm Losing You / (Find A) Reason To Believe

*Never a Dull Moment*
(released 1972, Mercury 6499 163)
True Blue / Lost Paraguayos / Mama, You Been On My Mind / Italian Girls / Angel / Interludings / You Wear It Well / I'd Rather Go Blind / Twistin' The Night Away

*Sing It Again, Rod*
(released 1973, Mercury 6499 484)
Reason To Believe / You Wear It Well / Mandolin Wind / Country Comfort / Maggie May / Handbags And Gladrags / Street Fighting Man / Twistin' The Night Away / Lost Paraguayos / (I Know) I'm Losing You / Pinball Wizard / Gasoline Alley

*Smiler*
(released 1974, Mercury 9104 001)
Sweet Little Rock 'N' Roller / Lochinvar / Farewell / Sailor / Bring It On Home To Me / You Send Me / Let Me Be Your Car / (You Make Me Feel Like) A Natural Man / Dixie Toot / Hard Road / I've Grown Accustomed To Her Face / Girl From The North Country / Mine For Me

*Atlantic Crossing*
(released 1975, Warner Bros K56151)
Three Time Loser/ Alright For An Hour / All In The Name Of Rock 'N' Roll / Drift Away / Stone Cold Sober / I Don't Want To Talk About It / It's Not The Spotlight / This Old Heart Of Mine / Still Love You / Sailing

## FACES

### Singles

Flying / Three Button Hand Me Down
    (released 1970, Warner Bros WB8005)
Had Me A Real Good Time / Rear Wheel Skid
    (released 1970, Warner Bros WB8018)
Stay With Me / Debris
    (released 1972, Warner Bros K16136)
Cindy Incidentally / Skewiff (Mend The Fuse)
    (released 1973, Warner Bros K16247)
Poolhall Richard / I Wish It Would Rain
    (released 1973, Warner Bros K16341)
Cindy Incidentally / Memphis / Stay With Me / Poolhall Richard
    (released 1974, Warner Bros K16406)
You Can Make Me Dance, Sing Or Anything / As Long As You Tell Him
    (released 1974, Warner Bros K16494)

### Albums

*First Step*

(released 1970, Warner Bros WS3000)

Wicked Messenger / Devotion / Shake, Shudder, Shiver / Stone / Around The Plynth / Flying / Pineapple And The Monkey / Nobody Knows / Looking Out The Window / Three Button Hand Me Down

*Long Player*

(released 1971, Warner Bros WS3011)

Bad 'N' Ruin / Tell Everyone / Sweet Lady Mary / Richmond / Maybe I'm Amazed / Had Me A Real Good Time / On The Beach / I Feel So Good / Jerusalem

*A Nod is as Good as a Wink to a Blind Horse*
(released 1972, Warner Bros K56006)
Miss Judy's Farm / You're So Rude / Love Lives Here / Last Orders
Please / Stay With Me / Debris / Memphis (Tennessee) / Too Bad /
That's All You Need

*Ooh La La*
(released 1973, Warner Bros K56011)
Silicone Grown / Cindy Incidentally / Flags And Banners / My Fault
/ Borstal Boys / Fly In The Ointment / If I'm On The Late Side / Glad
And Sorry / Just Another Honky / Ooh La La

*Coast to Coast/Overture and Beginners*
(released 1974, Mercury 9100 001)
It's All Over Now / Cut Across Shorty / Too Bad / Every Picture Tells
A Story / Angel / Stay With Me / I Wish It Would Rain / I'd Rather
Go Blind / Borstal Boys / Amazing Grace / Jealous Guy

## RONNIE WOOD

**Singles**
I Can Feel The Fire / Breathe On Me
    (released 1974, Warner Bros K16463)
If You Don't Want My Love / I Got A Feeling
    (released 1975, Warner Bros K16618)

**Albums**

*I've Got My Own Album to Do*

(released 1974, Warner Bros K56065)

I Can Feel The Fire / Far East Man / Mystifies Me / Take A Look At The Guy / Act Together / Am I Grooving You / Shirley / Cancel Everything / Sure The One You Need / If You Got To Make A Fool Of Somebody / Crotch Music

*Now Look*

(released 1975, Warner Bros K56145)

I Got Lost When I Found You / Big Bayou / Breathe On Me / If You Don't Want My Love / I Can Say She's Alright / Caribbean Boogie / Now Look / Sweet Baby Mine / I Can't Stand The Rain / It's Unholy / I Got A Feeling

**KENNEY JONES**

**Single**

Ready Or Not / Woman Trouble

    (released 1974, GM GMS027)

# BIBLIOGRAPHY

Bangs, L. (1988) *Psychotic Reactions and Carburetor Dung*. Vintage Books.

Baybutt, A. (producer/ director) (2001) *Rod Stewart: Wine, Women and Song*. BBC TV.

Bradley, L. (1999) *Rod Stewart: Every Picture Tells a Story*. Aurum Press.

Brown, L. (producer, Granada TV) (1995) *My Generation: The Small Faces*. Channel 4 TV.

Carson, A. (2001) *Jeff Beck: Crazy Fingers*. Backbeat Books.

Cox, R., Russell, D. and Vamplew, W. (2002) *Encyclopedia of British Football*. Frank Cass.

Davis, S. (1985) *Hammer of the Gods*. Pan Books.

Dellar, F. (1981) *NME Guide to Rock Cinema*. Hamlyn.

Frith, S. and Goodwin, A. (eds) (1990) *On Record*. Routledge.

Gorman, P. (2001) *In Their Own Write*. Sanctuary.

Hattersley, R. (1997) *Fifty Years On*. Abacus.

Hebdige, D. (1979) *Subculture: The Meaning of Style*. Methuen.

Hennessy, P. (1992) *Never Again*. Vintage.

Hewitt, P. (1995) *Small Faces: The Young Mods' Forgotten Story*. Acid Jazz.

Kureishi, H. and Savage, J. (1995) *The Faber Book of Pop*. Faber & Faber.

Levy, S. (2002) *Ready, Steady, Go!* Fourth Estate.

Lydon, J. (1993) *Rotten*. Coronet Books.

McLagan, I. (1998) *All the Rage*. Sidgwick & Jackson.

Miller, J. (1999) *Almost Grown*. William Heinemann.

Napier-Bell, S. (2001) *Black Vinyl White Powder*. Ebury Press.

Norman, P. (1982) *Shout!* Corgi Books.

O'Brien, L. (1995) *She-Bop*. Penguin.

Pidgeon, J. (1976) *Rod Stewart and the Changing Faces*. Panther.

Rawlings, T. (1999) *Rock on Wood*. Boxtree.

Sabin, R. (ed.) (1999) *Punk Rock So What?* Routledge.

Savage, J. (1991) *England's Dreaming*. Faber & Faber.

Shelton, R. (1986) *No Direction Home*. Penguin.

Sked, A. and Cook, C. (1993) *Post-War Britain*. Penguin.

Thompson, H. (series producer) (1996) *Dancing in the Street*. BBC TV.

Twelker, U. and Schmitt, R. (2002) *The Small Faces and Other Stories*. Sanctuary.

Whitburn, J. (1995) *The Billboard Book of Top 40 Albums*. Billboard.

http://www.creemmedia.com

# NOTES

**Chapter 1: Never Had It So Good**

1. Reported in Hennessey (1995), p. 275.

2. *NME* interview, 1971.

3. Quoted in Hewitt (1995), p. 26.

4. Ibid.

5. Ibid., p. 29.

**Chapter 2: A Chaotic Lesson in Bullshitting**

1. Quoted in Levy (2002), p. 199.

2. Brown (1995).

3. Hebdige (1979), p. 52.

4. Ibid.

5. Quoted in Hewitt (1995), p. 151.

6. Ibid., p. 26.

7. Quoted in Twelker and Schmitt (2002), p. 29.

8. Quoted in Hewitt (1995), p. 27.

9. Quoted in Pidgeon (1976), p. 12.

10. Ibid.

11. Ibid.

12. Quoted in Pidgeon (1976), p. 13.

13. Quoted in Hewitt (1995), p. 40.

14. Quoted in Baybutt (2001).

15. Ibid.

16. Ibid.

17. Quoted in Pidgeon (1976), p. 47.

18. Quoted in Rawlings (1999).

**Chapter 3: The Stonedest Men in Town**

1. Quoted in Hewitt (1995), p. 42.

2. Ibid.

3. Ibid.

4. Ibid.

5. Brown (1995).

6. Quoted in Hewitt (1995), p. 42.

7. Ibid., p. 43.

8. Ibid., p. 44.

9. Ibid., pp. 44, 46.

10. In fact, as late as 1980 groups like The Clash were still playing Lewisham Odeon.

11. Brown (1995).

12. Quoted in Hewitt (1995), p. 46.

13. Ibid., p. 47.

14. Ibid.

15. Ibid.

16. Ibid.

17. Ibid.

18. Ibid.

19. Ibid.

20. Ibid.

21. Ibid.

22. McLagan (1998), p. 29.

23. Ibid., p. 52.

24. Ibid.

25. Quoted in Twelker and Schmitt (2002), p. 37.

26. Quoted in Hewitt (1995).

27. Quoted in Pidgeon (1976), p. 19.

28. Quoted in Hewitt (1995), p. 50.

29. Ibid., p. 56.

30. Ibid.

31. Ibid., pp. 50–51.

32. McLagan (1998), p. 66.

33. Quoted in Hewitt (1995), p. 51.

34. Brown (1995).

35. Quoted in Hewitt (1995), p. 53.

36. Ibid.

37. Ibid., p. 57.

38. Ibid., p. 59.

39. Ibid., p. 63.

40. Ibid., pp. 59, 61.

41. Ibid., p. 59.

42. Ibid., p. 68.

43. Ibid.

## Chapter 4: The Industry of Human Happiness

1. Quoted in Hewitt (1995), p. 71.

2. Ibid.

3. Brown (1995).

4. Ibid.

5. McLagan (1998), p. 91.

6. Ibid., p. 92.

7. Quoted in Hewitt (1995), p. 75.

8. Ibid.

9. Ibid., p. 76.

10. Quoted in Levy (2002), p. 94.

11. Brown (1995).

12. Ibid.

13. Ibid.

14. Quoted in Hewitt (1995), p. 92.

15. Quoted in Pidgeon (1976), p. 27.

16. Brown (1995).

17. Ibid.

18. Napier-Bell (2001), p. 28.

19. McLagan (1998), p. 73.

20. Quoted in Hewitt (1995), p. 98.

21. Quoted in Twelker and Schmitt (2002), p. 50.

22. Quoted in Hewitt (1995), p. 98.

23. Ibid., p. 100.

24. Quoted in Twelker and Schmitt (2002), p. 51.

25. Quoted in Sked and Cook (1993), p. 225.

26. Quoted in Hewitt (1995), p. 101.

27. McLagan (1998), p. 108.

### Chapter 5: Happy Days Toy Town

1. Quoted in Hewitt (1995), p. 116.

2. Quoted in Pidgeon (1976), p. 32.

3. Ibid.

4. Ibid.

5. Ibid., p. 33.

6. Quoted in Hewitt (1995), p. 123.

7. Ibid.

8. McLagan (1998) p. 127

9. Quoted in Hewitt (1995), pp. 125-6.

10. Sabin (1999), p. 187.

11. Quoted in Pidgeon (1976), p. 33.

12. Ibid., p. 34.

13. McLagan (1998), p. 136.

14. Ibid.

15. Ibid., p. 138.

### Chapter 6: Thin

1. Quoted in Carson (2001), p. 71.

2. Baybutt (2001).

3. Quoted in Rawlings (1999), p. 73.

4. Quoted in Carson (2001), p. 70.

5. Ibid., p. 72.

6. Ibid., p. 75.

7. Ibid., p. 81.

8. Quoted in Pidgeon (1976), p. 50.

9. Ibid., p. 51.

10. Quoted in Rawlings (1999), p. 96.

11. Quoted in Carson (2001), p. 91.

12. Baybutt (2001).

13. Quoted in Carson (2001), p. 91.

14. Ibid., p. 92.

15. Ibid., p. 93.

16. Ibid.

17. Quoted in Pidgeon (1976), p. 65.

18. McLagan (1998), p. 159.

19. Quoted in Carson (2001), p. 94.


**Chapter 7: Face to Faces**

1. Brown (1995).

2. Quoted in the *NME* (1970).

3. Baybutt (2001).

4. Quoted in Sked and Cook (1993), p. 232.

5. See Hebdige (1979).

6. Ibid., p. 57.

7. Hattersley (1997), p. 177.

8. Quoted in Rawlings (1999), p. 114.

9. Ibid.


**Chapter 8: Starting the Party**

1. Speaking to the *NME* in 1973.

2. Quoted in Twelker and Schmitt (2002).

3. Quoted in Pidgeon (1976), p. 60.

4. Quoted in Rawlings (1999), p. 119.

5. McLagan (1998), p. 168.

6. Ibid., p. 169.

7. Ibid., p. 173.

8. Quoted in Rawlings (1999), p. 120.

9. McLagan (1998), p. 162.

10. Ibid., p. 163.

11. Baybutt (2001).

12. Ibid.

13. Quoted in Rawlings (1998), p. 121.

14. Ibid., p. 123.

15. Ibid.

16. Baybutt (2001).

## Chapter 9: Feel So Good

1. Quoted in Rawlings (1999), p. 130.

2. Ibid.

3. Ibid.

4. Ibid., p. 131.

5. McLagan (1998), p. 178.

6. Quoted in Twelker and Schmitt (2002), p. 123.

7. Quoted in Rawlings (1999), p. 135.

8. Ibid.

## Chapter 10: Every Picture Tells a Story

1. Quoted in Pidgeon (1976), p. 71.

2. Baybutt (2001).

3. Ibid.

4. Quoted in Pidgeon (1976), p. 71.

5. Speaking to the *NME* (1972).

6. McLagan (1998), p. 187.

7. Baybutt (2001).

8. Ibid.

9. Thompson (1998).

10. McLagan (1998), p. 181.

11. Bradley (1999), p. 11.

12. Gorman (2001), p. 193.

13. Baybutt (2001).

14. Ibid.

15. Baybutt (2001).

16. Quoted in Rawlings (1999), p. 143.

17. Baybutt (2001).

18. Ibid.


**Chapter 11: Never a Dull Moment**

1. Baybutt (2001).

2. Quoted in Rawlings (1999), p. 142

3. Ibid.

4. Hebdige (1979), p. 60.

5. Ibid., p. 61.

6. McLagan (1998), p. 192.


**Chapter 12: Borstal Boys**

1. Baybutt (2001).

2. Ibid.

3. Ibid.

4. Rawlings (1999), p. 155.

5. Quoted in Pidgeon (1976), p. 101.

6. Ibid.

7. Quoted in Rawlings (1999), p. 157.

8. *NME* (1973).

9. Quoted in Rawlings (1999), p. 157.

10. *NME* (1973).

11. McLagan (1998), p. 206.

12. *NME* (1973).


**Chapter 13: A Spiv or a Teddy Boy**

1. McLagan (1998), p. 203.

2. Baybutt (2001).

3. Quoted in Rawlings (2002), p. 160.

4. Baybutt (2001).

5. McLagan (1998), p. 203.

6. Ibid., p. 205.

7. Baybutt (2001).

8. McLagan (1998), p. 205.

9. Quoted in Twelker and Schmitt (2002), p. 131.

10. *NME* (1973).

11. Ibid.

12. McLagan (1998), p. 213.

## Chapter 14: A Study in Disintegration

1. *NME* (1974).

2. Ibid.

3. McLagan (1998), p. 222.

4. Quoted in Rawlings (1999), p. 170.

5. *NME* (1974).

6. Ibid.

7. Ibid.

8. Ibid.

9. Ibid.

10. Ibid.

11. Ibid.

12. Ibid.

13. Baybutt (2001).

14. *NME* (1974).

15. *NME* (1975).

16. Ibid.

## Chapter 15: Music for Housewives

1. Quoted in Pidgeon (1976), p. 110.

2. Ibid.

3. Quoted in Rawlings (1999), p. 173.

4. Ibid., p. 174.

5. Baybutt (2001).

6. Ibid.

7. Baybutt (2001).

8. Quoted in Pidgeon (1976), p. 112.

9. *NME* (1975).

10. Quoted in Rawlings (1999), p. 180.

11. Quoted in Pidgeon (1976), p. 113.

12. London *Evening Standard* (1/8/1975).

13. Baybutt (2001).


**Chapter 16: I'll Just Stay Here**

1. Quoted in Rawlings (1999), p. 180.

2. *Creem* (1975).

3. London *Evening Standard* (1975).

4. McLagan (1998), p. 236.

5. Quoted in Rawlings (1999), p. 181.

6. *Rolling Stone* (1975).

7. *Melody Maker* (1975).

8. *Rolling Stone* (1975).

9. *Melody Maker* (1975).

10. Baybutt (2001).

11. McLagan (1998), p. 246.


**Epilogue: 'Last Orders, Please'**

1. Baybutt (2001).

2. Sked and Cook (1993), p. 329.

3. Baybutt (2001).

4. Ibid.

5. Ibid.

6. Ibid.

7. Ibid.

8. Ibid.